D1524881

BUREAUCRACY
AND
CHURCH REFORM

BUREAUCRACY
AND
CHURCH REFORM

The organizational response of the Church of England to Social Change
1800 – 1965

BY

KENNETH A. THOMPSON

OXFORD
AT THE CLARENDON PRESS
1970

Oxford University Press, Ely House, London W. 1

GLASGOW NEW YORK TORONTO MELBOURNE WELLINGTON

CAPE TOWN SALISBURY IBADAN NAIROBI DAR ES SALAAM LUSAKA ADDIS ABABA

BOMBAY CALCUTTA MADRAS KARACHI LAHORE DACCA

KUALA LUMPUR SINGAPORE HONG KONG TOKYO

PRINTED IN GREAT BRITAIN

PREFACE

THE central theme of this book is the process by which a specific religious body, the Church of England, has adapted its organization in response to changes in the larger society. The perspective adopted is that of the sociology of religion, which views religion primarily as an institutional phenomenon, with a definite and established structure (goals, means, value orientations, sanctions) built around and sustaining one or more specific functions. Thus religion is viewed in its empirical, organized aspect, within the institutional framework of society, without thereby intending any pejorative implications regarding the *esse* of the Church.

Two developments in that framework over the last century and a half have had a crucial impact on the Church of England in its institutional aspect. The first development was the differentiation of institutions, as they became more specialized and delimited in their functions. The second development was the growth of instrumental orientations in modern society—the increased prevalence of a 'rationality' based on cause-and-effect thinking that is preoccupied with immediate, empirical ends, and pragmatic tests. On the level of organizational structure this entails the establishment of highly rational bureaucracies; on the level of ideology it calls for the maintenance of legitimations that are adequate for such bureaucracies.

The problems created by these developments for religious bodies have given rise to many controversies, but few empirical, sociological studies. Hence, the *Report of the World Council of Churches Commission on Institutionalism and Unity*, published in 1961, called for case studies of 'The sociological and ecclesiological significance of the increasing power of administrative boards and secretariats, and their changing relations to the traditional authority-structures of the churches'.[1]

[1] World Council of Churches Faith and Order Commission Report, *The Old and the New in the Church*, London, SCM Press, 1961, p. 91.

Various explanations have been offered for the failure to provide such studies. Thus, a recent, and influential, theoretical treatise on the sociology of religion suggested that:

> In view of the pervasiveness of bureaucracy on the contemporary religious scene and the general acknowledgement of this by those involved in it, it is remarkable how little attention has been given to it by sociology-of-religion research as compared, for instance, with the attention lavished on the local parish. One plausible explanation of this is the fact that so much of this research has been sponsored by the religious bureaucracies themselves, whose pragmatic interest was precisely in the achievement of their goals 'on the outside', *not* in reflection upon their own functionality.[1]

This case study of organizational developments in the Church of England represents one sociologist's modest contribution to that necessary research, and to analysis of the complex and delicate business of church reform. Also, although it was in no way sponsored by the Church, this research could certainly not have been undertaken without the co-operation and help of the officers of the Church Assembly and its departments.

I am especially grateful to Sir John Guillum Scott, the Secretary of the Church Assembly, and those other members of its staff, who patiently answered all my questions, and gave me guidance and access to the relevant documentary material in the Assembly's archives. Special permission to consult the later papers and correspondence of Archbishops R. T. Davidson and William Temple, at Lambeth Palace, was given by the present Archbishop of Canterbury, and by Mrs. Temple, the widow of the late Archbishop.

My greatest debt is to my mentor at Oxford, Dr. Bryan R. Wilson, of All Souls College, who showed me by example what is required in the ideal teacher. To Professor Ilya Neustadt and Dr. Percy S. Cohen I am indebted for much advice and encouragement in the early stages of this research. I would also like to thank Mr. J. R. Torrance, Dr. David Martin, and Professor Henry Chadwick, who read most of the manuscript at some stage and offered valuable suggestions.

[1] Peter L. Berger, *The Sacred Canopy*, New York, Doubleday, 1967, p. 209.

Finally, I have to acknowledge my dependence on my wife, Margaret, for inspiration and support at all times during the preparation of this book. Responsibility for my interest in the Church of England must be borne by my parents, who have devoted their lives to its service.

Needless to say, none of the above is in any way responsible for the opinions expressed and conclusions reached in this book.

KENNETH A. THOMPSON

Massachusetts, 1968

CONTENTS

ABBREVIATIONS

C.C.C.	Chronicle of Canterbury Convocation
P.C.C.	Proceedings of Church Congresses
P.C.A.	Proceedings of Church Assembly
Unpub. Lam. MSS.	Unpublished letters and papers at Lambeth Palace Library (Archbishop Davidson's collection, unless otherwise stated)

INTRODUCTION

THIS study deals with the need which arose in the nineteenth century for the Church of England to adapt its organization to a rapidly changing social structure. The role of the Church was changing, and its administrative apparatus was unadjusted to the new circumstances of its operation. Any adequate solution to the Church's organizational problems had to take account not only of instrumental requirements, but it had also to overcome problems raised with regard to the values of the organization. The principal problems examined are those of authority, co-ordination, and control within the organization.

The history of the Church of England's organizational response to social change will be divided into three phases: (1) the nineteenth century will be summarized as a period of *ad hoc* adjustment; (2) the period from the last decade of the nineteenth century up to, and centring on, the passing of the Enabling Act of 1919, which created the Church Assembly, will be viewed in terms of the emergence of a coalition of diverse groups in one church reform movement; (3) the third phase discussed is that of the formation and development of the Church Assembly organization. The main focus of the study is on the Church Assembly and its relation to the process of church reform which had its origins in the era of the Reform Act of 1832. That process can itself be analysed on three levels: (*a*) that of the relations between the Church and society; (*b*) that of the Church's own organization; (*c*) that of the roles involved in the life of the Church—bishops, clergy, laity—and the relations between them. The analysis is mainly concentrated on the second level—that of the Church's own organization, although it begins in Chapter I with a discussion of the more general level, and Chapter VIII includes a more extended discussion of changes in roles.

The nineteenth century was a period of rapid evolution of social institutions. Increasing differentiation and complexity of organization arose as institutions adapted to a changing social environment. This differentiation, on the societal level, was a prerequisite for the enhancement of the adaptive capacity of institutions. The main problem for the Church, at this level of analysis, was its relations with the State. In its operation in society, the Church needed to evolve new agencies to achieve its ends. In principle, it should have been possible for the established Church to do this by inducing the State to extend the facilities that it already made available to the Church, or to provide new ones. The alternative—and in practice this is what gradually happened—was for the Church to promote the development of new organizational arrangements that had varying degrees of integration with its own existing structure. With regard to a set of values to support the operations of its organization, the Church seemed to have a choice. It could respond to internal and external change by either appealing to the dominant values of the wider society to legitimate its functions and its structural changes (this response would tend, on balance, to emphasize the continued interdependence of Church and State), or else it could revive and reassert dormant elements in its own value system, and so tend to legitimate and perhaps accentuate its autonomy in relation to the State.

At the organization level the Church of England's development was a part of that larger process which Kenneth E. Boulding has described as the 'organizational revolution', and it was characterized by a growth in complexity, scale, and rationality.[1] For conceptual purposes it is convenient to distinguish, as Boulding does, between factors on the 'demand side' and those on the 'supply side' in this development. On the 'demand side' the factors more immediately conditioning the organizational response of the Church can be enumerated as follows:

(1) Demographic changes, urbanization, and the problem of maintaining social order in the towns.

(2) Increasing competition between rival religious bodies in a 'market' which was tending to regard all religious bodies as entitled to equal status.

[1] K. E. Boulding, *The Organizational Revolution*.

(3) Political changes which undermined the financial dependence of the Church on the State.

(4) The need for the Church to develop a sense of responsibility in its laity (especially middle-class laymen) for its financial support and management, and for its defence against its critics.

The 'supply side' is represented by improvement in the skills of organization—communications, transport, specialization, statistical and budgetary techniques.

It has been suggested that an essential condition for this development in organization, especially from a traditional type of organization to the modern form of rational bureaucracy, is an increased command over monetary funds by an organization, both in the means of administration and in remuneration.[1] The bureaucratic official normally receives a fixed salary paid in money, instead of being dependent on sources of income which are privately appropriated and which can be called benefices. Benefices typically involve payments in kind, and the receipt of a benefice implies the appropriation of opportunities for collecting various dues. The significance of this for the organizational development of the Church of England over the last century can be seen in the gradual sale of glebe-land formerly attached to benefices, the decline of private sources of clerical income, and the commutation of tithe, which created a need for supplementation from central funds, and so of central organization and control. This will be seen to have been part of a general trend in the development of the Church from a communal (*Gemeinschaft*) basis, to an associational (*Gesellschaft*) form. This process is related to the increase in scale and complexity of organization as it occurs in the structural differentiation of modern society.[2]

At the level of the performance of the role of the clergy, the change from local and private sources of income to central monetary payments (salaries, pensions, grants for

[1] M. Weber, *The Theory of Social and Economic Organization*, pp. 335 and 339.

[2] Cf. Ferdinand Tönnies, *Gemeinschaft und Gesellschaft*, Leipzig, 1887; reviewed by R. Heberle, 'The Sociological System of Ferdinand Tönnies: "Community" and "Society"', in Harry Elmer Barnes (ed.), *An Introduction to The History of Sociology*, pp. 227–48; and Emile Durkheim, *The Division of Labour in Society*.

maintenance and dilapidations) was in the direction of reducing the clergy to salaried, dependent status, and increasing executive roles at the centre. The development was resented by many clergy (already uncertain of their role) and produced a reluctance to accord full authority to the Church Assembly which was believed to epitomize that development. It also resulted in a failure on the clergy's part to communicate Church Assembly information to the local membership, or to elicit self-identification of the laity with the central organization.

The trend of development from *gemeinschaftliche* organization to *gesellschaftliche* not only altered the role of the clergyman in his relations with superiors, but it also altered his functions on the parochial level. Instead of being the charismatic or traditional leader of a communal group, the parish priest tended to become a co-ordinator and administrator for a proliferation of specialized interest groups. The urban church had not the status of an *ecclesiola in ecclesia*, but competed for a critical clientele and provided associational activities in its local branches of supra-parochial organizations. The nineteenth century onwards was a period of rapid growth and spawning of supra-parochial organizations to meet the challenge presented by the increasingly urban, industrial population. If the resulting change in roles and status of clergy and laity were to be characterized quite simply it would be by the use of the terms 'salaried administrator' and 'critical client' respectively. At least, such has been the trend. The interest of this study lies not in these role changes as such, but in their relation to the organizational changes, with particular reference to developments associated with the Church Assembly. The development of the Church Assembly organization will be shown to have been conditioned by the attitudes and fears which had been created by prior developments in central organization, especially the fear of bureaucracy.

Having indicated the three levels of analysis, it remains to sketch some of the historical developments which will be considered. At the general level, it will be shown that what little instrumental adaptation there had been in the Church prior to the Reform Act of 1832 had been along the lines of extending the work of existing agencies. After the Reform Act, for a time, the adaptation passed into the hands of the Ecclesiastical Commission set up by the Government. The reformers thought the Church might achieve a new security, to replace the loss of its privileged position caused by the repeal of the Test Acts and other changes, if the State could be involved in the Church's administrative reform to fit it for a continuing national function. In terms of values the reformers seized on 'utility'—the key value of the contemporary middle class. Bishop Blomfield (the arch-reformer), Robert Peel, Archbishop Whately, and even the *British Critic*, the organ of the old High Church party, justified reform in those terms.

The Oxford Movement arose ostensibly because the structural changes in the Church were initiated by an authority no longer formally exclusively Anglican (i.e. Parliament). In effect the Tractarian protest was a product of the *de facto* relegation of the Church to a subordinate position, brought about by the trend towards structural differentiation and increasing institutional plurality in society. The Tractarians were concerned less with instrumental adaptation than with the threat to the distinctive values of the Church which such adaptation accentuated. Although the reformers appealed to the predominant current value in society, in order to preserve the status of the national Church, the Catholic party wished to stress the autonomy of the Church by emphasizing its own distinct values. The Tractarians argued against the Ecclesiastical Commission's activities in the roomier framework of the Church as a spiritual society.

The early split in the church reform movement between what might be called the 'instrumental' and 'autonomist' elements was important in all subsequent stages of reform. The efforts to reconcile these two postions will appear as a central feature of the events leading up to the creation of the Church Assembly and the central administrative structure, as described here. What is posited is that there was a tension in the Church's development between instrumental adaptation and the values that the Church espoused; this was especially evident in crises over authority. In terms of internal and external relations, the instrumental reformers were active on the practical side, in efforts to improve the efficiency of the Church's functioning, the comprehensiveness of its contribution to the national life, and its own internal comprehensiveness. They sought to preserve as much as possible the status of the national Church. The autonomists were active throughout in seeking to heighten the sense of churchmanship (self-consciousness of the institution), and to define more clearly the distinctive values of the Church, and, in effect, to make it a more exclusive body. This attempt, in turn, gave rise to strain within the autonomist group itself because it threatened to reduce the Church of England to a denominational type of religious body. In Chapter VI this will appear as a central focus of debate in the movement to set up the Church Assembly, and in Chapter VIII it will be related to the church-sect typology and to sociological discussion of the tendency for religious bodies in modern society to develop a form of organization and outlook which is characteristic of the denomination rather than of the encompassing church or separatist sect.

The organizational developments which took place in the Church of England, and the social changes which gave rise to them, will be compared and contrasted, where possible, with parallel developments in other religious bodies. The sociological case study of the American Baptist Convention, carried out by Paul M. Harrison, will provide relevant data for one such comparison.[1] The growth of central organization in both the Church of England and the American Baptist Convention was part of the 'organizational revolution' as defined by Boulding, and similar social factors were operative in both cases. These social changes posed problems for the churches which could be handled only by a formal structure which incorporated principles of authority and modes of organization typical of the rational bureaucracies found in all spheres of modern, Western society. The adoption of such modes of organization created severe conflict between older and newer principles of authority in religious bodies, because their organization, or polity, was expected to be a manifestation of their doctrinal

[1] P. M. Harrison, *Authority and Power in the Free Church Tradition.*

systems. In the American Baptist Convention, the Baptist belief in the local congregation as the seat of ultimate authority conflicted with the accumulation of power in the hands of the officials of the central organization, and so those officials were accorded only a provisional authority, which was not fully legal, nor based on ecclesiastical tradition, but pragmatic and expediential. In the Church of England the various central agencies, the growth of which will be described, contained a mixture of principles of authority, and the precise mixture in each will be related to the origins of the agency, and to the constant endeavour to maintain a division of power, and a balance between the different groups and parties which made up the Established Church.

The history of the various central agencies in the Church of England's organization is presented in terms of origins and growth stages, as the organization was transformed by its evolution of new ways of dealing with a changing environment. The most important aspect of that transformation was the evolution of autonomous church agencies to take the place of the former dependence on the State. The traditional dependence of the Church of England on the State, and the progressive reluctance and inability of the State to continue that support, are illustrated by the tendency for state subsidies, church rates, Parliamentary commissions and legislation, to give way to voluntary contributions, structural development within the Church's own organization, and the advent of policy-making and representative councils at different levels within the Church. The practical requirement of co-ordination and rationalization of these proliferating bodies, and the need for representation in policy-making for the different parties and interests in the Church, were contributory factors in the development of the Church Assembly.

Chapter IV deals with the development of representative assemblies in the Church of England. The democratic consciousness fostered by middle-class habituation to democratic government created a desire for representation on the part of the Anglican laity and, perhaps more significantly, a consciousness on the part of church defenders that the only way of staving off disestablishment (and disendowment) was by reforming the Church along democratic lines. Those who were mainly concerned to stress the Church's autonomy did not mind disestablishment so much, although they varied from the more dogmatic who welcomed it, to the moderates who thought it ought not to be embraced until all else had failed. Reformers who were mainly concerned with the instrumental efficiency of the organization regarded such a prospect as destructive of the very nature of the Church of England. The Church Assembly solution, however, was able to attract wide support because it offered the instrumental reformers a cure for the Church's operational problems, especially that of getting church legislation passed; whilst it offered the autonomists some prospect of self-government. (Even if this had to include lay representation, at least they could insist on the maximum qualification for the lay representatives and perhaps even for the electors.)

Weber suggested that the growth of formally rational, bureaucratic organization was closely associated with an increasing dependence on central monetary funds for administration and remuneration. The development of such organization is a major feature in Chapter III in the discussion of the parts played by the Ecclesiastical Commission and Queen Anne's Bounty. It also features in the development of diocesan and central boards of finance, which set the character of the system of administration associated with the Church Assembly, described in Chapters VI and VII. It is worth quoting, at this point, the report of the Archbishops' Committee on Church Finance, 1911, which led to the setting up of diocesan boards of finance and the Central Board of Finance (the latter was to become the financial organ of the Church Assembly). The report gives some indication of the factors which gave rise to the new system, and of the fears which existed with regard to the possible dysfunctions of such a process of rationalization:

> Our investigations have convinced us that there is an urgent and pressing need for a sound financial system for the Church, based on clearly defined principles.
>
> The present position is a natural result of conditions which deserve study. Historically in England the diocese preceded the parish, but as Christianity gradually spread through the country, owners of land gave endowments for resident clergy, and thus parishes were formed

and the parochial system became strong. Endowments were never given to the Church as a body, nor even to the diocese. They were given to endow a bishopric, a parish, a monastery, or a capitular body. So long as the population was small and the endowments fairly adequate the want of an organized financial system was not felt. The expenses of the parish churches were till present times met from Church Rates. Each parish managed its own affairs and there was comparatively little corporate life. The Bishop visited his diocese from time to time, but the difficulty of communication between one part of the diocese and another made it impossible to establish the diocesan representation of clergy and laity which is now felt to be essential to Church life. The natural result was an exaggerated parochialism which could not see beyond the needs and rights of the parish and was wholly incapable of dealing with changed conditions. As the population grew and ancient endowments proved altogether insufficient a multitude of unofficial societies, institutions and funds gradually sprang up, designed to meet parochial needs for which the Church as a body had failed to make provision. . . . No mere arbitrary association of men or agencies can meet the needs of the entire body.[1]

The report recommended the development of an organized system of finance. In the absence of such a system, it stated, church members would never acquire a sense of responsibility, which previously had been rendered unnecessary by endowments and church rates.

In view of the previous history of strain between instrumental adaptation and values, and the later criticisms that the new system of administration had promoted bureaucratization, it is significant that the report should have ended by stating:

In reviewing the recommendations which we have now made we are conscious that an obvious criticism of them lies in the appearance which they may be thought to present of too easy a faith in the efficiency of machinery and organization. It is, indeed, not improbable that, when the Church of England awakes to the deficiency of her existing financial machinery, there will be a tendency—not unusual in large societies—to the opposite extreme of over-organization. That tendency can, we believe, safely be left to the broad common sense of churchmen to deal with when it arises. But in the meantime it is precisely the existing lack of organization that has so deeply impressed us. . . .[2]

[1] *Report of the Archbishops' Committee on Church Finance*, 1911, pp. 3–4.
[2] Ibid., p. 57.

The history of the administrative and financial organization of the Church of England reflected a persistent tension between instrumental efficiency, achieved through the agency of a small executive body of professional administrators, and the need for legitimation of its actions, and the representative formulation of policy and control over its implementation. In the first period of church reform the creation of the Ecclesiastical Commissioners, and the revival of Convocations, represented separate attempts to solve problems of adaptation. In the case of the Ecclesiastical Commissioners it was adaptation for the purpose of achieving greater instrumental efficiency, whereas Convocations were revived not primarily to promote efficiency but for the purpose of reasserting the Church's distinctive values and its own intrinsic authority. No attempt was made to provide a comprehensive system of organization which would bring together these separate functions. The result was that on the one hand the Ecclesiastical Commissioners were accorded only a very limited authority, whilst Convocations could exercise little control over the policies and administration of the various instrumental agencies. Problems of authority and representative control with regard to the Ecclesiastical Commissioners are illustrated by a description of the recurrent efforts to make the controlling board more representative and effective, whilst at the same time allowing more discretionary powers to the salaried officers in order to make the work more efficient. The reasons for Convocations' failure to develop into the central governing authority over the Church's organization are discussed in Chapter IV in the context of a description of the Church's search for an acceptable system of representative government.

The emergence of Church Assembly promised greater legislative efficiency to the instrumental reformers and the restoration of authority and self-government in the eyes of the autonomists. The process of forming a coalition of these interests (especially the role of the Life and Liberty Movement), the reasons for the compromise structure which emerged, and the subsequent effects of these factors on the working of the Assembly and its organization, are discussed in Chapters V, VI, and VII.

Although the history of changes at the level of roles in the Church is not dealt with separately, it is suggested that the increase in central organization and the greater dependence of the clergy on that organization, constituted a change in the role and status of the clergy, which has contributed to the failure of the Church Assembly to provide a comprehensive solution to the Church's organizational problems.

The clergy's fear of loss of security and independence at the hands of the growing central organization, and the desire to maintain their professional autonomy, made them reluctant to accord the Church Assembly organization the authority it required. The preference of some clergy for Convocations, over against Church Assembly, reflected this apprehension. Convocations had the advantage of not being associated with any bureaucratic administrative structure. This was an important consideration for those who thought that secular criteria of efficiency and utility were inappropriate in a religious body at a time when the most pressing need was for it to realize its corporate distinctiveness. This was part of the tension involved in the process of organizational adaptation. As part of the differentiation of institutional domains within the social structure, the Church, like other institutions, had to develop its autonomous administrative and governmental organization. But it had also to relate itself to other institutions, if its activities were to have any social relevance, and so, in its functioning, it was often evaluated according to common operational criteria.

As a national religious establishment, the Church of England contained a wide variety of religious parties, principles of authority, and sectional interests. In every stage of growth in the Church's organization, to be described in subsequent chapters, both instrumental adaptation and the assertion of particular values were rendered subordinate to the maintenance of the basic identity of the Church of England, which rested on this comprehensiveness.

PART ONE

I

THE PROBLEM AND ITS SETTING AT THE BEGINNING OF THE NINETEENTH CENTURY

SOCIAL CHANGE AND THE CHURCH'S NEED TO ADAPT

THE organizational response of the Church of England to changes in nineteenth-century society was demanded by the rapid process of social evolution in Britain. All organized departments of national life were becoming more highly differentiated in their internal structure as part of their adaptation to new circumstances. The process was one which more sharply limited and defined the areas of institutional operation. Two events in the single year 1836 were symptomatic: the setting up of the Tithe Commission and the Registrar-General's Office. Prior to this men still paid one-tenth of the fruits of their labour to the Church, and still registered at the parish church all deaths, births, and marriages. 'But in a capitalistic society tithes in kind were an anachronism and the parish register a very faulty statistical record.'[1]

The norms according to which institutions functioned ceased to be so diffuse, and institutions increasingly adopted norms which were directly related to their own functions and operations. The basis of institutional operation was ceasing to be the mixed feudal and aristocratic assumptions of traditional society, and were increasingly the rational

[1] David Roberts, *Victorian Origins of the Welfare State*, pp. 49–50.

principles of the modern world. As institutions became more specific in their function, so they gained a certain autonomy, and so their inter-relation also was governed by different assumptions from those which had prevailed in the past. Thus the norms of particular institutions were 'substantively rational' in the way in which that term has been employed by Max Weber, only in relation to the institutional context in which they applied; they ceased to be relevant outside it.

The Church in modern society did not escape this development and could not avoid the process of functional rationalization.

> She, too, gains an extraordinary amount of internal autonomy, while the validity of her norms becomes relativized, as much as this goes against the original overarching significance of her religious representations.[1]

The eighteenth-century Church of England was closely intertwined with the secular order at all levels and by so existing it served the function of sanctifying the established order, and in return the State succoured the Church. The demographic, constitutional, and social changes which swept over English society in the first four decades of the nineteenth century seriously weakened these traditional ties and threatened to destroy the substance of the partnership altogether. If the Church was to survive as an Established Church it would have to adapt its organization to the changed circumstances.

DIFFERENCES OVER VALUES AND PRIORITIES

The main alternatives open to the Church were either to elicit new, or an extension of existing, state provisions for its benefit, or to promote a structural growth of autonomous instrumental agencies with varying degrees of integration to its own system. Whichever organizational changes were advocated, they required legitimation by an appeal to appropriate values. The values appealed to could be either those dominant in contemporary society, which would emphasize

[1] T. Luckmann, 'On Religion in Modern Society: Individual Consciousness, World View, Institution', in *Journal for the Scientific Study of Religion*, vol. ii, 2, Spring 1963, p. 158.

the continued interdependence of Church and State, or dormant values exclusive to the Church could be revived and reasserted, thus accentuating and legitimating the Church's autonomy.

Recourse to the former strategy represented an attempt to salvage the overarching quality of the values that legitimated the Church's organization and its functioning, by seeking at least a minimum of consensus over key temporal goals and values. The consequent organizational structures derived their procedural character and their evaluative criteria from this frame of reference. This strategy facilitated instrumental reforms but invited criticism from groups such as the Nonconformists, and working-class radicals, that reacted against the secular values and goals to which it appealed, and also from internal groups who wished to stress the autonomous and transcendental element in the Church's values and goals. For the latter, 'autonomist', groups the overarching (or pre-eminent) nature of the Church's values was provided precisely by their transcendental reference.

The reforms associated with the formation of the Ecclesiastical Commissioners in the 1830s can be characterized as having been mainly concerned with instrumental adaptation and they originated at the highest levels of the Church and State hierarchies. The methods were those prevalent in secular government administration and in so far as there was any reference to particular values it was to values that emphasized the Church's usefulness to society, especially in maintaining social control and stability.

In contrast, the organizational prescriptions which emerged through the Oxford Movement may be regarded as having been concerned with an adaptation of values in response to the Church's changed position in society. They originated in hierarchical levels below those of the top administrative rank, among theologians. They were concerned with the *raison d'être* of the Church as a distinct, corporate entity, and were addressed primarily to the clergy as the responsible bearers of the organization's legitimate authority, based on a routinized charisma mediated by bishops standing in the Apostolic Succession. It was the stress on this autonomous source of legitimation of authority which led to the revival of Convocations and the addition of a larger clerical element to the controlling board of the Ecclesiastical Commissioners.

PROBLEMS OF AUTHORITY

The process of routinization of charisma[1] in an institutionalized form is not as unitary and unproblematic as the theological doctrine of the Tractarians seemed to suggest. The institution has to adapt itself to the requirements of everyday administrative routine, and so the authority of office holders depends not only on their standing in a valid succession, but also on their acting in accordance with legal precedents and rational administrative procedures, which have been institutionalized.

The routinization of charisma often gives rise to formal organization with bureaucratic structure. New offices tend to develop as new functions arise. Moreover, precedents established in action lead to a transformation of existing offices. The general contours of the administrative structure tend to reflect the problems and functions in response to which the structure developed.[2]

Max Weber suggested that there are two possible directions of legitimation of the authority of routinized charisma: these are the traditional and the rational-legal.[3] Later criticisms of these suggest that the dual category can be divided and the rational and legal elements analytically separated. Although the two sources of legality and rationality may reinforce each other, so that a legal code is subject to rationalization, and a process of rationalization may be furthered by legal codification, an important distinction can be made in terms of rational-legal and rational-pragmatic legitimation.[4] The latter type seems to be an 'expediential authority', not fully legal and not traditional, but dependent on success in achieving assigned goals. The Church of England's constitution developed as a mixture of all these

[1] 'The concept that charisma may be transmitted by ritual means from one bearer to another or may be created in a new person.' Max Weber, *Theory of Social and Economic Organization*, p. 366.

[2] T. F. O'Dea, *The Sociology of Religion*, pp. 93–4.

[3] Weber, op. cit., ch. 3.

[4] P. M. Harrison, *Authority and Power in the Free Church Tradition*, pp. 207–12.

elements, and reflected its chequered history. Whilst the Western Church's early appropriation of Roman law provided it with a legal bureaucratic model, in the Church of England this had been modified and complicated by statute law and custom. In the nineteenth century this mixed constitution was to present problems for all who sought to give an ideal definition of the basis on which it should rest.

At the beginning of the nineteenth century the Church of England was a vast aggregation of legal corporations.

> As a medieval institution the Church was in many ways a network of rights, privileges, traditional duties, with normally, circumscribed powers for its officers who had often to act judicially rather than by direct administrative act.[1]

This situation was typical of a time when most of what are now regarded as administrative functions were then entrusted to judicial bodies and carried out by strictly legal processes.

> The contribution of unwritten rules to the practical running of a constitution was scarcely recognized, and so far as such rules were recognized, they were condemned as illegal practices, tending to corruption or despotism. The laws of England, virtually, *were* the constitution, and the Church of England was but one—the largest single one by far, but still only one among many—of the legal establishments which formed it.[2]

With the creation of the Ecclesiastical Commissioners the Church of England increasingly received delegated powers from the State for its own agencies and their officers, so that administrative action inside the Church increased. Although this administration was still circumscribed by legal enactments, nevertheless the exercise of discretionary powers was permitted and so, therefore, was the growth of elements of rational-pragmatic bureaucracy.

The mixed bases of legitimation of the administrative agencies of the developing organization were to produce characteristic problems in each of them. Whereas the main dysfunctions of the predominantly legal bureaucracy tend to be rigidity and incapacity to experiment or innovate, the

[1] G. Kitson Clark, *The Making of Victorian England*, p. 154.

[2] G. F. A. Best, *Temporal Pillars*, p. 37.

typical dysfunctions of rational-pragmatic administration arise from appropriation of control over policy by experts. Efficiency requires the minimization of dysfunctions, whilst legitimation requires constant reference of the decisions of experts to rules (legal legitimation), precedent (traditional legitimation), or pragmatic criteria (rational-pragmatic legitimation). In the Church, the extent to which the principle of legitimacy based on law operates is dependent upon the support which the enacting body secures from the different theological and interest groups.

This in turn raises the problems of representation of such groups in assemblies and boards of control, and of theological validation of such bodies. Limitations on the legitimation based on precedent depend on the balance of power between conservative and innovatory groups. Rational-pragmatic legitimation is limited according to the position which the subject matter to which it is applied occupies on the sacred/profane scale as evaluated by the potential critic.

THE ORGANIZATIONAL REVOLUTION

The developments in the Church of England's organization must be set within the context of what Kenneth E. Boulding has described as an 'organizational revolution'.[1] It entails a growth in complexity, scale, and rationality. According to Weber this development of the modern form of the organization of corporate groups in all fields is nothing less than identical with the development and continual spread of bureaucratic administration.

> Its development, largely under capitalistic auspices, has created an urgent need for stable, strict, intensive, and calculable administration. It is this need which gives Bureaucracy a crucial role in our society as the central element in any kind of large-scale administration. Only by reversion in every field—political, religious, economic, etc.—to small-scale organization would it be possible to any considerable extent to escape its influence.[2]

On what Boulding calls the demand side for this development can be included the factors listed by Harrison in

[1] K. E. Boulding, *The Organizational Revolution*, p. 16.

[2] Weber, op. cit., p. 338.

discussing the causes of organizational developments in the American Baptist Convention. These were: increasing competition between religious bodies; the needs of an expanding missionary enterprise; urbanization; and the emergence of the labouring classes as a significant force.[1] To these may be added, in the case of the Established Church of England, constitutional changes, and, in the early nineteenth century especially, a rapid growth in population.

In the first half of the nineteenth century the population of England and Wales almost doubled, and the proportion of the population living in towns of over 20,000 inhabitants increased from a quarter to a half of the total population.[2]

From the point of view of the State, the problem was that of maintaining social cohesion in the face of a rising tide of poverty and distress in towns lacking adequate government, services, and police forces. From the point of view of the Church, the problem presented itself as one of maintaining the traditional disciplines of church attendance in parishes which were almost literally swamped by the new population, living only a little way above the subsistence level. The distinction between these two problems is somewhat artificial as the partnership between Church and State in this period was very close. For instance a legal maxim current at the time stated that 'Christianity is part of the law of England', and in 1832 over a quarter of the Justices of the Peace were clergymen. Thus the spread of 'heathenism' in the overcrowded industrial parishes was seen as one aspect of the menace of poverty and lawlessness, and in either case the parish was the administrative unit which was left to cope with the problem as well as it could.[3]

INADEQUACIES OF THE OLD ORDER

The rapid population changes and the urbanization process combined with the Church's long-standing deployment problems of pluralities and absence from livings to reveal the weakness of the Church's claim to fulfil the functions of an Established Church. In 1827 it was reported

[1] Harrison, op. cit., pp. 43–4.

[2] Kitson Clark, op. cit., p. 66; and A. F. Weber, *The Growth of Cities in the Nineteenth Century*, p. 46.

[3] R. A. Buchanan, 'Methodism and the Evangelical Revival', in W. S. F. Pickering (ed.), *Anglican-Methodist Relations, Some Institutional Factors*, pp. 39–40.

that of the 10,500 beneficed clergy in the Church of England and Wales, about 4,500 were absent from one living which they held.[1]

Pluralities and absence from livings did not necessarily require organizational innovations for their solution, and the legislation against them early in the century had some success, so that by 1848 the number of absentees had been reduced to about 2,000.[2] But they combined with the new conditions created by social changes to provide ammunition for the Church's critics (such as the Utilitarian journalist John Wade and his notorious *Extraordinary Black Book* of 1831), and strengthened the determination of those sympathetic towards constructive change in the Church itself.

Not only were the instrumental agencies of the Established Church inadequate in their present state to meet its practical commitments, but the constitutional revolution between 1828 and 1832 served to undermine the legal basis of the Establishment. The repeal of the Test and Corporation Acts destroyed the formal principle of Anglican monopoly in offices of State and municipalities; Catholic Emancipation admitted Roman Catholics to the legislature; and the Reform Act gave greater political strength to the intellectual and sectarian enemies of the Establishment. The Utilitarian Radicals and the rapidly increasing Protestant Dissenters were thus able to join forces in a campaign against the Established Church.

THE CHURCH BUILDING COMMISSIONERS

The response of conservative churchmen towards the challenge presented by the social changes was to seek modest adjustments by using traditional agencies. The legislation against pluralism and absence from livings was typical of the traditional dependency on the State for solving Church problems. Another variation of the conservative approach was exhibited in the church extension movement under the direction of the High Churchmen.

The Church Building Commissioners were a deeply conservative

[1] Kitson Clark, op. cit., p. 152. [2] Ibid.

body, and their assumptions were those of the *ancien régime* of before 1830. Their policy had been shaped between 1818 and 1825, when a degree of respect was paid to existing interests that crippled their potentialities for usefulness and had already by the forties come to seem unnecessary, even mistaken.[1]

The Church Building Commissioners directed their operations rigidly in accordance with the maze of Church Building Acts (twenty-one were passed between 1818 and 1856). In so doing they were able to reassure themselves as to their unswerving constitutionality and legal legitimacy.

The conditions under which the insertion of new churches into the parochial structure was conducted was thus unsatisfactory—rigid, acephalous, hectic, uneconomic. The church extension movement exhibited all the characteristic failings of those partnerships between official, 'central' direction and voluntary, 'local' enterprise which were so often the nineteenth century's response to the demands of the new society; but it exhibited them to a peculiar degree, because the weight lay more than usually on the voluntary, 'local' side.[2]

The more innovatory Ecclesiastical Commissioners were to be similarly hampered by this restrictive organizational device in their early years.

For full efficiency they needed to be sovereign masters in their own house. By the sixties they had become so. But in their early years they often had to share control and the making of policy with deans and chapters and bishops and their subordinates. . . .[3]

THE ECCLESIASTICAL COMMISSION

The Ecclesiastical Commission was set up by the short-lived Tory Government of Sir Robert Peel in 1835 and it continued under Lord Melbourne. It began as a commission of inquiry and had a mixed composition of important clerical and lay members. The appointment of a commission has been called a favourite Benthamite device, but in this case the proposed radical attack was forestalled by the Tories and the

[1] Best, op. cit., pp. 355–6.

[2] Ibid. In these dealings the deans and chapters, and the bishops, tended to represent local and financial interests.

[3] Ibid., p. 368.

more progressive of the episcopate under the joint leadership of Peel and Charles James Blomfield, Bishop of London, who used it as a device for constructive reform.[1]

The reports which it issued eventually produced legislation reorganizing dioceses and episcopal revenues, dealing with pluralism and non-residence, reducing cathedral chapters, and removing scandals of sinecures and nepotism. Under the Established Church Bill of 1836 the proposals for redistribution were put in the hands of the agency suggested in the Third Report—a permanent corporate body to be known as 'The Ecclesiastical Commissioners for England'. Their method of legislation was to be by Order in Council embodying schemes they had prepared. They could examine on oath and compel the production of documents. Clause 10 of the Act also enlarged their legislative capacity to include 'such Modifications or Variations as to Matter of Detail and Regulation as shall not be substantially repugnant' to the recommendations of the report.[2] From the start the Commissioners had a certain amount of discretionary power for the purpose of detailed administration.

Although reference has been made to the factors which made up the 'demand side' for the organizational developments in the Church of England in the first half of the nineteenth century, especially urbanism and the sociopolitical changes, it is necessary to examine other possible alternatives to the kind of organizational innovation which the Ecclesiastical Commissioners came to represent.

Mention has already been made of the Church Building Commissioners whose potentiality for innovation was vitiated by their conservatism and their dependence on voluntary, 'local' enterprise. They were eventually absorbed by the Ecclesiastical Commissioners, whose organization was more enterprising and efficient, being based on sustained expertise, and incorporating those characteristics of bureaucratic administration which led Max Weber to pronounce it superior to any other form in precision, stability, discipline, reliability, and calculability.

[1] Olive J. Brose, *Church and Parliament, The Reshaping of the Church of England 1828–1860*, p. 125.

[2] Best, op. cit., p. 307.

QUEEN ANNE'S BOUNTY

An alternative candidate to the Ecclesiastical Commissioners which might have undertaken the major role on the organizational response of the Church, was Queen Anne's Bounty. The Bounty was founded in 1704 when Queen Anne set up a corporation to take over her revenues from first-fruits and tenths and apply them to the augmentation of the poor clergy's incomes.

In the first three decades of the nineteenth century Queen Anne's Bounty was pre-eminent on the ecclesiastical side of Church and State. So much so that between 1820 and 1835 it seemed as if it might forestall the setting up of the Ecclesiastical Commission. It was improving its administration in these years. However, as Best has pointed out, the more ambitious plans which would have turned the Bounty into the business-like manager of large properties and trustee for the poor clergy (the position the Ecclesiastical Commissioners were to occupy forty years later) were not implemented.[1] Its conservative traditionalism and dependence on the State made it an unsuitable candidate for the more autonomous, rational bureaucracy that the Church required as its central financial executive, capable of sustained redistribution and redeployment of its resources.

THE ACCUMULATION OF STATISTICS— A FACTUAL BASIS FOR REFORM

On the other hand, Queen Anne's Bounty did play an important role in supplying some of the facilities for the organizational revolution as it applied to the Church. For the development of a rational-legal bureaucratic organization it was necessary that there should be an increased reliance on central funds and also an increase in statistical information.[2]

The development of statistics and numerical calculation in the Church of England was part of a general trend. The development of the new discipline of statistics in nineteenth-century Britain was closely associated with the Utilitarians. It was first used extensively in Britain by Sir John Sinclair

[1] Ibid., pp. 209–13.

[2] Max Weber, op. cit., p. 64,

in his 'Statistical Account of Scotland' (1771–99).[1] The Statistical Society of London (later the Royal Statistical Society) was founded in 1834, and in the first issue of its Journal in 1838 it stated:

> It is indeed truly said that the spirit of the present age has an evident tendency to confront the figures of speech with the figures of arithmetic; it being impossible not to observe a growing distrust of mere hypothetical theory and *a priori* assumption, and the appearance of a general conviction that, in the business of social science, principles are valid for application only inasmuch as they are legitimate induction from facts, accurately observed and methodically classified.[2]

It is significant that Richard Yates, who has been described as the best of the writers on Church reform in the early decades of the nineteenth century, entitled his Second Letter to the Earl of Liverpool, published in 1817, *The Basis of National Welfare, considered in reference to the Prosperity of Britain, and safety of the Church of England: with an examination of the Parliamentary Reports on Education, the Police, the Population of Parishes and the Capacity of Churches and Chapels.*

This concern for statistics and a factual basis as part of an empirical and pragmatic approach to Church reform he considered essential for the same reasons as the Utilitarian statisticians.

> The complicated and difficult questions in which these subjects abound, are so variously treated, and apprehended, even by the most celebrated enquirers, in so contradictory a manner that Abstract Reasoning upon such points must still be unsatisfactory; and practice founded upon its conclusions alone, must be liable to unexpected dangers. The most rational Politicians and judicious Statesmen allow, that the Reformations and the Improvements of Society, to be safe and effectual, must like the real improvements in physical science, be deduced from the observation of Facts, and conform to the lessons and guidance of Experience.[3]

Sir William Scott's Act of 1803, dealing with the non-residence of the clergy, contained a clause requiring the bishops to return annually to the Privy Council a statement

[1] Leslie Stephen, *The English Utilitarians*, vol. i, p. 80.

[2] Quoted in Nathan Glazer, 'The Rise of Social Research in Europe', in Daniel Lerner (ed.), *The Human Meaning of the Social Sciences*, p. 50.

[3] Richard Yates, *The Basis of National Welfare . . .*, p. 3.

of the conditions prevailing in the benefices under their care. The Council was also given other ecclesiastical tasks and a new office had to be created to undertake them. The Council also received Church reports from the archbishops of the use they had made of their powers (conferred by Scott's Act) to hear appeals from their provincial bishops' decisions to refuse licences of non-residence. This branch of the Privy Council Office 'soon turned into a kind of miniature Ministry for Ecclesiastical Affairs'.[1] A continued development in this direction might have given the Church of England a legal bureaucracy of the type which developed in some of the Scandinavian state churches.

The partnership of Church and State in Church administration functioned in this initial stage to provide the first statistical and financial resources, and these were necessary for even the most rudimentary budgetary processes if the Church was to deploy its resources to meet the increasing demands being made upon it.

Parliamentary grants between 1809 and 1816, and 1818 and 1820, for relief of poor clergy by Queen Anne's Bounty, extended the Bounty's usefulness as a central administrative agency and facilitated central budgeting, as did the additional information which it obtained from a survey of benefices under £150 a year. In 1812 two further sets of information were collected and tabulated by the Privy Council's ecclesiastical officer, on church accommodation in populous parishes, and of numbers and salaries of licensed curates.[2] There was no great improvement on these sources of information until the Commission of Inquiry into Ecclesiastical Revenues (1832–5). The extension of the existing function of the two traditionally based administrative agencies had been the first cautious step in the direction of supplying the factual basis for the Church's organizational revolution.

MODELS FOR THE ORGANIZATION

Models for the organizational reforms were suggested by different groups in the Church according to their general ideological and theological orientations.

[1] Best, op. cit., p. 200. [2] Ibid., pp. 202–3.

The conservative High Churchmen of the Hackney Phalanx, the lay members of which were merchants, financiers, and generally men of affairs below the top political rank (although not without influence with Conservative leaders), realized that some show of readiness to reform was necessary to forestall the Establishment's foes. Their scheme for a Royal Commission of Inquiry in 1831 proved too mild to satisfy anyone but their own supporters. It would have been composed entirely of clergy and would simply suggest 'the best practical remedies for the evils of translations, of unseemly commendams, and offensive pluralities'.[1] Even more cautious and respectful of existing interests were the property-holders of the second rank of the clerical hierarchy, the deans and chapters.[2]

The High Churchmen and capitular conservatives favoured organizational procedures in which the principles of voluntarism, respect for existing ownership, and localism, were predominant. Even Watson's plan for a Royal Commission of Inquiry insisted that the commissioners should all be ecclesiastics, existing rights should be considered sacred, and redistribution voluntary.[3] The capitular conservatives especially were against the mode of distribution proposed by the Ecclesiastical Commission because it disregarded the principle of locality and adopted centralization rather than some system of diocesan or regional synods or boards.[4]

But the rapid accumulation and convergence of factors on both the 'demand side' and the 'supply side' for organizational revolution allowed for no alternative to the Ecclesiastical Commissioners to anyone

> . . . who really tried to see the Church and nation as a whole, not abstractly nor in terms of conventional rhetoric, but in the modern way, with the aid of maps, committees, circular inquiries, and tabulated statistics.[5]

[1] Edward Churton, *Memoir of Joshua Watson*, vol. ii, pp. 3–7.

[2] See the memorials from deans and chapters to the Ecclesiastical Commission, Parliamentary Papers, 1837–8, vol. xxxviii, especially that from the Dean and Chapter of Lincoln.

[3] A. B. Webster, *Joshua Watson*, pp. 85–6.

[4] Best, op.cit., pp. 334–5. This was to be a frequent criticism against subsequent developments in the Church's organization, as will be seen.

[5] Ibid., p. 347.

THE ADVOCATES OF REFORM

It was members of the Evangelical Party who were most zealous in advocating reform.

In many respects their aims were identical with those of the High Church party. But since they knew that they could not trust the reform of abuses to the apathetic conservatism of the High Churchmen, they sought the intervention of the State.[1]

Although the Evangelicals had been suspect by constitutionalists in the Church in the eighteenth century because of their propensity for ecclesiastical irregularity, during the French Revolution and the war years they became firm believers in the Church's function of maintaining social order.[2] Yet the conservative High Churchmen constantly attacked the Evangelicals and excluded them from positions of authority in the Church. The Evangelicals did not hold the high view of the visible Church which was the doctrine of the High Churchmen, and their first loyalty was to the great invisible Church.

Their membership of the latter was by faith and conviction of its truth; but for an Established Church they produced no arguments except those drawn from high-minded expediency.[3]

The Evangelical organ *The Christian Observer* took to advocating reform and attacked the High Church idealization of the country parish.[4] Halévy has suggested that there were close affinities between Benthamite Utilitarianism and Evangelicalism and that one of the fundamental paradoxes of English society was 'the partial junction and combination of these two forces theoretically so hostile'.[5]

Many of the pamphlets and articles written on Church reform by moderate Evangelicals exhibit this combination of Evangelical passion for spiritual efficiency and Utilitarian rationalistic criteria for evaluating it. When they

[1] E. Halévy, *A History of the English People in the Nineteenth Century*, Paperback edn., 1961, vol. iii, pp. 137–8.

[2] Cf. Charles Smyth, *Simeon and Church Order*, pp. 250, 295–7, and *The Christian Observer*, vol. xv, 1816, pp. 443–65.

[3] G. F. A. Best, 'The Evangelicals and the Established Church in the Early Nineteenth Century', in *The Journal of Theological Studies*, vol. x, pt. 1, April 1959, pp. 64–5.

[4] *The Christian Observer*, vol. xv (1816) p. 479.

[5] Halévy, op. cit., vol. i, bk. 3, pp. 586–7.

examined the instrumental side of the Church's organization (as distinct from basic Christian doctrines) they were able to justify such rationalistic criteria by their legitimation of Establishment in terms of expediency.

The Evangelicals could advocate, but they were not in positions of the top rank where they could implement reform.

Leadership in the Church might have been expected to come from the archbishops, but they tended to be neither young and energetic enough to lead, nor administratively able. Charles Manners Sutton (1755–1828), Archbishop of Canterbury since 1805 and until he died aged 73, was grandson of the 3rd Duke of Rutland, and valued his rank, but seems to have provided little leadership, and in administrative affairs 'had a horror of becoming a parliamentary accountant'.[1] He was succeeded in 1828 by William Howley, already aged 62, who held the primacy until 1848, when he died aged 82. He had been tutor to the Prince of Orange at Oxford, and was reserved, conservative, and unwilling to give a lead.[2] The Archbishop of York from 1808 to 1847 was Edward Venables Vernon, sixth son of the 1st Lord Vernon. (In 1831 he assumed the surname of Harcourt, having succeeded to the estates of that family.) His main contribution seems to have been in managing his own diocese.

Howley, who was archbishop in the key period of the early nineteenth-century reform, in his Primary Visitation Charge in 1832 replied to the Church's critics by pointing out that if the present clergy were compared with those of former times and not with those of an ideal model they would be found to be superior, and boasted of 'the increase both in numbers and efficiency of Institutions for pious and charitable purposes under the more immediate patronage of the Church'.[3] It was a typically conservative attitude to defects and reform in Church organization and even ended by echoing Burke and insisting that, 'A system again far short of theoretical perfection may be exquisitely adapted to

[1] M. H. Port, *Six Hundred New Churches*, p. 16.

[2] Webster, op. cit., p. 80, states that until the appointment of A. C. Tait in 1868, Lambeth was not only without a policy, but also the extreme age of the Archbishop often prevented even an energetic opportunism.

[3] Archbishop Howley, *Primary Charge*, p. 8.

the combination of circumstances in this mixed state of things'.[1]

It fell to the outstanding administrator on the Bench of Bishops, Blomfield of London, to collaborate with Peel (and later with the Whig administration) in creating the Ecclesiastical Commission, and subsequently, by his constant attendance and administrative ability, he was to become the chief architect in its development.

Blomfield and Peel differed from the more aristocratic conservatives in Church and State by their lesser attachment to the aristocratic principle of non-accountability. To the aristocratic conservative

> The practical utility of an institution or office, more or less measurable and admitting public accountability, was not so much a bad test in their eyes as no test at all. What was right in principle was right in practice; and what was right in practice *must* be the most 'useful thing going'.[2]

Peel was able to salvage the fortunes of the Conservative Party by his greater sensitivity to the forces which were making for change, and with Blomfield was able to set in hand the equally necessary developments in the Church's organization by way of the Ecclesiastical Commission. In order to accomplish this organizational change in the Church it was necessary to set an empirical goal by which the most efficient means for its attainment could be evaluated by rational–empirical criteria.

Blomfield was clear as to what that empirical goal and its legitimation should be. In a sermon, *On the Uses of an Established Church*, he said:

> The strongest of arguments for an Established Church is this: that it is the only, or at any rate the most efficient, instrument of instructing the people in the doctrines of religion, and of habituating them to its decencies and restraints.[3]

Once the empirical goal of maintaining social order and stability was defined it was possible to legitimate organizational reforms in utilitarian terms:

> It is undoubtedly incumbent upon us to do all in our power to

[1] Ibid., p. 16.
[2] Best, *Temporal Pillars*, p. 183.
[3] G. E. Biber, *Bishop Blomfield and His Times*, p. 149.

render the Established Church efficient in the highest possible degree; and if any changes can be made in the actual distribution of its resources, which would have a clear and unquestionable tendency to increase its usefulness, and which are not inconsistent with the fundamental principles of its polity, we ought surely to carry them into effect, even if it be at the expense of those ornamental parts of the system, which have their uses, and those by no means unimportant; yet not so important as they should be suffered to stand in the way of improvements calculated to enhance and give lustre to the true beauty of the Church—the beauty of its holy usefulness.[1]

Blomfield and the Ecclesiastical Commission have been regarded as 'one of the evidences of Benthamite administrative centralization'.[2] The Commission owed its form as a permanent body more directly to the Commissioners suggested by the 1st Lord Henley (an Evangelical, and he also married Peel's sister) whose very popular *Plan of Church Reform* was first published in 1832 and ran into several editions. It was also influenced by the precedent of the Irish Church Commissioners set up in 1833 on the recommendation of Richard Whately, the Archbishop of Dublin. Nevertheless the Ecclesiastical Commissioners were as much a product of the *Zeitgeist* as the Poor Law Commission, the Committee of Council for Education, and the Board of Health.[3]

REACTION TO THE REFORMS

The new bureaucratic organization with its empirical goals and with norms which sought to maintain a supra-institutional reference and overarching significance by their appeal to contemporary utilitarian values, was bound to suffer at the hands of subsequent movements devoted to reassessment and reassertion of the Church's distinctive transcendental values. The High Church organ, *The British Critic*, sympathetic to reform in 1832, became the advocate

[1] C. J. Blomfield, Bishop of London, *Charge*, 1834, quoted in A. Blomfield, *A Memoir of Charles James Blomfield D.D., Bishop of London*, p. 140.

[2] Brose, op. cit., p. 2.

[3] Best describes the Ecclesiastical Commission in these terms and as 'the manifestation in the ecclesiastical sphere of the general reforming spirit of the age; professional, pious, and (in no precise sense) utilitarian'. Best, op. cit., pp. 399–400.

of 'no compromise' in the hands of the Tractarians and in 1841 condemned Peel (whom Blomfield had singled out as the one man on whom the Church could ultimately depend)[1] because 'from beginning to end his career was one of shifts and expedients'.[2]

Even Blomfield's own biographer, writing in 1857, reflected the success of the Oxford Movement's assertion of the Church's corporate autonomy and transcendental values:

> Bishop Blomfield, the earlier part of whose career coincided with the period of transition through which the relations between the Church and State have reached their present aspect, may indeed stand excused before the tribunal of history, if he continued to rely on the ancient relations between Church and State for some time after they had changed their character, and to cherish the hope that by making a partial surrender of her rights and possessions, and by endeavouring to commend herself to the minds of utilitarian statesmen by her usefulness as an instrument for the maintenance of social order and peace, the Church might so far conciliate the State as to induce a hearty co-operation between them for the same common good. But after the experience of his failure, those to whom the interests of the Church are committed, would be without excuse, if they should continue to look to the action of the Government and the Legislature for measures which shall increase her efficiency.[3]

This judgement on the Ecclesiastical Commission was premature, and it has continued to play an important part as the largest financial agency in the Church's organization. Whilst its constitution has functioned as a symbol of the established status of the Church, it has acquired sufficient autonomy in its functioning to be able to legitimate itself as an integral part of the Church's own organization. At the same time it will be seen to have maintained a degree of independence which prevents the consolidation of a monolithic bureaucracy such as appears in religious bodies which have developed a central organization as part of a movement from sect to denomination. This latent function can best be understood in the context of the constant tension and dialectic between those who canvass different types

[1] A. Blomfield, op. cit., p. 102.
[2] *British Critic*, vol. xxx, July 1841 ,p .59.
[3] Biber, op. cit., p. 414.

of legitimation of the constituent parts of the Church's developing organization, and their relation to actual or potential sectarian, denominational, and *ecclesia* elements in the Church of England.

SOCIOLOGICAL OBSERVATIONS ON THE LOGIC OF REFORM, AND ITS CRITICS

The factors which facilitated the growth of rational-legal bureaucratic organization in the Church of England, and the problems which this presented, if the Church was to maintain its own distinctive values and goals, can be understood by considering Max Weber's distinction between the formal and substantive rationality of economic action:

> A system of economic activity will be called 'formally' rational according to the degree in which the provision for needs, which is essential to every rational economy, is capable of being expressed in numerical, calculable terms, and is so expressed. . . .
>
> On the other hand, the concept of substantive rationality is full of difficulties. It conveys only one element common to all the possible empirical situations; namely, that it is not sufficient to consider only the purely formal fact that calculations are being made on grounds of expediency by the methods which are, among those available, technically the most nearly adequate. In addition, it is necessary to take account of the fact that economic activity is oriented to ultimate ends (*Forderungen*) of some kind, whether they be ethical, political, utilitarian, hedonistic, the attainment of social distinction, of social equality, or of anything else. Substantive rationality cannot be measured in terms of formal calculation alone, but also involves a relation to the absolute values or to the content of the particular given ends to which it is oriented. In principle, there is an indefinite number of possible standards of value which are 'rational' in this sense.[1]

In addition to tracing the advance of formal rationality in the Church's different administrative agencies and the facilitation of this process by the acquisition of statistical data and the accumulation of central funds (to both of which Queen Anne's Bounty and the Ecclesiastical Commission were the chief early contributors), it is also necessary to analyse the substantive rationality of each agency. Such an

[1] Max Weber, op. cit., p. 184.

analysis must take account of the different configurations of ultimate values which prevail in each agency, and the relation of these values to the historical and environmental forces which brought the agency into being and shaped its character. The relation of these values to the policy-makers and administrators in each agency is also significant. The amount of power gained by the full-time administrators will be seen to be of crucial importance in determining the extent to which a bureaucratic form develops in an organization.

The degree of formal rationality possible in an organization is not unrelated to the particular values which are dominant both within the organization and in the contemporary society. Some values are more congruent with formally rational administrative methods than others. Utilitarian ends and values are particularly productive of norms of organizational functioning which can be implemented by formally rational means such as numerical calculability.

Talcott Parsons's discussion of Pareto's criteria of logical action provides some indication of why this should be so. He points out that the ultimate ends of intrinsic means–end chains of reasoning must have an empirical location, because if the end is transcendental it cannot be said that the means employed are inappropriate, but only that there is no criterion for determining, logico-experimentally, whether the means are appropriate or not.[1] Logico-experimental criteria can only be applied on the intermediate, temporal level below that of any point of transcendental reference. In religious organizations, however, especially in those of the church type, extensive accommodation of such intermediate goals and values is always occurring and inviting the charge of 'compromising' with the secular, from dissatisfied groups appealing to transcendental goals and values. The Oxford Movement's attitudes to church organization will be examined as such a group, and the group responsible for creating and developing the Ecclesiastical Commissioners will be examined for their susceptibility to utilitarian goals and values.

In examining the organizational images and metaphors favoured by different church groups and theological parties

[1] Talcott Parsons, *The Structure of Social Action*, p. 256.

it is necessary to be clear about the relation of transcendental ends to means and especially to means–end chains.

> There seem to be two logical possibilities. First, a given transcendental end, like eternal salvation, may be held by the actor to imply one or more ultimate empirical ends as a necessary means to it. . . . (But) the 'theory' cannot be entirely logico-experimental, since one element at least, the transcendental end itself, is not observable even after the action. Hence not only, as in the case of an ultimate empirical end, is the end itself given, but the link between the last empirical link in the means–end chain and the ultimate transcendental end is nonlogical, since a scientifically verifiable theory can establish an intrinsic relation only between entities both of which are observable.[1]

Thus even the setting of a compromise, temporal and empirical goal such as, for example, by the Ecclesiastical Commissioners in strengthening the parochial unit as an agent of social control and stability, although the means for its attainment facilitated the adoption of a formal, rational organization, and could be tested by logico-experimental criteria, the empirical goal itself could not be evaluated in its relation to the transcendental goals by a similar means–end chain of reasoning.

Parsons has suggested a second logical possibility for relating transcendental ends to means:

> Secondly, a transcendental end may be pursued directly without the intervention of an empirical end and an intrinsic means–end chain leading up to it. In so far the means–end relation cannot by definition be intrinsically rational. The question then arises whether it is merely arbitrary or there is a selective standard of the choice of means involved. . . . there is at least one alternative selective standard, what has been called the symbolic. The term the 'symbolic means–end relationship' will be used whenever the relation of means and ends can conveniently be interpreted by the observer as involving a standard of selection of means according to 'symbolic appropriateness', that is, a standard of the order of the relation of symbol and meaning, not of cause and effect.[2]

[1] Talcott Parsons, *The Structure of Social Action*, pp. 257–8.

[2] Ibid. In the present context of considering organizational functioning the distinction between 'symbolic-appropriateness' and logico-experimental criteria is useful for the light which it throws on the particular problems presented by the transcendental goals and values contained in the substantive rationality of religious organizations. It does not ignore the point made by Peter Winch, in his discussion

These two logical possibilities for evaluating the relation between transcendental ends and the means employed by an instrumental agency, both occur in criticisms of organizational forms and procedures in the Church of England. The term 'bureaucratization' (in the derogatory sense) will be shown to have been used at different periods and of different aspects of the Church's organization. It will be seen to compound criticisms of the empirical goals that had been adopted, and also of the incongruity of the organizational form in relation to particular theological ideals about organization.

F. W. Dillistone, in analysing the six main ideal types of organization which have been stressed in the Christian Church, provides an illustration of these two sources of evaluation—the interposed empirical goal and symbolic congruence—as found in the preference of many Christians in modern times for the 'organic' ideal type.

> Thus at a time when there is much dissatisfaction with over-specialization it is natural for men to turn back nostalgically to the middle ages when society seems to have been remarkably integrated and when every section seems to have found its own particular function to fulfil within the life of the unified whole. To these two attractions of a general kind must be added the particular fascination which this view holds for the Christian because of its relation to the New Testament conception of the Body, Divinely originated and sustained, then organic structures and categories must be of peculiar importance to Christian theologians and sociologists.[1]

The present form of the Church of England's organization can be understood and explained only when its history is seen as a process of evolution. In this process instrumental adaptation to changing social circumstances required the acceptance of empirical, temporal goals, which facilitated the

of Pareto, that science and religion each have their own criteria of intelligibility. Cf. Peter Winch, *The Idea of a Social Science*, pp. 95–103. However, it does suggest that a religious symbol cannot be broken down very easily into specifiable, empirical conditions without generating controversy. The reason for this has been given by Paul Tillich: 'Religious symbols are distinguished from others by the fact that they are a representation of that which is unconditionally beyond the conceptual sphere; they point to the ultimate reality implied in the religious act, to that which concerns us ultimately.' (Paul Tillich, 'The Religious Symbol', in F. W. Dillistone (ed.), *Myth and Symbol*, p. 17.)

[1] F. W. Dillistone, *The Structure of the Divine Society*, p. 169.

adoption of bureaucratic structures and their appropriate operational criteria of effective functioning. A dialectical process has constantly been generated, however, by the Church's unrelinquishable commitment to transcendental goals and values.

Critics of the organization have constantly appealed to these transcendental elements and have criticized the inadequacy of both the intermediate goals and the means employed—the former because it falls short of transcendental goals and values and involves a compromise, the latter because they are alien to the ideal types of organization evaluated favourably according to symbolic appropriateness.

On what Boulding calls the 'supply side' of the organizational revolution, the raw materials and devices necessary for organizational development in the general rational-legal bureaucratic direction included the accumulation of statistical data and of central funds. It also required sufficient consensus about an empirical goal to allow those who were in a position to secure adaptation of the Church's structure (those at the top of the Church and State hierarchies) to evaluate the effectiveness of the methods proposed.

It is the relation between these necessary components of a system of budgeting, and their reconciliation with the criteria of symbolic appropriateness which are applied to the transcendental goals and values incorporated in tradition, theology, and ideal types of polity, which will be shown to constitute many of the problems associated with the development of Queen Anne's Bounty, the Ecclesiastical Commissioners, the revived Convocations, diocesan conferences, and Church Assembly and its offices.

The significance of the budgetary process has been described by Weber:

> Where rationality is maximized, its basis for an individual or for a group economically oriented in this way is the 'budget' (*Haushaltsplan*), which states systematically in what way the means which are expected to be used within the unit for an accounting period—needs for utilities or for the means of production—can be covered by the anticipated income.[1]

The development of Queen Anne's Bounty, to a lesser

[1] Max Weber, op. cit., p. 187.

extent, and the creation of the Ecclesiastical Commissioners, to a greater degree, introduced central budgeting into the Church of England's own organization and was based on the application of formally rational calculations with a concomitant increase in the use of numerical methods. But budgeting in substantive rational terms also required discussion of ends and goals—which was a source of conflict between church parties, and required 'political' decisions involving compromise (and hence the need for representative controlling boards and assemblies). At the same time it invited criticism of the methods on ethical, ascetic, or aesthetic grounds.

On all these grounds

> . . . the merely formal calculation in money terms may seem either of quite secondary importance or even as fundamentally evil in itself, quite apart from the consequences of the modern methods of calculation.[1]

Subsequent criticisms of 'bureaucracy' or 'centralization' in the Church of England have stemmed from any one or several of these sources: dissatisfaction with budgetary allocations to different purposes (or interest groups); uneven representation of different groups on boards or assemblies; inadequate control by representative bodies over administrative agencies; failures in communication due to the use of different 'languages' in terms of substantive rationality; and with the use of rational-legal methods in a religious organization.

[1] Ibid., p. 186.

II

THE EARLY NINETEENTH-CENTURY CHURCH PARTIES

ATTITUDES OF THE CHURCH PARTIES TO REFORM

ALTHOUGH the Church of England in the nineteenth century was faced with the necessity of adjusting its organization to meet changing social conditions, its organization was affected, like other religious movements, by that quality of religious ideology—its absoluteness—which made any reforms vulnerable to the charge of undermining the truth which was believed to be embodied in its polity.[1] It was over the relationship between organization and ideology, and their respective contents, that the church parties fought and flourished, to such an extent that the *Westminster Review*, disseminator of the law of progress, pronounced that 'M. Comte's law stands aghast'.[2]

Whatever may have been the consequences of the nation's embroilment in religious party controversy for M. Comte's law during the nineteenth century, it had important consequences for the form of organization which the Church of England developed. The church parties constituted an 'intervening variable' between differentiation and organization in the process described by Glock and Stark:

> It is, of course, evident that organization and differentiation tend to occur together. The more an institution concerned with values is differentiated from other institutions within a society, probably the more complex the society, and likely, the greater strain towards formal organization to increase the institution's power to maintain itself and reach its goals. However, . . . organization and differentiation do not always occur together, and hence can be treated as distinct variables.[3]

The nineteenth century was a period of increasing differentiation of institutions in Britain, so that the organi-

1 Cf. B. R. Wilson (ed.), *Patterns of Sectarianism*, pp. 10–11.

2 *Westminster Review*, January 1851, vol. liv, p. 442.

3 Charles Y. Glock and Rodney Stark, *Religion and Society in Tension*, p. 12.

zation of the Church of England experienced pressures to develop even more explicitly as a discrete institutional unit *vis-à-vis*, for example, political, economic (especially property), and family institutions.[1] Like any other institution, the Church as a social system, if it was to preserve at least a minimum degree of integration, required some consensus over its norms, values, and beliefs.[2] In a situation in which specific institutional norms were increasingly replacing diffuse societal norms, it was inevitable that the Church should seek to reassess her own norms of operation, the character of the values which they embodied, and the belief system necessary to make those values viable and rational.

The first period of church reform was primarily one of reassessment and reform of the norms of operation and the Ecclesiastical Commissioners were the chief instrumental agency charged with implementing those new norms. But institutional reform could not proceed without generating a reappraisal of values, which defined the ends towards which the means were directed, and of the belief system which provided their rationale.

In a period of relative stability, such as the larger part of the eighteenth century had been for the Church of England, there was seldom occasion to question the norms governing the Church's operation (the same norms often served both Church and community, especially at the local level),[3] and so the high degree of consensus over norms, values, and beliefs, inhibited any growth of church parties. The main exception was that of the evangelical movement which led to the Methodist schism, and it was partly the intractability of the norms in this period which precipitated that schism. That the values and beliefs of evangelicalism were not incompatible with allegiance to the Church of England was demonstrated by the Church Evangelicals. It is significant,

[1] Cf. G. E. Biber, *Bishop Blomfield and His Times*, pp. 207 ff., for examples of how this affected the Church of England constitutionally and in matters such as births, marriages and deaths, poor relief, and education.

[2] Because these terms undergo slight changes in meaning in common usage it is not possible to define them in any exclusive sense, but in general it can be said that norms deal with means, values with ends, and beliefs with their rationale. Cf. Glock and Stark, op. cit., p. 173.

[3] Biber, op. cit.; N. J. Figgis, 'William Warburton', in W. E. Collins (ed.), *Typical English Churchmen From Parker to Maurice*, pp. 216 f.

however, that the Evangelicals provided the only organized party at the end of the eighteenth century. But because they were considered suspect in their adherence to the norms of church order, they were distrusted in the Church and excluded from higher offices.[1] Like the Whigs, the Evangelicals adopted the criterion of expediency for legitimating the norms of the Established Church.[2]

It was the looseness of the attachment of Evangelicals to the normative order of the Church, as perceived by the High Churchmen, that reactivated the latter into a party in reaction at the end of the eighteenth century. (The danger was heightened for High Churchmen because they mistakenly grouped the Church Evangelicals with the dangers of radicalism and Dissent.[3]) Tension between Protestant and Catholic elements in the Church had been controlled in the eighteenth century by the stress on tradition to secure some normative consensus.[4] The term 'High Church' had received its meaning just before the Revolution of 1688, and indicated strictness in observing the rules of the Church. The suspected irregularities and enthusiasm of Evangelicals encouraged by reaction the 'stiff quality' in High Churchmen.[5] The High Church stress was potentially stronger when the Tories were in office, and so the long ascendancy of the Tories at the turn of the century allowed the High Church to exercise a strong influence in the affairs of the Church. Their influence can be characterized as being directed towards the integrative functions in the Church, stressing the primacy of the normative order, and prepared, when necessary, to make both goals and values subservient to established procedure. 'Any deviation from the traditional normative pattern appears to them as a threat to the integrity of the total system.'[6]

1 Their response was to proliferate voluntary societies as an organizational device for exerting their influence. See Ford K. Brown, *Fathers of the Victorians*, pp. 4–6.

2 G. F. A. Best, 'The Evangelicals and the Established Church in the Early Nineteenth Century', in *The Journal of Theological Studies*, vol. x, pt. 1, April 1959, pp. 63–78 (esp. pp. 64–5).

3 Charles Smyth, *Simeon and Church Order*, pp. 250, 295–7; also the *Christian Observer*, vol. xv, 1816, pp. 443–65.

4 Owen Chadwick, *The Mind of the Oxford Movement*, p. 15.

5 Ibid., p. 27.

6 Sister Marie Augusta Neal, *Values and Interests in Social Change*, p. 16. Sister

The High Church was not a unified party at the beginning of the nineteenth century. It developed a more active and even mildly reformist wing in the Hackney Phalanx, but the wider High Church spectrum stretched from the successors of the non-jurors to the merely 'orthodox'. In general:

> They belonged to an age when the clergy represented the Church, and the Church the nation, or at least that part of the nation which did not live in towns and was connected with the land.[1]

Such an outlook as they possessed was ill fitted for reforming the normative ordering of the Church to meet the needs of the changing social structure of England. In their eyes established dispositions and property rights were sacred because hallowed through time. When faced with proposals for reform by the Ecclesiastical Commission in the 1830s many High Churchmen considered that such institutional changes and innovations were far worse than the conditions they were intended to deal with. This was strongly felt in the ranks of the capitular conservatives.

> That there are populous benefices with very inadequate endowments, is equally a matter of notoriety and regret . . . but the method proposed for solving this means that the bounty of the founders is *pro tanto* perverted from its original design; one patron enriched at the expense of another; payments made to the church in one place applied to spiritual purposes in another; and property concentrated and converted into money; so rendering it less safe from rapacious usurpation than lands scattered and divided, committed to the immediate guardianship of several unconnected owners.
>
> In the recommendations relative to minor corporations in cathedrals we find a contempt for the rights of property, a defiance of the respect due to the memory of our founders, and an open avowal of indifference

Neal's study of clergy in the Catholic archdiocese of Boston suggested that the way role incumbents respond to pressures to change that which is currently institutionalized is characterized by a general orientation to change or non-change, to values or interests, and according to the individual's primary concern for one or other of four system problems: adaptation, goal attainment, integration, or pattern maintenance. However, the value-interest dichotomy seems to be a misnomer, because the 'interest oriented' are simply those functionaries who are oriented either to the control of the system, or to preservation and reinforcement of the normative structure. For a more highly formalized discussion of these system problems see T. Parsons, *et al.*, *Theories of Society*, vol. i, pp. 38–41.

[1] F. Warre Cornish, *The English Church in the Nineteenth Century*, vol. i, p. 63.

to the constitution of choral establishments, which fill us with unfeigned astonishment and sorrow.[1]

Any deviation from the traditional normative pattern appeared as a threat to the entire system:

> In truth, many of the staunchest Friends of the Establishment have a sort of Religious Respect for whatever is old, and connected with established Habits or preconceived Opinions, and they dread all Changes for this further Reason, that they are aware what Advantages may be taken of them by those whose only object is to destroy.[2]

The existing normative order 'possessed a natural, inalienable, and irrefutable title to deference' in the eyes of conservative churchmen,[3] whilst to debate the merits of the values embodied therein, or to discuss publicly their rationale, would only weaken that system. But, by the 1830s, the Dissenters' attacks on the injustice of the Establishment, as tested by Christian values and beliefs, had become altogether stronger as a result of the statistical evidence produced by critics inside and outside the Church as to the inefficiency of the Church's functioning even in fulfilling the minimum obligations which might justify its establishment. The Church's own accumulating statistics provided ammunition for those critics who were skilled at using such information. To the Utilitarians it provided ample evidence of the Established Church's inefficiency and redundancy.

> The Church of England system is ripe for dissolution. The *service* provided by it is of a bad sort: inefficient with respect to the ends or objects professed to be aimed at by it: efficient with relation to divers effects which, being pernicious, are too flagrantly so to be professed to be aimed at.[4]

Bentham went on to use the statistical evidence which the Church did possess (Non-Residence Returns) to show how its very lack of other statistics was a sign of the Church's inutility for the State:

[1] Memorial from the Dean and Chapter of Lincoln, January 1837, to the Commission on the State of the Established Church, in *Parliamentary Papers*, 1837–38, vol. xxxviii. Cf. the memorials from Lichfield and Winchester.

[2] Letter of Lord Liverpool to Bishop Tomline, 24 January 1821, Brit. Mus. Add. MSS. 38289, fols. 45 ff., quoted in Best, *Temporal Pillars*, p. 177.

[3] Best, op. cit., p. 172.

[4] Jeremy Bentham, *Church-of-Englandism and Its Catechism Examined*, pp. 198–9.

> Necessary to the performance of duty in this line is the possession of a corresponding stock of information in that line of appropriate science, which may be termed *Pastoral Statistics*. . . . Inherent in the constitution of the Church of England may be seen to be the branch of ignorance correspondent and opposite to this science: call it anti-pastoral ignorance.[1]

There followed a Benthamite eulogy on the happy position of the Church of Scotland, which had the statistical information provided by Sir John Sinclair. The Utilitarian criticisms were put into popular form by John Wade in his *Extraordinary Black Book* and the available statistics used (or misused) to condemn both the Church's inefficiency and the injustice of its operations.

The conservative churchmen's mental image of the Church's organization related to the rural parish, which was part of the very fabric of traditional English social structure. Tradition provided whatever legitimation was required, although in the previous period of relative stability it was seldom considered necessary to theorize about its ideological basis. If necessary, theological legitimation could always be provided by reference to Richard Hooker's theory of the union of Church and State, set out in his *Of the Laws of Ecclesiastical Polity*.[2] But events had been steadily rendering that theory difficult to maintain. The presence of Dissenters had been tolerated as a deviation from the theory that was not too severe a threat to its continued persuasiveness, provided they remained few in number. Industrialization, however, brought a growth of towns and an expanding middle class which were fertile ground for the rapid spread of Dissent. Whilst the sects could be founded on new norms of procedure more appropriate to the times, and the older denominations were relatively free to adapt their norms, the Church of England was entangled with statutes, and her clergy with civic functions, which limited her freedom of action and yet were an intrinsic part of that system which conservative churchmen considered inviolate.

Those High Churchmen who were conservative and yet active could seek to reactivate the traditional norms of

1 Ibid., pp. 216–17.
2 8th Book, posthumously published 1648.

operation, and to do this they needed to attract aid from the Government. To some of them it seemed only necessary to appeal to tradition and obligation to persuade the Government to act generously. Both the Church Building Commissioners and Queen Anne's Bounty benefited from government grants up to the 1820s.[1] The admission of Dissenters to the House of Commons as of right, after the repeal of the Test Act in 1828, undermined the theoretical legitimation of state aid to the Church on the basis of Hooker's union of Church and State. Churchmen active in political circles realized that more attention would have to be paid to wooing public opinion.

Lord Henley justified his influential *Plan of Church Reform* not by appealing to law and privilege as the grounds on which the Church position rested. Rather, the Church must depend on

> . . . the habits and affections of the people, strengthened and confirmed by her own growing desire to work out her purity and efficiency and by her faithfulness in the discharge of the great trust which is committed to her hands.[2]

To those conservatives who refused to acknowledge the increasing power of public opinion, the only recourse was to fall back on the aristocratic principle of non-accountability and the view that church property was private property. But this attitude was difficult to maintain in conjunction with an effort to secure the continuance of the State's help in maintaining the Church's pre-eminence over other religious bodies.

A famous theoretical justification for maintaining this pre-eminence had been produced in the eighteenth century by William Warburton in *The Alliance Between Church and State: Or, The Necessity and Equity of an Established Religion and a Test Law Demonstrated in Three Books*. Warburton argued that to raise man from his Hobbesian state of nature it was necessary for the State to enter into alliance with a religious body which could act as the moral instructor of the people. The ensuing benefits would be found mainly in

[1] Biber, op. cit., pp. 165–6.

[2] Lord Henley, *A Plan of Church Reform*, 4th edn., p. 53.

the preservation of order and stability in society. It differed from Hooker's theory in emphasizing that Church and State were two independent, sovereign bodies, which voluntarily entered into alliance for their mutual benefit. Despite the breach in the theory caused by the repeal of the Test Act, it could still justify the Church receiving favoured treatment from the State provided the Church recognized that in this exchange it must set as its dominant goal the rendering of some service which public opinion valued. 'Utility' was the value most prized by the middle classes. Warburton's theory equated utility with truth and so provided some kind of religious rationale for its use as a criterion for evaluating the Church's functioning.

> That Truth is *productive* of Utility, appears from the Nature of the Thing. Observing Truth, is acting as Things really are: He who acts as Things really are, must gain his End; all Disappointment proceeding from true or false Principles, the Conclusion that follows must be necessarily right or wrong. But gaining the End of acting is Utility or Happiness; Disappointment of the End, Hurt or Misery. If then Truth produces Utility, the other Part of the Proposition, that Utility *indicates* Truth, follows necessarily.[1]

Of the more active High Churchmen, excluding those charged with episcopal authority, the Hackney Phalanx were somewhat more in touch with the world of commerce and political affairs where such criteria were in the ascendant.

> They all shared a common outlook in a remarkable way: they were all High Church, they were all Tories, they were all middle-class, they co-operated in the same humanitarian and charitable projects and in the same business projects as well, they read the same devotional books, and they owned a serious and influential periodical, the *British Critic*, in which to publish their views.[2]

The group had already, before the crisis of the 1830s, played an important part in the church extension and church education movements. They were moderate conservatives —welcoming new initiatives but fearing innovations. On the proposals of the Ecclesiastical Commission they tended to take a middle line between the extremes (although their

[1] Ibid., pp. 92–3.

[2] A. B. Webster, *Joshua Watson, The Story of a Layman 1771–1855*, p. 18.

caution would probably have rendered their objectives unattainable). They desired the objectives of a more equal distribution and a more complete circulation of the ministrations of the Church throughout the country, but agreed with the more conservative High Churchmen that there was a danger 'of ultimately centralizing in the metropolis the whole power and jurisdiction of the Ecclesiastical Establishment.'[1]

Thus the moderate conservatives could go some way towards accepting the utility principle as a legitimation for the goal of an Established Church,[2] but they were too attached to the traditional normative order of that Church to employ the same criterion in reforming the system by innovation. The *British Critic* proclaimed that it was 'little disposed to go in quest of novelties' and placed its main hope 'in the judicious combination of existing principles and agencies'.[3] The even more conservative *British Magazine*, founded and edited by the High Churchman Hugh James Rose, devoted itself to opposing church reform and alluded unfavourably to the *British Critic* for its sympathy towards reformers.[4]

But if the outstanding man of the Hackney Phalanx, Joshua Watson, deserved the description of being 'more at home on a committee than on a crusade', and at a time when 'it was committees which were needed',[5] so too did his fellow supporter of the established normative order Rose. They both wished to revive the established normative order so as to prevent it being over-turned by state interference, but at the same time they were orientated towards preserving integration and stability in the Church. In contrast, the Oxford Movement's leaders were more oriented towards reviving latent traditional values and beliefs of the Church and to restoring whatever patterns had implemented the expression of those in the Church's period of greatest strength—which to them was the Middle Ages.[6] They were not

[1] *British Critic*, vol. xxi, no. xlii, 1837, p. 514.

[2] Ibid., vol. xxii, no. xliii, 1837, p. 251.

[3] Ibid., no. xliv, 1837, p. 487.

[4] W. L. Mathieson, *English Church Reform 1815–1840*, p. 81.

[5] Webster, op. cit., p. 31.

[6] H. J. Laski, *Studies in the Problem of Sovereignty*, pp. 74–5.

'London men' nor men involved in business and national politics, and their major experience was concentrated within the ecclesiastical system. Their emphasis was not on the articulation of the church system with society, but on the articulation of the system with the supernatural which acted through the system.

Newman regarded Hurrell Froude as, like himself, committed to asserting first principles irrespective of their consequences, unlike Rose and the High Churchmen:

> . . . Froude had that strong hold of first principles and that keen perception of their value, that he was comparatively indifferent to the revolutionary action which would attend on their application to a given state of things; whereas in the thoughts of Rose as a practical man, existing facts had the precedence of every other idea, and the chief test of the soundness of a line of policy lay in the consideration of whether it would work.[1]

Likewise his description of William Palmer, as lacking in depth, and, in effect, incapable of abandoning himself to a charismatic movement, which was what the Oxford Movement was during Newman's time:

> . . . coming from a distance, he never had really grown into an Oxford man, nor was he generally received as such; nor had he any insight into the force of personal influence and congeniality of thought in carrying out a religious theory,—a condition which Froude and I considered essential to any true success in the stand which had to be made against Liberalism. Mr. Palmer had a certain connexion, as it may be called, in the Establishment, consisting of high Church dignitaries, Archdeacons, London Rectors, and the like, who belonged to what was commonly called the high-and-dry school. They were far more opposed than even he was to the irresponsible action of individuals. Of course their *beau idéal* in ecclesiastical action was a board of safe, sound, sensible men. Mr. Palmer was their organ and representative; and he wished for a committee, an Association, with rules and meetings, to protect the interests of the Church in its existing peril.[2]

Warburton's theory of the Alliance had been oriented towards the articulation of the systems of Church and State, in which exchange the principle of 'the greatest utility' was

[1] J. H. Newman, *Apologia Pro Vita Sua*, p. 106.
[2] Ibid., pp. 108–9.

the best criterion for producing 'Truth'. For Warburton this orientation was what preserved an Established Church from falling into the errors of sectarianism or religious autonomy, in which religious values were formulated solely with reference to the supernatural or transcendental criteria, unhindered by the necessity for translating them into intermediate temporal goals:

> Let us then consider the Danger Religion runs, of deviating from Truth, when left in its natural State, to itself. In those circumstances, the men of highest Credit are such as are famed for greatest Sanctity. This Sanctity hath been generally understood to be then most perfect when most estranged from the World, and all its Habitudes and Relations. But this being only to be acquired by Secession or Retirement from human affairs; and that Secession rendering Man ignorant of Civil Society, and of its Rights and Interests; in Place of which will succeed according to his natural Temper, the destructive Follies either of Superstition or Fanaticism; we must needs conclude that Religion, under such Directors and Reformers, and God knows these are generally its Lot, will deviate from Truth, and consequently from a Capacity, in proportion, of serving Civil Society.[1]

Unlike a sect, an Established Church was ill fitted and unused to legitimating its norms of organization by immediate reference to theological principles. The skeleton of its structure could no doubt be related to a theological belief system, but its actual system of organization and administration could only be legitimated either by reference to tradition, or to a rational criterion such as social utility. The conservatives had tried to take their stand on tradition, but it could not appease a public opinion which was mobilized in new urban areas and among groups which did not share that tradition. Men of affairs, who to different degrees were concerned about the relation of the Church to the wider society, could not ignore public opinion, and so adopted the criteria provided by the utility principle. This was the position of Bishop Blomfield and Robert Peel, the chief architects of those reforms which gave the Church a new centralized administrative agency in the Ecclesiastical Commissioners.[2]

Even a High Churchman like Gladstone could not escape

[1] Warburton, op. cit., pp. 93–4.

[2] Best, op. cit., pp. 175–6.

the suspicion of a moderate Tractarian such as Keble that he was concerned with the Church's temporal goals and the use of utilitarian criteria to evaluate the means for their attainment. Keble reviewed Gladstone's *The State in its Relations with the Church*, in the *British Critic* (after it had been taken over by the Oxford Movement), and warned:

> . . . it seems to us not obscure, that the conservative tendencies of the very best public men require to be watched, in this matter of the conditions of an establishment, by persons more exclusively concerned with the spiritual integrity of the Church.
>
> We observe, what greatly confirms us in this idea, that even the high-minded writer before us has not been quite able to keep his language clear of a certain utilitarian tone: we mean not utilitarian in any low or offensive sense, but simply as devoting somewhat too much of regard to intelligible and visible results in our estimate of a system, the purposes whereof we are confessedly so very ignorant of. . . .
>
> Now the life of a statesman must of necessity be spent very much in calculations of expediency, and in measuring things by their visible results: and the habit of thought so generated may sometimes be unfavourable to that particular exercise of faith, the necessity of which in all church questions we have now tried to point out. . . .[1]

Keble went on to suggest that the separation of Church and State had virtually taken place, but that Gladstone, because of his position, was reluctant to admit it. If, as Keble believed at that time, and Newman and Froude would have asserted all the more forcefully, temporal goals or purposes of the church system were elusive of definition, and the alliance of Church and State was dissolving, then they were justified in adopting as their criteria for the Church's normative structure purely autonomous criteria close to first principles. It was this assertion of autonomous values that gave the Oxford Movement during its charismatic phase under Newman's leadership, a quasi-sectarian character in the eyes of church leaders.[2]

[1] *British Critic*, vol. xxxvi, no. lii, 1839, pp. 369–70.

[2] Gladstone wrote to Manning, 5 April 1835: 'I think with you that if, in contemplating the state and destinies of the Church, we set out from that point of view which has reference to what we may call her sectarian interests, it is impossible to avoid lamenting her connection with the State, which in greatly enlarging the extent must also materially diminish the purity of her communion. But I find from more considerations than one a more than countervailing weight of reason and utility which induces me to banish this thought of discontent almost as soon as it

The Oxford Movement had little interest in a State which had become secularized. Thus Dr. Pusey wrote to Gladstone in 1849:

> What the State is to do when it casts off the guidance of the Church, and is to act upon some heathen principle, I know not what; some abstraction or ideal of its own, and to have education theories, etc., of its own, is no concern of mine.[1]

Later in the century developments in the Catholic party in the Church of England were to give a new interest in working out a *modus vivendi* for an Established Church in which the heirs of the Oxford Movement had developed a new social concern the principles of which they could not escape applying to the Church's own norms and values. In particular, they were to realize that true catholicity required the restoration and involvement of the working classes in the Church's government. Even the *Tracts for the Times* did not reject the established status of the Church, but they did reject the test of utility. 'It is this idea of a Church as a *societas perfecta*, founded upon a definite and statutable creed, which so clearly lies at the basis of the Tractarian antagonism to the State.'[2]

Gladstone valued the Establishment more than the Tractarians, and wrote in order to vindicate its norms, 'but he did so just at a time when it was ceasing to be possible to continue the realization of those norms as they had been established in England'.[3] Although he came to see that it was impossible to maintain a perfect union of Church and State, he was more positive than the Oxford Movement in seeking to preserve as much of it as possible. He wrote to Newman:

> My language has always been, 'Here is the genuine and proper theory of government as to religion; hold it as long as you can, and as far as you can.' Government must subsist; and if not as (in strictness) it ought, then as it may.[4]

has been tangibly entertained.' Quoted in D. C. Lathbury, *Correspondence on Church and Religion of William Ewart Gladstone*, vol. i, p. 23.

1 In H. P. Liddon, *Life of Edward Bouverie Pusey*, vol. iii, p. 184.

2 H. J. Laski, op. cit., p. 87.

3 A. R. Vidler, *The Orb and the Cross*, p. 137.

4 Lathbury, op. cit., vol. i, p. 72.

Gladstone was concerned with the co-existence of Church and State to the extent that he wished to legitimate the Church's norms according to principles which would be not just autonomous religious values and beliefs, but would also overarch the different systems. He agreed with Warburton's recognition of Church and State as distinct and separate societies, but Gladstone could not accept that civil government was concerned only with the body and property; he wished, unlike Warburton, to base the adoption of a national Church not just on public utility, but on the State's capacity for acknowledging truth. The theory which he used to justify this was based on the notion of the moral personality of groups, and so of the State's ability and duty to recognize and pursue truth.

But many of the 'instrumentalists' in the Church, who supported the Establishment and had the responsibility for its functioning, were more likely to defend its norms on traditional or utilitarian grounds than on theoretical speculation. Thus Lord Selborne in his *A Defence of the Church of England Against Disestablishment*, referring to Gladstone's theory, wrote:

> I do not, and cannot, take my stand on any mystical view such, e.g., as that the State is 'a person', with a corporate conscience, 'cognisant of matter of religion'.[1]

The process of institutional differentiation, which began to make itself felt most acutely for the Church of England in the third decade of the nineteenth century, resulted most immediately in reform of the normative structure of the Church. But its effects on the values and beliefs of the Church as they rationalized and legitimated that organization, were increasingly felt. The bishops, and those lay churchmen who held high political office, had to defend the Established Church against the charge that it had no utility. The Utilitarian James Mill applied the criterion of social utility to its revenues, as did the Dissenter M.P., Faithfull, who found 'that the Church, as by law established, is not recommended by practical utility'.[2]

[1] Lord Selborne, *A Defence of the Church of England Against Disestablishment*, 1886, p. 72.

[2] *Hansard*, New Series, vol. xxiv, p. 802; and vol. xvii, 1833, p. 178.

Bishop Blomfield who, like Peel, was a son of the middle classes and not of the aristocracy, could not fall back on the aristocratic principle of non-accountability, and so his defence appealed to the dominant values of the Church's middle-class opponents. Peel also spoke in his Tamworth Manifesto of his desire

> . . . to remove every abuse that can impair the efficiency of the Establishment, to extend the sphere of its usefulness, and to strengthen and confirm its just claims upon the respect and affections of the people.[1]

He and Blomfield became so closely united in their church reform that a contemporary dubbed Blomfield 'an ecclesiastical Peel'.[2]

It was their agency, the Ecclesiastical Commission, which had the practical task of making the instrumental changes in the Church's organization. The process of institutional differentiation provided the pressure for a development of more formal organization in order for the institution to maintain itself and to attain its goals. But the nature of the subsequent organization depended on the possible definitions of its essential character as an institution, and of its goals. The process of differentiation, and the possible responses towards increasing autonomy can be observed in other cases parallel to that of the Church of England. H. J. Laski drew attention to the striking parallel between the Oxford Movement and the Disruption of 1843 in the Established Church of Scotland:

> That of Oxford, in the narrower sense, begins in 1833 and ends with the conversion of Newman in 1845; that of which Chalmers was the distinguished leader begins in 1834 with the abolition by the General Assembly of lay patronage, and ends in 1843 with the secession of those who refuse to accept what they term an invasion of their peculiar province by the State. In each case, as was well enough admitted by contemporaries, the attempt was made—and in the case particularly of Presbyterianism, this lay at the very root of its theory—to work out a doctrine of the Church which, neglecting the State, gave the Church the general organization of a perfect society.[3]

1 Quoted in Best, op. cit., p. 297.

2 A. Blomfield, *A Memoir of Charles James Blomfield*, 2nd edn., 1864, p. 219; also P. J. Welch, 'Blomfield and Peel: A Study in Co-operation between Church and State, 1841–1846', in *Journal of Ecclesiastical History*, vol. xii, 1961, p. 74.

3 Laski, op. cit., pp. 112–13.

In trying to define the autonomous identity of the Church, Newman had to assert its exclusiveness—and to do this was to adopt a sectarian principle which threatened the traditional character of the Church of England as a national Church. For Chalmers, in the Church of Scotland, the result was the formation of a new sect, whilst for Newman and his fellow secessionists it meant joining an already existing body (the Roman Catholic Church), and for the remaining Anglo-Catholics it involved some compromise. Contemporaneous parallels with the Disruption and the Oxford Movement on the continent of Europe, suggest that adjustment to the process of institutional differentiation causes conflict in religious bodies over the degree to which a substantive rationality based on autonomous principles should be adopted.

Whether the result was the setting up of a new sect by the advocates of autonomous principles, or else a compromise solution, was influenced by the type of theological system, and the extent to which its main principles prescribed the normative structure of the organization. The secession from the Dutch National Church led by Dr. Abraham Kuyper in 1839, and that from the State Church of Geneva under the leadership of Merle D'Aubigne in 1849, were the result of movements devoted to the restoration of autonomous, or pure, religious principles in established Churches. These movements, like that in Scotland, took place in countries with Calvinist Established Churches. In Lutheranism and Anglicanism there was less sympathy towards *Freikirchentum*.[1]

The doctrine of the Church of England did not clearly prescribe the normative structure of the Church's organization. The pressing necessity for the Church of England to adapt to changing conditions recommended a process of rationalization—but what was at issue was the type of rationality on which this should be based. William Palmer described the problem as perceived by the Tractarians: there was

> . . . no principle in the public mind to which we could appeal; an utter ignorance of all rational grounds of attachment to the Church; an

[1] J. H. S. Burleigh, *A Church History of Scotland*, p. 353.

oblivion of its spiritual character as an institution not of man but of God; the grossest Erastianism most widely prevalent especially among all classes of politicians.[1]

Newman, above all, perceived that it was the source of the legitimation of authority in the Church that was at issue. He therefore addressed his Tracts primarily to the clergy. The first Tract, *Thoughts on The Ministerial Commission*, set the question out plainly: 'On what are we to rest our authority when the State deserts us?' The answer was equally clear: 'OUR APOSTOLICAL DESCENT . . . APOSTOLICAL SUCCESSION.'

They have been deluded into a notion that present palpable usefulness, produceable results, acceptableness to your flocks, that these and such like are the tests of your Divine Commission. Enlighten them in this matter . . . magnify your office.[2]

The application of this sole principle of legitimation would have given the Church of England a charismatic bureaucracy which would have been very different from the organization which developed between the formation of the Ecclesiastical Commissioners and the creation of the Church Assembly, with its complicated balance of powers and mixed sources of authority. Those bishops and prominent laymen who had to undertake most of the reforms will be seen to have pursued a policy of which pragmatism and expediency were unavoidable ingredients by virtue of that very quality of heterogeneity which gave the Established Church its necessary breadth (and ambiguity). The *ad hoc* character of the nineteenth-century Church reforms was a consequence of this.

In the first half of the nineteenth century, however, the Oxford Movement reduced the issue to one of choosing between two sources of legitimacy for the authority of the Church. Tract 1 exhorted the clergy: 'Choose your side'. Tract 3 informed them:

In a day like this there are but two sides, zeal and persecution, the Church and the world; and those who attempt to occupy the ground between them at best will lose their labour, but probably will be drawn back to the latter. . . . Speculations about ecclesiastical improvements

[1] W. Palmer, *A Narrative of Events*, 1883 edn., pp. 99 f.
[2] *Tracts for the Times*, vol. i, Tract 1, pp. 2–4.

which might be innocent at other times, have a strength of mischief now.[1]

Tract 4, by Keble, was entitled *Adherence to the Apostolical Succession The Safest Course.*

A comprehensive solution which sought to gather together instrumental reforms under one agency and at the same time preserve the integrity of the Church's values by creating a centre of authority which would satisfy both Church and State was impossible to arrive at in the circumstances. An attempted solution along the same lines as that essayed in the formation of the Church Assembly seems to have been offered by the Chancellor of Bangor, John Warren, in 1837. He considered the alternatives of a commission, such as that suggested by Archbishop Whately, and the revival of Convocation, which had been suggested at different times and was subsequently taken up by High Churchmen. The first he considered unsuitable because it would be under the influence of Parliament, and the second he rejected on the grounds that it would place the whole power of legislating for the Church in the hands of the clergy. Warren saw the tendency in these two schools to devote themselves either to the much-needed instrumental reforms or to reasserting the Church's own values and autonomous authority:

> But in order to preserve the purity of our Church, and at the same time to give it energy and efficiency, it appears to be desirable that the management of its internal affairs should be placed in the hands of a synod, composed partly of clergy and partly of laity, but entirely members of our own communion.[2]

The solution ignored the favourite source of legitimation of conservative High Churchmen—tradition, and the *British Critic* reviewer rejected it on those grounds.[3]

What was needed was a shared symbolism in relation to church polity which would sanction instrumental adaptation, and also cohere the different value emphases of the church parties. But when it came to testing a proposed

[1] Ibid., Tract 3, *Thoughts on Alterations In the Liturgy*, pp. 4–5.

[2] John Warren, *An Address to Members of the Church of England; both Lay and Clerical on the Necessity of Placing the Government of the Church in the hands of Members of its Own Communion*, 1837, pp. 17–20.

[3] *British Critic*, vol. xxii, no. xliv, 1837, pp. 474–93 (p. 487).

system by reference to its symbolic-appropriateness, the symbols employed by the different parties reflected their concern for different system problems (such as coexistence with the State to preserve the Establishment, or restoration of autonomous principles), and diverse evaluations were produced. Hooker's symbolism of the corporate unity and identity of Church and State might satisfy those who saw the Church only in its local and rural aspect, where less had happened to disrupt the unity of the structure; but for those concerned for the towns and national affairs, the former relations between Church and State could not be taken for granted. Warburton's symbol of an 'Alliance' consciously or unconsciously informed the thinking of many in the latter group. It had the advantage that it could legitimate the Establishment status of the Church, and, at the same time, legitimate the popular 'Utility' principle which allowed for flexibility and rationalization in adapting the organization. The Oxford Movement, however, emphasized principles which could not be so symbolized. It has been described as a part of that larger movement in which 'Romanticism was rising up against utilitarianism'.[1]

Coleridge, another herald of that wider movement, drew a distinction between the national Church and the universal, supernatural Christian Church, but left in obscurity the connection between the English branch of the universal Church and the actual hierarchic national Church. The Oxford Movement, in their concern to assert the supernatural qualities and transcendental principles embodied in the Church, ignored Coleridge's double characterization, so that for them the English Church in its hierarchy and its priesthood was, without reservation and limitations, the English branch of the universal, supernatural Church. Thus every attack on the external order of the Anglican Church became a kind of sacrilege.[2] It was because reform of the Church involved action by the State that the Oxford Movement saw it as a denial of the autonomous principles of the Church,

[1] Eugene Stock, *The History of the Church Missionary Society*, vol. i, p. 286.

[2] S. T. Coleridge, *On the Constitution of Church and State according to the Idea of Each*, 1830; also Yngve Brilioth, *The Anglican Revival: Studies in the Oxford Movement*, pp. 64–8.

and the attack on its external order as disregard for the indissoluble connection and proximity, between the supernatural order and its embodiment in the institutionalized Church.

The confrontation which developed between the church parties was a 'clash of symbols' that was to frustrate for the rest of the century any comprehensive church reform based on a consensus of views on means, ends, and values in the Church. The same High Church reviewer who had rejected John Warren's plan for a mixed legislative assembly for the Church, on the ground that novelties were distasteful to High Churchmen, could nevertheless deplore the growing partisanship and opposition of single principles.[1] But nothing deterred Newman from leading a movement to fight the rationalistic pragmatism of the new middle class, under the banner of the Church as the embodiment of transcendental values and supernatural qualities.[2]

Under Newman's leadership the Oxford Movement had the character of a value-oriented movement—'a collective attempt to restore, protect, modify or create values in the name of a generalized belief'.[3] Its generalized belief was that liberalism was the insidious enemy which was threatening to destroy the Church (especially through Government interference in the Church), and that the relativistic view of truth which liberalism promoted could only be defeated by asserting the supernatural authority of the Church, conveyed to its priests and bishops through Apostolical Succession. As a value-oriented collective movement, it represented a 'compressed' way of attacking the problems causing strain in the Church; it paid little attention to working for the implementation of specific reforms on the appropriate levels at which the strains were being experienced. It believed that the acceptance of its generalized belief would itself solve many of the problems.

Newman himself seems to have realized the shortcomings

1 *British Critic*, vol. xxii, no. xliv, 1837, p. 487.

2 Cf. H. W. Fulweiler, 'Tractarians and Philistines: The Tracts for the Times Versus Victorian Middle Class Values', in *Church History* (the Historical Magazine of the Protestant Episcopal Church of America), vol. xxxi, March 1962, no. 1, pp. 36–53.

3 Neil J. Smelser, *Theory of Collective Behaviour*, p. 313.

of such a movement and he confessed them in a letter to the Bishop of Oxford:

> There has been another, and more serious peculiarity in the line of discussion adopted in the Tracts, which, whatever its merits or demerits, has led to their being charged, I earnestly hope groundlessly, with wanton innovation on things established. I mean the circumstance that they have attempted to defend our Ecclesiastical system upon almost first principles. The immediate argument for acquiescing in what is established is that it *is* established: but when what has been established is in course of alteration (and this evil was partly realized and feared still more, eight years since) the argument ceases, and then one is driven to considerations which are less safe because less investigated, which it is impossible at once to survey in all their bearings, or to have confidence in, that will not do a disservice to the cause we are defending as well as a benefit. It seemed safe at the period in question, when the immediate and usual arguments failed, to recur to those which were used by our divines in the seventeenth century, and by those most esteemed in the century which followed, and down to this day. But every existing establishment, whatever be its nature, is a *fact*, a thing *sui simile*, which cannot be resolved into any one principle, nor can be defended and built up upon one idea. Its position is the result of a long history, which has moulded it, and stationed it, in the form and place which characterize it. It has grown into what it is by the influence of a number of concurrent causes in time past, and in consequence no one first principle can be urged in its defence, but what in some respect or measure may also possibly be urged against it. This applies, I conceive, as to all social institutions so as to the case of our religious establishment and system at this day. It is a matter of extreme difficulty and delicacy, to say the least, so to defend them in an argumentative discussion in one respect as not to tend to unsettle them in another. And all but minds of the greatest powers, or even genius, will find nothing left to them, if they do not attempt it, but to strike a balance between gain and loss, and to attempt to do the most good on the whole.[1]

It was precisely because the Oxford Movement brought into opposition single principles that it lost those High Church supporters who at first looked to it to stabilize the Church in a period of unsettlement. After Newman's secession the movement gradually became more institu-

[1] J. H. Newman, 'A Letter to the Rt. Rev. Father in God Richard, Lord Bishop of Oxford, On Occasion of No. 90 in the Series called The Tracts for the Times', 29 March 1841, in *Tracts for the Times*, vol. vi, pp. 11–13.

tionalized and adopted the system of committees with rules and meetings with which Newman had little patience. In 1860 a national organization was formed, the English Church Union. Much of its energy was taken up with defending its members against prosecutions for ritualism and in carrying on the defence against liberalism.

The Oxford Movement's contribution to the Church followed from its character as a value-oriented movement: it prepared the Church of England for a necessary development of corporate self-consciousness and self-evaluation which were essential if it was to function in its changing position in society. The aggressive strategy of the movement of opposing single principles on the level of generalized beliefs, disqualified it from making immediate contributions to instrumental reforms, whilst at the same time it fermented party strife and intensified the strains experienced by the Church as it adapted to social change. The party itself began to split up as it became more institutionalized, until a severe split occurred between those older leaders who reacted towards conservatism, and the *Lux Mundi* group of the 1880s, who began to assimilate liberalism and engage in the task of further instrumental reform in the Church.[1]

Instrumental reforms in the organization of the Church tended to lack a general theory to legitimate them which did not appear to involve merely a rationalization based on the principle of expediency. In practice, if the Church was to maintain its Established status there had to be a certain element of expediency in all its reforms; but the effect of the value-oriented Oxford Movement was to expose the Church's lack of any self-governing power which could initiate policies, rather than have policies forced on the Church. The Ecclesiastical Commission had been intended by those whose concern was with material church reform as a permanent executive board, which would make good this lack, without running the risk of exacerbating church divisions which the proposed revival of Convocation might entail. The Ecclesiastical Commissioners, however, were

[1] Cf. W. R. Ward, 'Oxford and the Origins of Liberal Catholicism in the Church of England', in C. W. Dugmore and C. Duggan (eds.), *Studies in Church History*, vol. i, 1964, pp. 233–52.

denied the necessary authority to develop rapidly into a powerful executive. To the High Churchmen, and conservatives in general, their norms forfeited traditional legitimation by ignoring the principles of localism, voluntaryism, and the sacredness of property rights. To those who inclined toward the Oxford Movement's stand for autonomous religious principles as the legitimation of authority, the norms of the Ecclesiastical Commissioners appeared to be based too much on expediency.[1] This is not surprising in view of the major concern of those responsible for the actual reforms to improve the efficiency of the church system as it articulated with that of the State. In general the reforms were pragmatic and not ideological. As Blomfield pointed out:

> Many and powerful are the arguments by which we may prove our right to the attention and respect of individual Christians and our claims upon the support and protection of the State. But they will fail to produce conviction in the minds of the greater part of mankind, if unaccompanied by the more conclusive proof of *usefulness*. In spite of all the reasons which are to be urged in behalf of our excellent Church, —the purity of her doctrines; the wisdom of her discipline; her legitimate authority; the unbroken succession and right ordination of her ministry; the excellence of her constitution and formularies:—yet if there be a failure in activity and zeal on the part of the clergy, the Establishment must sink beneath them. But it will never cease to be respected and maintained, while it is *useful*. . . .[2]

On the whole, the bishops and laymen who led the Church during this crisis were empiricists who acted within the context of each situation, and who accepted the ambiguity of a National Church in a pluralist society. But what was

[1] G. F. A. Best, 'The Constitutional Revolution 1828–32 And Its Consequences for the Established Church', in *Theology*, vol. lxiii, no. 468 (June 1959), pp. 226–34 (pp. 228–9).

[2] Biber, op. cit., p. 60. In contrast Pusey, in opposing the Ecclesiastical Commission's proposals for cathedrals, stated, 'We have, in this statement, purposely confined ourselves to the one main principle of the *sacredness* of foundations; the arguments, from their utility or necessity, have never been answered; but we do not wish to defend them on these grounds. This would be to appeal to the judgement of man, as though, if he thought them useful, they were to be retained, if he on the scant measure of the present day, thought otherwise, to be destroyed. We do not take men as arbiters, we appeal to One higher than they. The question of utility is not open; . . . we do not wish our cathedrals to be left on grounds of utilitarianism; but we claim them on grounds of eternal justice. . . .' *British Critic*, 1838, vol. xxiii, pp. 561–2.

needed in the long term was a theory which could reconcile expediency in adapting the norms (the concern of the reformers) with legitimation in terms of religious principles (the emphasis of the Oxford Movement). Legitimation on the grounds of expediency alone was too Whiggish to be acceptable for long in the Church, and it carried with it doubts as to the future stability of the Church–State relationship, as the Whig idea of the Church was that of 'a sect raised to the eminence of an establishment by the favour (and self-interest) of the State'.[1]

Macaulay rejected Gladstone's attempt to provide a theory of Church and State on the Whig grounds that: 'We consider the primary end of government as a purely temporal end, the protection of the persons and property of men.'[2] For the Whigs:

> The great difference as they saw the matter, between the state and any church was, that while there was no doubt about the ends and operations of a state, there was much doubt as to the ends and operations of a church.[3]

Although the Evangelicals' social concern made them responsible, along with the Utilitarians, for forcing the Whigs into the role of 'improvising architects of that most rambling of structures the Victorian administrative state', they had no definite political philosophy, 'only a clear and consistent Christian philanthropy'.[4] They occupied a similar position with regard to the improvement and legitimation of the Established Church.

> The work of the Church of England was important to the Evangelical scheme, more for its diffusive contribution to the general righteousness than for its centrality as a divinely appointed vehicle of truth.[5]

[1] M. J. Jackson and J. Rogan, *Thomas Arnold: 'Principles of Church Reform' with an Introductory Essay*, p. 15.

[2] Lord Macaulay, 'Gladstone on Church and State', a review of Gladstone's *The State in its Relations with the Church*, in the *Edinburgh Review*, April 1839, vol. lxix, pp. 221–80 (p. 273).

[3] G. F. A. Best, 'The Whigs and Church Establishment in the Age of Grey and Holland', in *History*, vol. xlv, 1960, pp. 103–18 (p. 113).

[4] David Roberts, *Victorian Origins of the Welfare State*, p. 99.

[5] Best, 'The Evangelicals in the Established Church in the Early Nineteenth Century', op. cit., p. 66.

They preferred to work through their own societies, although Bishop Law of Chester might brand these as 'dangerous to the State and the Establishment', and Dr. Pusey attacked them vehemently.[1] The Evangelicals resisted the pressures generated by the Oxford Movement that they should allow their work to be done by the Church in her corporate capacity.[2] Macaulay's low ground of expediency on which to rest the legitimation of an Established Church accurately reflected his Evangelical upbringing as the son of a prominent member of the Evangelical 'High Command'.[3]

The problem facing church leaders, who had to attain goals and yet maintain integration, was to define the temporal goals and norms of operation of the Church in terms of legitimate theological principles, which at the same time did justice to the ambiguous situation of an Established Church, and did not relate purely to autonomous values of a sectarian type. The thought of Thomas Arnold was to prove increasingly influential among such leaders. Arnold sought to provide a theory which avoided the mysticism of Gladstone's theory and yet went beyond the low view of some of the Whigs and of Warburton's 'Alliance'. He believed that the ends and operation of the Church need not be in doubt as his Whig friends feared, provided they were not shrouded in mysticism. Thus he opposed the Oxford Movement for creating a sharp division between sacred and secular and narrowing the Church down to a sect. He wanted the Church to comprehend the life of the whole nation, as in Hooker, although he disliked the 'priestly and ceremonial religion' that appeared in Hooker's Fifth Book.[4] He was much influenced by S. T. Coleridge's ideas, especially that of the clergy of a national Church being directly called upon to Christianize the national life in the widest sense.[5]

Lord Henley's *Plan of Church Reform*, published in 1832, drove Arnold to publish his own *Principles of Church Reform*

[1] Stock, op. cit., pp. 134 and 384. [2] Ibid.

[3] Ford K. Brown, op. cit., p. 6, and E. Stokes, *The English Utilitarians and India*, p. xiv.

[4] A. P. Stanley, *Life and Correspondence of Dr. Arnold*, Teachers' edn. 1901, p. 430; and Jackson and Rogan, op. cit., p. 35.

[5] C. R. Sanders, *Coleridge and the Broad Church Movement*, p. 113.

in the same year. Henley's plan was one of the most influential of the time and some of its proposals were adopted by the Ecclesiastical Commission, but to Arnold it was too narrow in its conception. His own plan contained suggestions which were to be implemented later, such as the institution of diocesan and general mixed assemblies of laity and clergy, but it was too novel for the time and it forfeited all support by its suggestion that the basis of the Church should be widened to include Dissenters.[1] Arnold's general theory sought to satisfy the demands of symbolic-appropriateness in legitimating the Church's system, by adopting a symbolism which made no division between the sacred and the secular. He shared with his earlier colleagues among the Oriel Noetics, the eighteenth-century tradition of ecclesiastical rationalism, which refused to accept the mystical authority of dogma, and was willing to raise questions which might be rationally answered. They were continuing the post-Reformation trend described by Hegel, in which states and laws manifested religion.[2]

Newman had repudiated his early association with the Noetics precisely because he was not prepared to forgo the Church's dogmatic claims and so place the Church on the same ground as other social institutions. Although the Arnolds might seek to symbolize the Church as a 'national society for the promotion of goodness', or 'a society for the putting down of moral evil',[3] to Newman this ignored its all-important transcendental reference. The idea that: 'Science, the modern *Zeitgeist*, could be shown to be actually the ally of religion if only religion would limit itself to the realm of morality,'[4] might seem a rational conclusion to Matthew Arnold, but it was exactly the same tendency that Newman had condemned in Peel.[5] Nevertheless, Matthew

[1] Cf. E. L. Williamson, *The Liberalism of Thomas Arnold: A Study of His Religious and Political Writings*, pp. 130–2; cf. also the *Quaterly Review*, l (January 1834), p. 560.

[2] Lionel Trilling, *Matthew Arnold*, p. 56.

[3] Williamson, op. cit., p. 149.

[4] Trilling, op. cit., p. 320.

[5] J. H. Newman, 'The Tamworth Reading Room' (Letters on an Address delivered by Sir Robert Peel, Bart., M.P., on the Establishment of a Reading Room at Tamworth, published in *The Times*, 5, 9, 10, 12, 20, 22, 27 February 1841, signed 'Catholicus', in G. Tillotson (ed.), *Newman, Prose and Poetry*, p. 91.

Arnold's attempt to symbolize the transcendent in the language of naturalism was one possible development from the influence which Thomas Arnold exerted. The broader aspects of that influence were to be found in the powerful group of religious liberals which after about 1850 became known as the Broad Church movement.

The name seems to have been chosen to describe the tendency of the liberals to favour toleration of religious differences and to de-emphasize the importance of formal doctrine. In sharp contrast to the Tractarians and other High Churchmen, the Broad Church party was generally receptive to the findings of modern Biblical criticism, favourably disposed to proposals for reform of the Church in the direction of increased lay participation of its government, and deeply concerned that the Establishment be maintained. Along with Coleridge, Dr. Arnold was unquestionably one of the important sources of this movement.[1]

The importance of the group for the actual development of the Church of England's organization derived from the crucial positions which its members and sympathizers held for long periods in the leadership of the Church. Although A. P. Stanley, as Dean of Westminster, was the most devoted disciple of Arnold, Archibald Campbell Tait, successor to Blomfield as Bishop of London (1856–68), and Archbishop of Canterbury (1868–82), and Frederick Temple, Bishop of London, (1885–96), and Archbishop of Canterbury, (1896–1902), were the two men most concerned with shaping the Church's organization who had been influenced by Arnold.[2]

Frederick Temple's son, William, successively Bishop of Manchester, Archbishop of York, and Archbishop of Canterbury, who led the Life and Liberty Movement which played a major part in the setting up of the Church Assembly, derived most of his early views of the church system from Arnold, and considered him the greatest Englishman of the nineteenth century.[3]

[1] Williamson, op. cit., p. 151; cf. Sanders, op. cit., pp .7–13, and W. J. Coneybeare, 'Church Parties', in *Edinburgh Review*, vol. xcviii (October 1853), pp. 273–342.

[2] Williamson, op. cit., pp. 152–7.

[3] F. A. Iremonger, *William Temple*, p. 93. (Although in his *Citizen and Churchman*, published in 1941, he showed that he had modified his views.)

A second influence on the later church reform, and subsequently on William Temple, was Liberal Catholicism, which involved for one section of the descendants of the Oxford Movement

> . . . a wholesale change from the deductive theology of the Tractarians with its imperatives against the world and all those things which liberalism accepted in the world, to an inductive theology which appealed to men for Christ by showing how the best and truest things led up to Him and found fulfilment in Him. At the same time religion appeared now as an interpretation of the world as well as of the Church, and the intense conservatism of Pusey and Keble was replaced by the radicalism of Scott Holland and Gore.[1]

In the earlier period of institutional differentiation, however, dissensus over norms, values, and beliefs limited the development of formal organization in the Church to one of *ad hoc* adjustment. The 'intervening variable' of the church parties has been discussed in terms of their respective orientations to change and to different system problems. To liberals like Arnold, whose primary concern was the function of adaptation of the church system, their main concern was the articulation of the system with the larger community. This meant that, although they identified with what they considered the ultimate values of Christianity, and so were acceptable to most people in the Church (although Newman seems to have had doubts about Arnold)[2] they had no binding commitment to any specific goals or norms, as traditionally defined and structured, if they seemed no longer functional for the expression to the world of ultimate values. Their favourable attitude to change, however, made them more acceptable to people less involved in the Church.[3] The Evangelicals had a similar orientation towards reform, although their attachment to the church system depended on whether there was a threat of social unrest (in which case they tended to be more conservative), whether they were under attack within the Church (thus inducing them to

[1] W. R. Ward, op. cit., p. 233.

[2] Cf. Meriol Trevor, *Newman*, vol. i, pp. 150–1.

[3] Arnold's *Principles of Church Reform* went through four editions within the first six months of its appearance in 1833, see Williamson, op. cit., p. 146; but it was rejected by churchmen as 'impracticable'—cf. the *Quarterly Review*, vol. l (January 1834), p. 560.

retaliate by pressing for reforms), and whether they were in areas where Evangelicals were strong in numbers and involved in diocesan administration and patronage.[1]

The Tractarians also had a value orientation, but it was to values traditionally stressed in the system by 'right-thinking' divines (and so neglected in the ecclesiastical rationalism of the eighteenth century). Their concern was to preserve whatever patterns had implemented the expression of those values in the past. In Neal's terms:

> The fact that in the course of time the former implementation might have become less effective is rather difficult for them to perceive, since their major experience is concentrated within the system.[2]

Thus Arnold criticized the Tractarians and High Churchmen because their apotheosis of the past as perceived within the confines of the system made it impossible for them to define the Church's temporal goals and purposes in terms acceptable to contemporary thought.

> Arnold maintained that a glorification of the past, in company with an ill-acquaintance with the present, had put the High Churchmen out of all touch with the *Zeitgeist*. . . .[3]

Instrumental reformers like Blomfield and those who assisted him in bringing about changes in the normative functioning of the organization, sought primarily to attain specific goals as defined by church functionaries like themselves. Their deep, binding commitment was to the goals, which they strove to attain by the most effective methods. To their normative-oriented, conservative critics, they seemed too disposed to jettison the traditional normative structure, whilst to their value-oriented critics they seemed prepared to make ultimate values subsidiary to the attainment of temporal goals.

But as Brose has pointed out in reviewing the references to the Church as an 'instrument of usefulness' in Blomfield's writings:

> It is always a temptation in assessing statements such as these, to say that such a ground of usefulness implies no real independence for

[1] Best, 'The Evangelicals in the Established Church . . .', op. cit., and *Temporal Pillars*, pp. 242–5; also Charles Smyth, *Simeon and Church Order*, pp. 250, 295–7.

[2] Neal, op. cit., p. 16.

[3] Williamson, op. cit., pp. 144–5.

the Church, but only its existence as a useful aid to the State, and hence to label them as Erastian in the most unfavourable sense of that word. But there is a distinction, I think, between attempting to relate the Church as an institution to society and saying that the Church's essential existence is determined by society.[1]

High Churchmen and conservatives in general were primarily concerned about the integrative functions in the Church, and stressed the primacy of the normative system. Deviations from the traditional normative pattern seemed likely to unsettle the whole system, consequently they were to be found expressing anxiety about changes, irrespective of whether they were advocated by Arnold, Evangelicals, Blomfield, or Peel, or else an unintended consequence of the value stress of Newman and the Oxford Movement.

An attempt at a more comprehensive solution to the problems of Church organization had to wait until the twentieth century. It required an increase in formally rational organization, especially in central financing, ministerial recruitment and training; but substantively rational legitimation could be attained only by a form of representative government and control that could secure a minimum of consensus among all parties. The fulfilment of these requirements waited upon the development of a shared orientation to change in sections of all parties, and the focusing of attention on a limited number of problems which could be translated into intermediate goals.

[1] Olive J. Brose, *Church and Parliament: The Reshaping of the Church of England 1828–1860*, p. 85.

III

THE ECCLESIASTICAL COMMISSIONERS AND QUEEN ANNE'S BOUNTY

MAJOR FACTORS IN THE DEVELOPMENT OF CENTRAL ORGANIZATION

THE need for central budgeting and planning agencies in the Church of England was a product of those general factors of social change which both deprived the Church of state financial aid, and eroded those administrative arrangements that it had previously shared with central and local government. This occurred at a time when demands were being made on the Church by the increasing competition from dissenting religious bodies and by critics who wanted it to utilize its resources more efficiently and equitably. It was also a time when the social problems presented by the growing labouring population in towns required a substantial missionary effort from the Church if it was to fulfil its social obligations as the Established Church.

The two central agencies which undertook these tasks, and which loomed so large in determining the pattern of subsequent church organization, were the Ecclesiastical Commissioners and Queen Anne's Bounty. The attitudes of the different church parties to such agencies have been discussed as an important factor in determining the type of rationale employed in legitimizing their powers and in shaping their structure. But both legitimation and structure were influenced not solely by theological considerations or the values of the parties involved, but also by the models of administration, and methods of controlling it, prevalent in the wider society, and by the exigencies of the situations in which these agencies had to operate in their formative years.

THE ECCLESIASTICAL COMMISSIONERS

Administrative boards were common in central government before 1832, and continued to be widely used until about

1855. This period has been seen as an interlude between the old eighteenth-century administration, almost completely independent of Parliament, and the closely controlled, 'responsible' administration of the later Victorian era, when ministerial administration was strengthened by civil service reforms and changes in Parliamentary procedure.[1] The Ecclesiastical Commissioners were set up in this earlier period. The failure to provide for clear ministerial representation of the Ecclesiastical Commissioners in the House of Commons facilitated their development of semi-autonomous and discretionary powers.

At first, however, the composition of the Commission seemed to threaten the Church with just such a centralized ministerial control. As a permanent body it grew out of the Commission of Inquiry set up by Peel in 1835 'to consider the state of the Established Church with reference to Ecclesiastical Duties and Revenues'. The original Commission had twelve members, five of whom were episcopal and seven laymen. In 1836 the first permanent Commission was appointed consisting of twelve members (the Tory ministers being replaced by Whigs), plus the Lord President of the Council; thus giving it eight laymen, the two archbishops, and three bishops. This composition weakened any authority it might have hoped to possess in the eyes of High Churchmen and conservatives. Even the *British Critic*, which had been sympathetic to reform, announced that, although 'a vast good may be done by effecting a more equal distribution and a more complete circulation of the ministration of the Church throughout the country', it added nevertheless,

> We do from our hearts deprecate its perpetuity: as a virtual government by a standing Commission, composed half of Clergy and half of laity, would indeed be an anomaly and a canker in an Episcopal Church.[2]

It held out hopes that private representations by the bishops

[1] F. M. G. Wilson, 'A consideration of the experience in Britain of administrative commissions represented in Parliament by non-ministerial commissioners, with special reference to the Ecclesiastical Commission, the Charity Commission and the Forestry Commission', unpublished D.Phil. thesis, Oxford, 1953, pp. ii and 30.

[2] *British Critic*, vol. xxi, no. xlii, 1837, pp. 514–15.

on the Commission might probably result in this being modified. It was not to be disappointed.

To the Oxford Movement, however, the Ecclesiastical Commission seemed set to become the Church's central governing body, and they recoiled in horror from the breach which this would make in the sacred edifice of the pure church system. Pusey maintained that the substitution of five Whig politicians for the four Tories showed 'the intention of the new ministry to make the Commission an instrument of power, and to maintain their authority on it'.[1] He had already forecast the result of this trend:

> . . . the Commission has shown no disinclination to receive multifarious duties; in a short time, if things go on thus, each ecclesiastical measure will be absorbed into the Commission; it will be our legislative, executive, the ultimate appeal of our bishops; it will absorb our Episcopate; the Prime Minister will be our Protestant pope.[2]

But this was to overestimate the Whigs' attachment to centralized administration. The fact that they were in office for fifteen of the twenty-one years following the Reform Bill meant that they had responsibility for reform in the administration of Church and State, and so they were often forced into centralization even as they spoke against it, for their *ad hoc* reforms expanded the total of central administration. And yet the immediate result was not a rationalized bureaucracy with clear lines of responsibility. Although the Utilitarians were more rational in their demands for a certain amount of efficient central government to promote administrative reforms, their plans were always modified by the more pervasive English attitude to administration which was based on the traditions of the Church, the Universities, and local government. Of men who had imbibed such traditions it has been said:

> Their anger against centralization could not prevent its growth, but it left an indelible mark on the resultant state. So great was Parliament's regard for local government and private enterprise that it limited the powers and personnel of the new departments. And since it had established these departments, as it had won the Empire, piecemeal and in almost absence of mind, they did not constitute a model of administrative organization.[3]

[1] *British Critic*, vol. xxiii, 1838, p. 561. [2] Ibid., p. 526.

[3] David Roberts, *Victorian Origins of the Welfare State*, p. 318.

When *The Times* inveighed against centralization and said it was a French notion, it was voicing the same dislike in the secular sphere of social reform as Bishop Phillpotts had expressed in the Church about the Ecclesiastical Commission in his famous Charge of 1836:

All is marked by what most of the wisest men around us consider to be the vice of modern legislation—all is 'centralization', as it is called; a word not more strange to our language, than the practice which it indicates, is foreign to our ancient habits and feelings. London, in short, is made to be all in all. In the present instance, one Board, seated in London, and composed of men, some of whom, and those the best qualified by experience, will necessarily be often, and for many months together, absent in the discharge of their own high duties as bishops, while a large portion of the remainder must be mainly occupied by their cares as statesmen—this one Board, practically reduced to London, would have to regulate in several most important particulars, the concerns of every diocese in England. Surely this ought not to be.[1]

If centralization seemed foreign to *The Times* and Bishop Phillpotts, then 'bureaucracy' was too distant and strange a notion to enter much into the discussions at this time. But these early criticisms of centralization included many of the objections to be raised in the Church against what later became known as bureaucracy. To conservative churchmen it represented the overthrow of the traditional norms of localism, voluntaryism, and individual rights and responsibilities with regard to property. To those with the value-orientation of the Oxford Movement, its norms seemed to depend on a rationale which was alien to the transcendental values of the Church. Thus Manning demanded to know of the Bishop of Chichester: 'Why, under an idea of centralization and efficiency, is the whole genius of the apostolic to be superseded by an external parliamentary board?'[2]

Manning and the Oxford Movement wished, 'to fall back on old principles, and to walk once more in the sure footing of primitive usage',[3] but the Ecclesiastical Com-

[1] Henry Phillpotts, Bishop of Exeter, *Charge delivered to the clergy of the Diocese of Exeter*, 1836, 2nd edn., p. 33; cf. *The Times*, 19 February 1845.

[2] H. E. Manning, *The Principle of the Ecclesiastical Commission Examined in a Letter to the Rt. Rev. the Lord Bishop of Chichester*, 1838, p. 30.

[3] Ibid., p. 43.

mission was conceived by its architects as an instrumental agency with clearly defined temporal goals, which permitted the evaluation of its norms of operation by the criteria of efficiency and utility:

> In order to give increased efficiency and usefulness to the Established Church, it is obviously necessary that we should attempt the accomplishment of two objects, which are indispensable to the complete attainment of that end. One is, to improve the condition of those benefices the population of which is of considerable amount, but which are now so scantily endowed as not to yield a competent maintenance for a clergyman; the other is, to add to the numbers of clergymen and churches, and so to make a more adequate provision for the religious instruction of a rapidly increased and increasing population.[1]

Although all parties might agree with these intermediate temporal goals, those who were primarily concerned with re-emphasizing transcendental values remained critical of the rationale which an organization such as the Ecclesiastical Commission required and promoted, with its this-worldly criteria of utility and efficiency. The paradox was that this sectarian emphasis on other worldly values, over against the Church-like tendency to compromise, and to accommodate secular patterns, emanated from the Catholic wing of the Church. (For some of them the need to preserve the Church's transcendence of the State was satisfied by seceding to the Roman Catholic Church in England, which set them free from the compromising responsibilities of a national Church.) Groups which felt some responsibility for the instrumental organization and its administration tended to direct their criticisms towards the methods of controlling the organization.

The strength of these combined criticisms resulted, in 1840, in the Ecclesiastical Commissioners being increased from thirteen to forty-nine (two archbishops, five members of the Government, all the bishops of England and Wales, three deans, six common law, equity, and ecclesiastical judges, and eight permanent lay Commissioners—six appointed by the

[1] *Second Report from the Commissioners appointed to consider the State of the Established Church, with reference to Ecclesiastical Duties and Revenues, P.P.* 1836, vol. xxxvi, pp. 1–44.

Crown and two by the Archbishop of Canterbury). This seemed to promise that a legitimate church control would be maintained over the organization. The *British Critic*, now in the hands of the Oxford Movement, declared: '. . . in all this we see indications of strength. We seem also to see a body whose passive resistance will be enough to save the Church from further innovation.'[1]

The predominance of bishops on the Commission might have settled the problem of legitimating the controlling powers of the Board, but it did not guarantee the effectiveness of that control. Even as an Inquiry Commission, power had tended to accumulate in the hands of a few, as the Archbishop of York's famous statement made clear: 'Till Blomfield comes, we all sit and mend our pens, and talk about the weather.'[2]

The work of inquiry, calculation, and tabulation was in the hands of the permanent staff under the increasingly powerful control of the Secretary, Charles Knight Murray, a lawyer:

> Thus Charles Knight Murray, the church's Edwin Chadwick, was part of the Ecclesiastical Commissioners from the start, as active and dominating in the management of their ordinary business as was Blomfield in their general meetings and committees.[3]

Efforts to increase the authority of the controlling Board by extending the representativeness of its composition were difficult to balance with the need to increase the organization's effectiveness and to secure effective control over its operations. There arose a constant tension between the requirements of efficiency, effective co-ordination and control, and the reconcilation of controlling power with legitimate (acceptably representative) authority. Two ideal-typical solutions that were sometimes advocated, but never successfully implemented, were ministerial control according to the pattern that has come to be associated with the Scandinavian state churches, in which there is a Government Board for Church Affairs, or an Ecclesiastical Department;

[1] *British Critic*, vol. xxix, no. lviii, 1840, p. 150.

[2] A. Blomfield, *A Memoir of Charles James Blomfield D.D., Bishop of London*, p. 167.

[3] G. F. A. Best, *Temporal Pillars*, p. 302.

and the denominational pattern of making the instrumental agency into a department of the denomination's representative assembly. These two patterns of organization, whilst appropriate to the ideal types of *ecclesia* and denomination, did not correspond to the actual ambivalent and transitional status of the Church of England, as it was torn between seeking to maintain its Established Church status, and, on the other hand, developing an autonomous organization in keeping with an increasingly pluralistic society.[1]

In its early years, the Commission failed to achieve either instrumental success and efficiency, or a satisfactory co-ordination and control of its activities. In 1850, *The Times* expected it to disappear altogether and reflected:

> If the memory of what it has been survives, it will be known as a board which, during thirteen years, disappointed no expectations because it never raised any, was mainly administered, so far as it was administered at all, by a class of men who thought it wrong in principle and opposed its formation; was resisted from the first by the interest it professed to defend; was unsound in its original organization; and had all its theoretical defects increased indefinitely, by unpardonable carelessness in its management.[2]

The three main tasks of the Commission were all fraught with difficulty and likely to stir up opposition. There was first, the suspension and reorganization of various capitular and episcopal estates; secondly, the augmentation of poorer livings and the endowment of new livings; and thirdly, the rearrangement, extension, and creation of parishes, dioceses, and other ecclesiastical districts.

The most effective and durable charge which opponents found they could use against the new organization in its discharge of these functions was that of 'centralization' and, later, 'bureaucracy'. Deans and canons, who had a con-

[1] An ideal type was defined by Max Weber as follows:
'An ideal type is formed by the one-sided accentuation of one or more points of view and by the synthesis of a great many diffuse, discrete, more or less present and occasionally absent concrete individual phenomena, which are arranged according to those one-sidedly emphasized viewpoints into a unified analytical construct. In its conceptual purity, this mental construct cannot be found anywhere in reality.' (Max Weber, *The Methodology of the Social Sciences*, p. 90.)
See below, pp. 214–18 and 224–5, for a fuller discussion of the ideal types referred to here.

[2] *The Times*, 7 February 1850.

servative attachment to the principles of respect for long-standing arrangements and localism, claimed that the new central administration would reduce them to mere stipendiaries. It was they, and a few like-minded bishops and less impecunious clergy, who developed the case against centralization and advocated decentralization. The dysfunctions which they attributed to the former can be summarized as: a high cost of management, a needlessly large staff, red-tape-ridden office procedures, and inhumanity in dealing with individuals.[1]

The separation of revenue from the episcopal estates in an Episcopal Fund, distinct from the Common Fund that was the only source of money for the augmentation of livings, lost the Commission some support among the lower clergy in its early years. The lower clergy's deprivation was made more acute by Peel's decision, in 1843, to respond to the recent Chartist unrest by insisting that the Commissioners create and endow a host of new parishes in populous areas. This increased burden to be borne by the Commission had the result that it was unable to continue its programme of general augmentation of stipends after 1844. The short-lived support among the lower clergy which the remodelling of the Board had achieved in 1840 was now threatened by its ineffectiveness in performing the function of improving the clergy's financial state.

The process of rationalization also stirred up another sector of opposition to the Commission. This was among church leaseholders. In addition to planning the creation of new bishoprics, and the redistribution of diocesan territories, the Commission had been charged with reforming episcopal finances, and with finding a substitute for the traditional system of subsidizing poor bishops by allowing them to hold livings, prebends, and deaneries in plurality. The Episcopal Fund was to pay the bishops according to a fixed scale, but this entailed taking a fixed annuity out of the variable incomes of the richer sees. However, the bishops' revenues tended to depend on a system of church leases based on fines for renewal rather than on fixed rent. Leases for lives were more unpredictable than leases for a number

[1] Best, op. cit., p. 422.

of years, but they brought larger profits, and so suited the richer landed bishops, who could afford to wait for them. A rational system of budgeting was the prerequisite of financial reform, and it was not attained until leases were converted into a more economical form in the 1850s. Until then leaseholders were one of the main sources of opposition to the Commission.

To the leaseholders and critics in Parliament it seemed that the large board of bishops and state dignitaries could exercise little control over the Commission's business, and that, although the bishops safeguarded and furthered their own interests, most of the business was completely in the hands of the Secretary and his staff. The leaseholders had the ear of the House of Commons Committee, which reported on the Commission, in 1848, and decided that the large nebulous board required a solid core or nucleus of permanent lay members.[1]

The North British Review, commenting on the standing of the Commission in the middle of the century, said: 'With the Church this barely solvent public office was looked at with much the same cordiality as the War Office was when our Crimean disasters were at the worst.'[2]

The small board of 1836–40 had been able to comprehend all the business, but as the work of the Commission grew in scale and complexity, the large board set up in 1840 had to place more and more reliance on the Secretary and his staff. The 1847–8 Select Committee recommended that steps be taken to prevent 'a larger power' being thrown 'into the hands of the officers of the Commission than is fitting should fall to their share'.[3]

It was clear that the Commission was becoming bureaucratic and yet it had not so far acquired the bureaucratic virtue of efficiency and instrumental success to commend it. When its Secretary, Murray, lost some of its funds by personal speculation in railway shares, this further dramatized its failures.

[1] *The North British Review*, March 1866, vol. xliv, p. 195.

[2] Ibid., p. 197.

[3] *Report from the Select Committee on the Ecclesiastical Commission*, *P.P.* 1847–8, vol. vii, p. iv.

The Times asked:

What has the Ecclesiastical Commission done since 1836? It has received and expended a great deal of money. Unhappily, it appears that the expenditure has been rather greater than the receipts. This is not surprising when we learn how its funds have been regulated. Balance, audit, account, were for nine years, it seems, words unknown to the Commission. In any case, the things they represent were wanting. The sole record of its pecuniary transactions were to be found in the mangled remains of the Secretary's check-book. That Secretary was an important personage. He grew with the growth of the body. At first an official who could be dismissed, a clause in an act of Parliament of which no one chooses to know the history, fixed him in his post for life. He thus became the constant element of the fluctuating whole. Bishops came and went, but the Secretary remained.[1]

Although there were forty-nine members on the Board, the 1847–8 Select Committee found that the average attendance at a meeting was ten or eleven, and the bishops usually outnumbered the lay members two to one.[2] This majority of bishops failed to placate the lower clergy, who felt that the bishops had used their increased power to further their own interests. The bishops' reputations had suffered, but that was not all.

One other interest has suffered, that of Commissions generally. We have one more fact for the long induction which is numbering instance after instance of the inefficiency of bodies of which the members are not responsible as individuals, and the entire structure is too loose and indefinite to insure their adequate discharge of a very limited amount of duty.[3]

One possible course of action at this early date, before the Commissioners became almost indispensable by virtue of the very quantity and complexity of their responsibilities and property ownership, was to decentralize and return to a congregational, or regional, autonomy. This might have been the most popular solution within the clerical ranks, but it did not commend itself to those leaders in Church and State who wished to make the Church useful and to keep it moderate, and free from control by rival church parties. If

[1] *The Times*, 7 February 1850.

[2] *Report from the Select Committee on the Ecclesiastical Commission*, *P.P.* 1847, vol. ix, Table of Attendances, Appendix H. 2; also, Best, op. cit., p. 382.

[3] *The Times*, 7 February 1850.

the Church was to maintain its established status and to fulfil its national responsibilities it could not resort to a sect or congregational type of organization, however attractive some aspects of such organization might be to conservative localists, or to theological parties which demanded that the church system conform to a theological ideal.

Those charged with responsibility for leading the Church had to come to terms with the sociological fact that social systems are always less consistent than cultural systems.[1] This is due to the fact that the means needed to attain all the goals of a social system are always larger than the means available, and also that some of those means cannot be devoted directly to the main goal activities, but have to be used for the creation or recruitment of further means, and for maintaining and servicing the units which do perform goal activities.[2] The logical consistency of a Church's doctrinal system is often preserved by isolating it from problems of polity, such as adaptation to the condition of the secular environment, and internal problems of conflict over scarce resources (including money and power). The temptation is always to castigate the Church because its polity does not truly express its theology. In the Church of England in the nineteenth century the temptation was particularly strong. To the clergy in general, and the theologians in the universities in particular, charged as they were with the fulfilment of the primary goal of the Church—the propagation of transcendental values—the central organization often seemed to be either an expensive irrelevance or, occasionally, a compromise with the enemy.

In order to fulfil its responsibilities in a time of rapid social change, the Church had no realistic alternative to centralization. A policy of decentralization to a limited extent was possible only after the formation of the Church Assembly, and the concomitant development of diocesan organization. The suggestion put to the Commissioners by the 1862–3

[1] A cultural (or symbolic) system has a mode of integration that may be called 'pattern consistency'. A social system, however, refers to a concrete system of social interaction. Cf. Talcott Parsons, *The Social System*, p. 15.

[2] Cf. A. Etzioni, 'Two Approaches to Organizational Analysis: A Critique and a Suggestion', in the *Administrative Science Quarterly*, vol. v, no. 2, September 1960, pp. 257–78 (pp. 258–9).

Select Committee, that they might be divided into fifty-two local boards based on counties or dioceses, was rejected by the Commissioners on the grounds that it would not meet the need for a central board for collection and redistribution, and that the result would be duplication and increased expense.[1]

The development of a bureaucratic form of central organization in the Ecclesiastical Commission was a natural outgrowth from the Inquiry Commission. Despite all his reservations about central government, Jeremy Bentham was true to his utilitarian philosophy in insisting that a centrally administered system of statistical information was necessary to make policy intelligent. And once a staff collected such information, it gave them an attachment to formal rationality which made them indispensable for solving empirical problems on the basis of inference from detailed evidence and technical appraisal. In turn, the bureaucracy amassed statistical data as a by-product of conducting administrative functions.[2] It was this accumulation of statistical information, and the expertise to interpret it and formulate policies based on factual data, that made the officers of the Ecclesiastical Commission indispensable to the Church.

The application of formal rationality is facilitated by the instrumental character of bureaucracy. It is instrumental in being a means to an end, and its rationality is based on seeking to do what has to be done as fully, quickly, and economically as possible. Its ends are supplied by the governing body, to which the bureaucracy is responsible. Although it may give advice on policy as well as operations, its obligation is to serve. However, although the norm of service was being institutionalized in the British civil service in the nineteenth century, and provided the model for the Church's own administrative staff, the problem of securing control over its administrative agencies was especially difficult for the Church since it lacked an autonomous governing body.

Until it developed such a government, the Church had to

[1] *Report from the Select Committee on the Ecclesiastical Commission, P.P.* 1862, vol. viii, pp. 18–19.

[2] Cf. Fritz Morstein Marx, *The Administrative State*, p. 39.

turn to secular models. Of the two available, the Benthamite Utilitarian principles of administration were the most akin to what Max Weber was to characterize as the ideal type bureaucracy. Whereas Whig theory maintained that it was important to make the exercise of power impersonal and collective through the agency of boards, committees, or benches of judges, the Benthamites argued that officials should be employed singly, so that they could be held responsible. Accountability could be achieved by publicity and official inspection. Thus Benthamite administration was based on individual agency, accountability, and systematic bureaucratic hierarchy. Its advantages lay in its speed, efficiency, regularity, and uniformity. To limit the abuse of power by reducing these advantages would be a case of 'cutting off the nose to spite the face'. The error of Whig theory, according to the Benthamites, was that it assumed that the exercise of control could be carried out by the division of powers that were set as a check against one another in the way that Montesquieu had advocated.[1]

Both sets of principles can be discerned in the Church of England's organization as it developed in the nineteenth century. A pure Benthamite bureaucracy might have developed had the Ecclesiastical Commissioners been represented by a responsible minister in Parliament, but this was not feasible at a time when the Church was being urged from within to assert her autonomy. In practice, the organization experienced a constant tension between the Whig requirement of a system of checks and balances and division of powers, and, on the other hand, the bureaucratic requirements of speed, efficiency, economy, regularity, and uniformity.

Despite the long term progress towards meeting these requirements, and the occasional suggestion, after the formation of a partially democratic governing body in the Church Assembly, that the Ecclesiastical Commission should be controlled by that body, the Whig principles remained strong.

Thus *The Economist* in two articles on the Church of England's finances in 1944 could conclude:

[1] Eric Stokes, *The English Utilitarians and India*, pp. 72–5.

The Church can now boast a division of powers which would have pleased Montesquieu, and which possess indeed many of the advantages he enumerated. Queen Anne's Bounty and the Ecclesiastical Commissioners are independent and disinterested bodies, with a tradition of benevolent administration and of personal attention, free from the dangers of over-centralization and bureaucracy which might affect a representative central authority. They are in no sense democratic.[1]

The development of the formal administrative organization in the Church of England was not, therefore, uniformly in the direction of a pure bureaucratic type with a single hierarchy and monocratic authority. The contemporary climate of opinion in the formative years of the organization favoured models of administration which involved a division of powers and the principle of collegiality. In the period in which the constitution of the Ecclesiastical Commissioners was being formed, administrative boards were being widely used, and in so far as this entailed bureaucratic organization, it was *bureaucratie* in the eighteenth-century French usage of Vincent de Gournay, and meant simply 'desk government'. By the time the late nineteenth-century German usage of *Bürokratie* had become generally accepted, with its more specific connotation of administration by single-headed departments, in contrast with organizations headed by collegial bodies such as boards and commissions, with each member equal, the Ecclesiastical Commissioners had already developed a constitution incorporating these elements. As Weber observed, however, the employment of collegiality in order to limit the power of individuals has constantly been under pressure to give way to the technical superiority of monocratic organization.[2]

In the Ecclesiastical Commission, the enlarged board of Commissioners established in 1840, with a clerical majority, was more representative than its predecessor, which had only thirteen members, but it was internally weak as attendance was irregular. In consequence, great influence was wielded by the Secretary. Russell's Government gave greater co-ordinative and controlling strength to it by adding a nucleus of paid members in 1850. This development in

[1] *The Economist*, 16 September 1944, pp. 373–4 (p. 374).

[2] Max Weber, *The Theory of Social and Economic Organization*, p. 402.

the constitution meant that there were in theory three collegial bodies within the organization: in addition to the full Commission there was a five-man statutory Estates Committee with certain exclusive duties, and there were the three Church Estates Commissioners—two paid and one unpaid—who had exclusive powers with regard to leasehold property. This latter provision was a guarantee of close, business-like control over the administration of the policy of rationalization, and it was a necessary concession to the church leaseholders, who criticized the amateur and ineffective control exercised by the Board.

The Estates Committee consisted of the three Church Estates Commissioners and two other members appointed by the Ecclesiastical Commissioners (one of them was to be a layman, and the other, by custom, was usually the Bishop of London). The Committee was given absolute charge over the Commissioners' property, and also, under a clause in the Act of 1850, the Commissioners could delegate to them any other part of their business, except the right to affix their common seal. This latter provision was to be widely used and a great deal of delegated power accumulated in the hands of the Estates Committee.

The need to introduce a strong, responsible, and business-like element into the Board was created by the inability of the bishops, who constituted the majority of the board after 1840, to supervise and control the staff, especially the all-important Secretary. The Commissioners had to satisfy two masters: the churchmen who demanded that they be primarily responsible to, and representative of, the Church, and on the other side Parliament and the leaseholders, who demanded of them efficiency, impartiality, and answerability to the State, as befitted an Establishment. Lacking an autonomous governing body, the church interest had been represented in the Ecclesiastical Commission by the episcopal majority on the Board. This might have given it some legitimacy in the eyes of churchmen, but it was unsatisfactory to a Parliamentary critic like Horsman, the Member of Parliament for Cockermouth. He described the situation in the Second Reading Debate on the Ecclesiastical Commission Bill of 1850:

The Bishops, besides the Ecclesiastical Commission, were also practically the managers of two other public boards—the Church Building Commission, and Queen Anne's Bounty—both established by Act of Parliament. The Church Building Commission was charged, like the Ecclesiastical Commission, with forming new districts, and contributing to the funds required. Its board consisted of forty-one members; but Mr. Jelf, the Secretary, told them that as they were mostly high functionaries engaged with other duties, the attendance was comparatively scanty, and the meetings rare. The business fell into the hands of the Bishops, and through them, as in the Ecclesiastical Commission, it fell of course entirely into the hands of the secretary, who, according to what seemed the standing rule of these ecclesiastical boards, united in his own person the offices of secretary and treasurer. From July to October there were no meetings at all, and during that time the secretary was both nominally and really the whole Commission. . . .

The Ecclesiastical Commissioners were 49, the Church Building Commissioners 41; but the Governors of Queen Anne's Bounty were upwards of 400. But the prelates again were practically the board, and the same system prevailed—only eight or nine meetings in the year, and always on Thursday, the same as the Ecclesiastical Commission. The same individual was of course secretary and treasurer, and he thus described the system: 'I control everything: when there is sufficient business to render a board necessary, I tell the Archbishop, and he summons a board, but "summons" are only sent to the bishops and the town-clerk of London.'[1]

Horsman suggested that the three boards should be combined, thus increasing efficiency and reducing expense, and that they should be run by laymen. Sir George Grey who, as Home Secretary in Lord John Russell's administration, acted as the nearest thing to a minister for ecclesiastical affairs, had also suggested to the 1848 Select Committee that the three boards might be combined and put under one general management. John G. Shaw Lefevre (one of the original Poor Law Commissioners and an Ecclesiastical Commissioner since 1846), to whom he made the suggestion, was favourably disposed, but could not answer for the other two boards.[2]

It was Russell, Grey, and Lefevre, who thought of applying the solution of paid Commissioners on the Board of the

[1] E. Horsman, M.P., 29 April 1850, *Hansard*, Third Series, vol. cx, pp. 948–9.
[2] *P.P.* 1847–8, vol. vii, Q. 943.

Ecclesiastical Commission as a means of securing a more responsible control of the business.[1] *The Times*, which opposed centralization in theory, but could not suggest an efficient alternative in practice, was not enamoured of this solution. The 1848 Select Committee's advocacy of three paid Commissioners (although subsequently, under the Act, only two were paid) coincided with the demise of the independent Poor Law Commission and the creation of the ministerial Poor Law Board.

The Times commented on the proposed reform of the Ecclesiastical Commission:

> Nothing of course without three *paid* commissioners! The mysterious Whig *Triumviri*, the solution of all difficulties, political, social, and moral, meet us as surely as the Fates or the Furies do the classical scholar.

It recognized, however, that men of business believed that full-time, paid officials were necessary—'The Great Unpaid are passing away'. Although it claimed to recognize an 'old friend' in this solution, it had to concede:

> But what help is there for it? The Apostles surrendered the 'serving of tables' to seven men of business chosen for the purpose, so we cannot object to a financial order of Ministers in these days.[2]

Complete state control over the administrative organization of the Church, as was to become the pattern in the Scandinavian established churches, was unacceptable in the Church of England which, under the pressure and inspiration of the Oxford Movement, was reviving its own autonomous values. But without an autonomous governing body, it could not control its bureaucracy according to the modern pattern of ministerial responsibility in which the single head of the department is answerable to the elected assembly. It had to depend on the older devices of division of powers and collegial control, although the latter principle had to be modified as the technical superiority of the paid Commissioners meant that, in practice, the formal equality of the members of the Board was not preserved.

The *Edinburgh Review*, which was apprehensive of the split between Church and State which the recent revival of

[1] Best, op. cit., p. 393.

[2] *The Times*, 17 November 1848.

Convocation threatened, welcomed the strengthening of the Ecclesiastical Commission by the inclusion of paid Commissioners:

It does in fact create a rudimentary *department of ecclesiastical affairs*; but with this advantage over a ministerial department, that the board would be independent of all party influence, its members being appointed for life. The small number of the board is also a recommendation, because it secures their acting with a due sense of individual responsibility. We should see the adoption of this measure with peculiar pleasure, because it is obviously a step towards re-establishment of some instrument of church government intermediate between Parliament and clergy. We have from time to time taken occasion to point out how much such an instrument is needed.[1]

The article seemed to recognize, however, that a department of ecclesiastical affairs in the form of a Commission was a compromise, and its suggestion as to what would be the ideal solution was a far-sighted forecast of the future Church Assembly and the role envisaged for it by those who wished to see it become the effective controlling body in church organization:

Its best form would, perhaps, be a body of representatives (whereof not less than half should be laymen), elected by the members of the Church of England. This might retain the ancient name, without the defects of Convocation. . . . Some organ of this kind is absolutely necessary, both to prepare church measures for the sanction of Parliament, and to superintend their execution. Till it exists there can be no thorough reform in our ecclesiastical machinery.[2]

Both its prognostication and its prescription were to be proved accurate by subsequent developments.

The new constitution did not solve all the Commissioners' problems, and between 1851 and 1866 it remained a subject of controversy. Its financial position was weak and prohibited large-scale augmentation of stipends until the early 1860s, and so the clergy gave it little support. The new Church Estates Commissioners gave some stability and efficiency to the Board, and together with the other two members of the Estates Committee and the Archbishop of

[1] *Edinburgh Review*, vol. xcix, January 1854, p. 117.

[2] Ibid., pp. 117–18.

Canterbury, they constituted the working body of the Commission.

Throughout the period no direct representation of the Board was established in Parliament—the Second Estates Commissioner, who was to become the regular representative, was not an M.P. until 1859. A difference between the Board and the Government concerning the Dean of York, in 1859/60, probably influenced the development of direct representation, and also helped to force the Board to become financially self-supporting. (Establishment expenses were not paid from public funds after 1866.)[1]

The Estates Committee, and especially the Church Estates Commissioners, progressively increased their power as the Commissioners delegated more of their own powers to them, and omitted to lay down general rules for their guidance as the 1850 Act had intended. Members of the Estates Committee undertook the bulk of the work of the Commission and were the most frequent attenders at Board meetings. Even at general meetings, the attendance of the bishops was irregular, with the constant exception of the Bishop of London and the Archbishop of Canterbury.[2]

The 1856 Select Committee on the Ecclesiastical Commission was impressed by the improvements in efficiency which the Commissioners had made, but they were somewhat puzzled by the control, if any, which the Board exercised over the Estates Committee. Lord Chichester, who, as First Church Estates Commissioner from 1850 to 1878, became in effect its chief executive, admitted that the Board delegated much of its business to the Estates Committee. Lord Robert Cecil inquired of him if there was any point in the Estates Committee referring matters to the Board at all. Chichester's answer was revealing. He said that he thought the Church and the public derived a benefit from the occasional presence of the bishops at the Board, and added that it gave satisfaction to the clerical members of the Church.[3] It was clear that efficiency was best served by delegating more and more power to the Church Estates

[1] F. M. G. Wilson, op. cit., p. iv.

[2] Ibid., p. 120.

[3] *Report from the Select Committee on the Ecclesiastical Commission*, *P.P.* 1856, vol. xi, pp. 1–504, Qs. 150–61.

Commissioners (in effect the two paid Commissioners—the First and Third), but that legitimization of their activities required the occasional attendance of the bishops at the Board to set their seal to the business prepared by the staff and the Estates Committee.

It began to seem as if the Commissioners were set to become the permanent central administrative organization in the Church. The amount of work being transacted was steadily increasing as the Commission found itself able to resume augmentations at about the same time as the Select Committee was sitting in 1856, and in the following year the powers of the Church Building Commissioners were transferred to them.[1] Bishop Tait said that 'it was becoming more and more the very centre of the establishment of the Church of England' and this accumulation of power seemed to worry him. He said that its business was solely to get ecclesiastical property back into good shape and then to hand it back—not to administer it 'to the end of time in an office in Whitehall Place'. He thought a period should be fixed after which the Commission should 'not cease to exist, but—fall into its proper position, that of regulating changes with regard to property, without holding the whole property in its hands.'[2]

The 1862–3 Select Committee's examination of the Ecclesiastical Commissioners was perhaps the last occasion on which the Commissioners were still sufficiently vulnerable to be overthrown by a coalition of localists and clerical critics. The Committee itself was opposed to centralized administration of augmentation and proposed that the application of surplus revenues should be transferred from the Commission to regional (diocesan) authorities. It wanted to restrict the Commission to management of property, thus narrowing its discretionary powers and its executive scope, and to place this in the hands of a small three-man board.

Lord Chichester's evidence again revealed the actual distribution of power in the Commissioners' office. Henry Danby Seymour, the Chairman of the Committee, asked him if the three bodies to which he alluded (the General Board,

[1] 19/20 Vic. c. 55.

[2] *Hansard*, Third Series, vol. clx, pp. 929–30, 9 August 1860.

the Church Estates Commissioners, and the Estates Committee) each had a separate staff, or if their decisions were all carried out under the same control.[1] Chichester's reply gave some indication of the increasing quantity of the Commission's work and of how it was distributed:

The Secretary is the officer of all three Boards and records their decisions, and is equally responsible for the working of all the departments. In the last year the number of decisions of the different Boards were the following: of the General Board, 355; at the General Board, Reports from the Estates Committee, 458; the decisions of the Estates Committee, 2,789; of the Church Estates Commission, 855; and the number of letters received last year was 16,785, and the number sent out 18,177; accounts exceeded £2,600,900; the number of files in the office, each of which may be called for at any moment, exceeded 26,000, the number of deeds registered exceeds 60,000.[2]

The evidence revealed in existence an organization possessing many of the characteristics usually included in definitions of bureaucracy, especially as these related to the spread of formalization, the extensive use of files, and legal formulation. It might have been expected that this would throw all power into the hands of the bureaucratic staff, and Chichester was asked if he did not think that with so large a Board great power must have necessarily devolved upon the Secretary and the permanent officers of the establishment. His reply exposed the true distribution of power as it existed then, and continued to exist, in the Ecclesiastical Commission:

It would probably be so to an inconvenient extent, if the Board were formally and actually the administrative body; but the real administrative power is, in fact, exercised by the Estates Committee, and it is only on very general questions, that is to say, the questions of general principle, that the Board interferes.[3]

This account was shown to be accurate by the searching investigation into the Commissioners' Office carried out by a Treasury Committee in 1859.[4]

The 1862 Select Committee included a majority of members who wanted to decentralize much of the Commission's work and their advocacy of localism was supported

[1] *P.P.* 1862, vol. viii, Q. 28. [2] Ibid.
[3] Ibid., Q. 43. [4] Ibid., Appendix, pp. 293–307.

by clerical critics who were either specifically concerned to restore powers to the cathedrals, or else objected to the non-spiritual values of the central organization.[1] Bishop Waldegrave of Carlisle was one who felt concerned about the unspiritual temper of central organization, and saw diocesan boards as a useful corrective:

> . . . with reference to the general question of the constitution and working of the Ecclesiastical Commission, I am of the opinion that the institution of local or diocesan boards is highly to be desired, not for the purpose of superseding, but for that of checking, the proceedings of the central office.
>
> It would have this great commendation—first, that it would enlist, all over the kingdom, hearty local co-operation, both clerical and lay, in the well-working of the Central Board; secondly, that it would constrain the Central Board to exhibit a more manifest interest in its spiritual objects. At present it deliberates, and speaks, and writes much too much as if the management of its property were its great function. Now, surely, the management of its property is but a means to an end, and that end the making better provision for cure of souls.[2]

Lord Chichester was able to point to the greater efficiency and economy of a central board in order to justify the Ecclesiastical Commission, and suggested that local boards would be either less efficient or more expensive.[3] Although the majority of the Select Committee introduced a Bill in favour of local boards (the Ecclesiastical Estates Bill of 1864) it was withdrawn without being debated. An alternative Bill drawn up by the three Church Estates Commissioners would have increased their own powers even further, but this transfer of further powers was so heavily attacked that it had to be dropped. The Bill which eventually emerged did, however, include a clause which reduced the quorum for meetings of the Estates Committee from three Commissioners, at least two of whom had to be Church Estates Commissioners, to just two Estates Commissioners.[4] This quorum, as laid down in the Ecclesiastical Commissioners

1 For examples see *P.P.* 1862, vol. viii, Qs. 288–91, 308–20; also, Best, op. cit. pp. 431–4.

2 *P.P* 1863, vol. vi, Appendix 15, pp. 190–1.

3 *P.P.* 1862, vol. viii, pp. 18–19.

4 F. M. G. Wilson, op cit., pp. 149–51.

Act, 1866, was probably meant to apply only to powers in respect of land, but in practice the same procedure was applied to decisions concerning all other assets, and even to control of staff and expenses of administration.[1]

The accumulation of power in the hands of the paid Estates Commissioners was really the result of trying to limit its accumulation in the hands of the permanent staff and especially the Secretary. The complexity of the Commissioners' business, and the need for long, continuous acquaintance with its affairs in order to be able to understand it, determined where control would lie. The Treasury Committee which investigated the duties and establishment of the Office in 1859 were warned that all power was accumulating in the hands of the Secretary, and so they undertook a 'rigid investigation'. They cleared him of the charge on the grounds that the two paid Commissioners' close attendance to the business checked the powers of the Secretary. The only practical suggestion made to them for increasing control was to appoint another paid Commissioner, who would give daily attendance for the purpose of exercising a constant supervision over the business. The Committee rejected the suggestion:

> It would lead to an entire alteration in the present system of conducting the business, and to a transfer to the resident Commissioner of many of the functions now discharged by the secretary. Whether any improvement would be obtained by such a transfer of duties is problematical; and it appears evident to us, that if a Commissioner should obtain that mastery over the business which would enable him to discharge the detailed duties with efficiency, he would, as a colleague, be less under the control of the Board, and would acquire a degree of authority much more independent than that which it sought to supersede.[2]

To have given way to the technical superiority of monocratic authority would have resulted in the erosion of the check on bureaucratic power provided by the element of collegiality in a board of equals. However, the First and Third Church Estates Commissioners, who were appointed

[1] See the *Report of the Archbishop's Committee on the Administration of the Church Commissioners for England* (hereafter referred to as the *Monckton Report*), 1963, p. 19.

[2] *Treasury Committee Report, P.P.* 1862, vol. viii, Appendix, pp. 293–307 (p. 299).

respectively by the Crown and the Archbishop of Canterbury, did in fact acquire a degree of authority and independence which was almost as great as that which the Secretary threatened to acquire in the early days. They were assisted in this by the intimate knowledge of its affairs which their salaried status and long service enabled them to acquire. Between 1850 and 1963 there were only 6 First and 13 Third Church Estates Commissioners; the Second Church Estates Commissioner, who by custom was an M.P. and appointed to his unpaid position by the Crown, tended to change more often, and the position was occupied by 31 different individuals over the same period.[1]

Because the Church of England was an Established Church, the problem of controlling its organization was not merely an internal matter, but also a matter of public interest. Until 1867 the leading question with regard to the Church was how it should be reformed, whereas from 1867 to 1914 the question was whether or not it should be disestablished. In 1866 it was still not unusual that a journal like *The North British Review* should devote a long article to examining the growth of the Ecclesiastical Commissioners, and especially to the problems of what would now be termed bureaucratization. It noted that from 1857 onwards the Commission's income had increased and that it was also a great firm for buying, selling, enfranchising, managing, draining, and improving land, for the building of parsonages, making new parishes, and numerous other duties. The only control over these activities, however, was exercised by the three Estates Commissioners, and this did not seem to promise adequate protection of the public interest. The *Review* asked:

> Yet can it be hoped, in the long-run, that a few gentlemen, however great their abilities, however sedulous their attention, can efficiently control all these great transactions, in which so many interests are involved? The professional actuary, in the intricate calculations of terminable rights, the professional surveyor, in all questions of purchase or sale, must have the advantage over those who are not versed in the same matters. Thus, whilst the general policy of the Commission is settled by Parliament, the details must ever be left to

[1] *Monckton Report*, p. 19.

the professional officers; and those who have the nominal control will have little power to direct the working of the Commission.[1]

The North British Review was concerned only with safeguarding the public interest and the exercise of public control over the Commission—it was less concerned with the position of the Commission within the Church, and of its control by legitimate Church authority. Its recommendations had a Benthamite flavour:

> We have shown that we are not inaccessible to the dangers of centralizing the control of a large amount of property. But the Committee makes no suggestion towards another scheme. In fact the multiplication of centres would be yet more dangerous. One office in London will be observed, criticized, examined by Parliament, checked by an efficient audit. A number of offices would be less responsible, less observed, more likely to be treated carelessly. The dangers that beset great pecuniary trusts must be met in this case by reducing the duties of the Commission to the simplest form, by prescribing a clear method of rendering the accounts, far more clear than the present mode, by careful auditors, and by reports to Parliament.[2]

Ideally, this model of organizational control would have been suitably completed by the appointment to the Board of a Minister responsible to Parliament—as Cardwell of the 1862 Select Committee had suggested to Lord Chichester.[3] But, as the discussion on that occasion revealed, such a device might secure state control, but it would not satisfy the desire of churchmen for representation on the Board. In practice, and in the absence of a representative governing body in the Church, there was no alternative to the compromise system of checks and balances based on the division of powers between staff, Church Estates Commissioners, Estates Committee, and the Board. However, the circumstances of the long-service and salaried status of the First and Third Estates Commissioners, and their ability to constitute a quorum on the Estates Committee, combined with the delegation of power from the Board to that Committee to make them the real power in the Church's main central administrative agency.

1 *The North British Review*, vol. xliv, March 1866, pp. 180–212 (p. 205).
2 Ibid., p. 211.
3 *P.P.* 1862, vol. viii, Qs. 447–50.

More recently the amalgamation of Queen Anne's Bounty and the Ecclesiastical Commissioners, when Church Assembly passed, and Parliament approved, the Church Commissioners' Measure of 1947, and the provision in the new constitution for the appointment of representatives of Church Assembly as Church Commissioners did not substantially alter the balance of power. The *Monckton Report* in 1963 referred to the feelings of powerlessness which these representatives experienced, and said these were connected with the immensely powerful and rather isolated position of the three Church Estates Commissioners.[1] A certain degree of decentralization with regard to augmentation of stipends became possible after the amalgamation, and on the basis of the financial machinery which had been developing in the dioceses since the First World War, but it did not substantially detract from the powers of the Commissioners.

Although the different agencies which came to make up the central organization of the Church of England possessed many of the structural characteristics of bureaucracy, the use of a deterministic theory of bureaucratic behaviour such as that advanced by Robert Michels or James Burnham would neglect the implications of the somewhat different patterns of bureaucratic response which were institutionalized during the period of separate growth of these agencies.[2] It is not inevitable that all the traits included in the 'type' will vary together in some determinable relation. Thus as Harrison has pointed out:

> The ideational background of any bureaucrat plays a determining role in the decision-making process; and the social and religious heritage of the Baptist bureaucrat may be radically different from that of the bishop in the Episcopalian hierarchy or from that of the civil servant in a state bureaucracy.[3]

The internal organization and staffing of the Ecclesiastical Commission's office was from the start closely linked to the civil service. The Treasury Investigation of its duties

[1] *Monckton Report*, pp. 28–9.

[2] See the discussion in Seymour M. Lipset, *Agrarian Socialism*, p. 271; also, Robert Michels, *Political Parties*, and James Burnham, *The Managerial Revolution*.

[3] Paul M. Harrison, *Authority and Power in the Free Church Tradition*, p. 144.

and establishment in 1859 reported that there was a total staff of 32, plus 6 supernumerary clerks. It said that the Order in Council regulating appointments to civil service offices was enforced, and that promotion from class to class was guided solely by reference to merit. (It added that on the whole the office was very efficient, but over-worked and under-staffed.)[1] The Commission itself reported that:

> For staff purposes, we are almost a branch of the Civil Service. Our staff is recruited by the same examinations, its salaries are those of the Civil Service, and the pension provisions... have always marched side by side with those of the Civil Service.[2]

Having passed the civil service examinations, a candidate could choose to enter the Ecclesiastical Commissioners' office. Once having entered, however, they were unlikely to leave, as status and pension rights were not transferable to other civil service departments.[3]

QUEEN ANNE'S BOUNTY

A description of Queen Anne's Bounty will show that it had developed in ways significantly different from the Ecclesiastical Commissioners. In 1901, the Commissioners' staff was 94. Queen Anne's Bounty had grown from a staff of 8 in 1837 and 13 in 1868, to 28 in 1900. The combined staff in the Church Commissioners' office in 1963 was 472. (Administrative expenses had risen from £34,764 for the Ecclesiastical Commission in 1900, to £680,000 in 1961–2.)[4]

Queen Anne's Bounty had a much smaller and more paternalistic organization than the Ecclesiastical Commission. No qualifications or examinations were stipulated for the staff. The Joint Select Committee on Queen Anne's Bounty

[1] *Treasury Committee Report*, op. cit., pp. 304–5.

[2] *Hansard*, Fifth Series, vol. cclxxx, col. 1689.

[3] F. M. G. Wilson, op. cit., p. 171; also the evidence of Mr. Alfred De Bock Porter, Secretary and Financial Adviser to the Ecclesiastical Commissioners, in the *Report of the Joint Select Committee on Queen Anne's Bounty, P.P.* 1901, vol. vii, pp. 313–479, Q. 581.

[4] Ibid., Q. 574; and the *Monckton Report*, p. 32.

recommended, in 1901, that if it continued separate from the Ecclesiastical Commission

> . . . its staff should be appointed and paid, as is the staff of the Ecclesiastical Commission, upon conditions more nearly alike to those applicable to members of the Civil Service doing similar work.[1]

Power was shared between the Secretary-Treasurer and the bishops until 1868, after which the customary dominance of the bishops on the Board tended to give way to that of a group of lay governors. From his appointment as Secretary to Queen Anne's Bounty, in 1832, to his retirement in 1871 aged 87 (from 1831 he was also Treasurer) Christopher Hodgson dominated the Bounty office and ran it as his own empire. A Select Committee on Queen Anne's Bounty, in 1868, found that most of the staff was old; that Hodgson supervised everything; that the Bounty did not come under the Civil Service or Superannuation Acts; that Hodgson's home, private office, and the Bounty office, were all mixed together.[2] (Best has even interpreted the evidence to mean that the Upper House of Convocation used to meet in Hodgson's drawing-room.)[3]

The 1868 Committee also found that, although the Board was 600, its affairs were under the control of a small number of bishops.[4] It was clear that the monopoly of administration in the hands of the Secretary-Treasurer, and the paternal control exercised by the bishops, was possible because of the smallness of the Bounty's business and responsibilities compared with the Ecclesiastical Commission. The Bishop of Carlisle, in evidence to the Committee, said he thought that Queen Anne's Bounty represented local interests better than the Ecclesiastical Commissioners 'because the bishop is much more a reality, as a power, at the Bounty Board than he is at the Ecclesiastical Commission'.[5] He admitted that this was possible because, whereas the Ecclesiastical Commission had £150,000 to distribute that year, Queen Anne's Bounty had only £10,000.[6]

[1] *1901 Committee on Q.A.B.*, op. cit., p. iv.

[2] *Report of the Select Committee on Queen's Anne's Bounty*, *P.P.* 1867–8, vol. vii, pp. 467–615 (p. viii).

[3] Best, op. cit., p. 228.

[4] *P.P.* 1867–8, vol. vii, p. iii.

[5] Ibid., Q. 735.

[6] Ibid., Qs. 724–5.

The Bishop of Oxford, another staunch supporter of Queen Anne's Bounty, also told the Committee that it was more 'paternal' to the clergy than was the Ecclesiastical Commission. He added:

> . . . in meaning that I meant no blame to the Ecclesiastical Commissioners, because I think it is the necessary consequence of so large a concern, that its real administration must fall into the hands of the men of business who manage the details.[1]

The dominance of the bishops on the Bounty Board persuaded the Bishop of Oxford that its constitution was more analogous to the constitution of the Church of England than the Ecclesiastical Commission, and therefore more advantageous.[2] Both he and the Bishop of Carlisle were against amalgamating Queen Anne's Bounty and the Ecclesiastical Commission.[3] He further maintained that it was unnecessary for the lay members of the Board to attend, and he agreed that the sense of his argument was that: 'The bishops are the directors and the laity the shareholders in the company.'[4] Despite this argument, the Committee recommended that the responsibilities of members of the Board should be more clearly defined and that laymen should attend more.[5]

Queen Anne's Bounty in this period was the agency which most closely resembled an episcopally based church bureaucracy with central administrators acting in conjunction with the bishops. Thus the Bishop of Carlisle said that Queen Anne's Bounty had an advantage in that it administered much of its work through the bishops and on their authority.[6]

As a result of the 1868 Committee's recommendations, however, and the disclosure that the Board had frequently failed to secure a quorum, the system of control changed. An Audit Committee was created in 1872 (known as the Finance Committee from 1875) and a Standing Committee was set up at the same time. A layman was always chairman of the Finance and Audit Committee, and it was with him that the governors corresponded between boards. A subcommittee of the Finance Committee, composed of three laymen, dealt with questions requiring immediate decision,

[1] *P.P.* 1867–8, vol. vii, p. iii., Q. 1005. [2] Ibid., Qs. 987–8.
[3] Ibid., Qs. 756 and 995. [4] Ibid., Q. 1020. [5] Ibid., p. iii.
[6] Ibid., Q. 769.

and their actions were subsequently endorsed by the Finance Committee. Although the Standing Committee was chaired by the Bishop of London, like the Finance Committee it was attended by a majority of laymen. Of the eleven regular attenders at the Board meetings over a typical period, 1897–9, seven were laymen and four bishops, and the two highest attenders were an M.P., Alderman Sir Joseph Savory, Bart., and a lawyer, Cyril Dodd.[1]

The advantage which Queen Anne's Bounty had possessed, in churchmen's eyes, over the impersonal bureaucracy of the Ecclesiastical Commission, was the predominance of the bishops and the authority which this gave to the Board, and also the fact that the Bounty devoted most of its slender resources to augmentation of the lowest stipends. But, after 1868, this advantage diminished as lay control increased and the organization become more complex. The passing of the old regime with the retirement of Hodgson in 1871, and the increasing participation of laymen on the Board, seemed also to reduce the bishops' attachment to the Bounty.

Archbishop Tait was particularly critical of the power possessed by the Secretary-Treasurer. At a meeting of the Board, in 1875, he strongly criticized a proposed increase in the Bounty's expenses and an increase in its staff, and also the proposal to alter the building at an unstated cost subject to the judgement of the Secretary-Treasurer. He wrote to the Bishop of London to say that they had already spent much without improving business efficiency over what it was in Hodgson's time—'though the result had certainly been to provide an admirable house at a very small rent for the Secretary'.[2] Tait said that the Board should be on guard against further expenditure, adding:

> I confess also that I thought we were come to a point when it was desirable not to let the Secretary lead us too much. I thought there was a danger of his becoming autocratic, having got rid of all the checks which restrained former secretaries from the presence and co-operation of the Solicitor, and I was the more afraid as I saw that a

[1] *Report of the Joint Select Committee on Queen Anne's Bounty*, *P.P.*, 1900, vol. viii, pp. 79–254, Qs. 75–128 and Appendix D.

[2] Unpublished letter to the Bishop of London, 7 August 1875, Archbishop Tait's Correspondence, vol. xcv, Lambeth Palace Library.

leading clerk, who was so notoriously on bad terms with the Secretary, was recommended first to be dismissed or pensioned off—and if that could not be done, to be passed over in the augmentation list. In fact all I wished and still wish to impress is the necessity for caution on the part of the Board and that they should let the Secretary understand that he cannot have everything his own way, so as to increase his power even at the risk of additional expenditure.[1]

When the Joint Select Committee examined Queen Anne's Bounty in 1900–1 the Bishop of London asked W. R. Le Fanu, the Chief Clerk (the Secretary-Treasurer had just died) whether the combined office of Secretary and Treasurer did not give its occupant too much power. Le Fanu's answer expressed the bureaucratic attitude very well: 'Not over the office certainly. The consolidation of the power in the hands of one man certainly tends to rapidity of business.'[2]

It seemed that the bishops feared increasing lay bureaucratic control more than did the laymen on the Select Committee. Sir William Anson suggested to Le Fanu that the Secretary-Treasurer could not become powerful because he was watched over by a body of governors, and added: 'In fact he is under more permanent supervision than the head of a Government department where the political chief changes from time to time.' Le Fanu hastened to agree.[3]

ADVANTAGES AND DISADVANTAGES OF THE DIVISION OF POWERS

The Joint Select Committee was in favour of Queen Anne's Bounty and the Ecclesiastical Commission amalgamating. The Bishop of London put it to Le Fanu that the Bounty's system of collecting first fruits and tenths from some 5,000 parishes and then paying the money out again, sometimes to the same parishes, appeared an extravagant way of proceeding, especially as the annual tenths payment was under £1 at times.[4]

The Committee decided that the arguments against amalgamation, such as the alleged loss of lay control involved, the greater expense of management by the Ecclesiastical

[1] Unpublished letter to the Bishop of London, 7 August 1875, Archbishop Tait's Correspondence, vol. xcv, Lambeth Palace Library. [2] *P.P.* 1900, vol. viii, Q. 179.

[3] Ibid., Qs. 228–30. [4] *P.P.* 1901, Qs. 417 and 421.

Commission, the probable increased influence of the Crown or the Government, and the fear of increasing the patronage of one combined body, were based on a misapprehension of the facts.[1]

For those bishops who were members of both boards, amalgamation would mean a considerable saving of timc. The bishops' diocesan administration and responsibilities had been increasing during the nineteenth century, and by the end of the century bishops who attended both central boards, such as the Archbishop of Canterbury, and the Bishops of London and Winchester, were prepared to welcome any plan which reduced their burden of administration.[2]

Both the Archbishop of Canterbury and the Secretary to the Ecclesiastical Commissioners gave evidence as to some indirect advantages which would result from amalgamation. In order to help the poorer clergy on dilapidation of parsonages and with glebe land a large capital fund was required and this Queen Anne's Bounty, unlike the Ecclesiastical Commission, did not possess. Also, the Bounty was legally confined to helping the poorest livings, whereas the Ecclesiastical Commission had a freer hand over its funds.[3] The Ecclesiastical Commissioners' administration was more rationalized in that they did not give grants merely on an income basis and without reference to size of population, as did the Bounty, but had a graduated scale of minimum stipends based on size of population which they gave grants to level up, and in keeping with this, they had built up a more detailed knowledge of the parishes.[4]

Not only were they more rationalized, but the Ecclesiastical Commissioners' payments were on a far larger scale. They told the 1900–1 Committee that their present additional grants to benefices amounted to £200,000 per year (plus £700,000 a year in permanent annuities to 6,000 livings) compared with the Bounty's £20,000–£30,000.[5] The Commissioners' staff were obviously as irked by the independence of the Bounty as the lay governors of the Bounty were by the Commission's desire to include them in their tidy system. One of the chief spokesmen for the lay governors, Mr. Cyril

[1] Ibid., p. ix. [2] Ibid., p. xv. [3] Ibid.
[4] Ibid., Qs. 77–8. [5] Ibid., Qs. 51 and 65.

Dodd, said that they were opposed to amalgamation because the Ecclesiastical Commission worked too much according to a 'system' of management, whereas Queen Anne's Bounty had a more 'personal' management.[1]

Despite the fact that the two central agencies overlapped in their membership and in some of their functions, they were very different in character and somewhat isolated from each other in their working. The 1900–1 Committee found that there was no direct communication between the two about their common business of augmentation.[2] The difference in their characters was revealed in the answers of their respective officers to the question of whether they saw different aspects of their work as business or philanthropy; the Ecclesiastical Commission office saw its work as business with an occasional dash of philanthropy, whereas the Bounty office could regard some of its work as philanthropy and not strict business.[3]

The dominant lay element on the Bounty Board opposed amalgamation, and a Bill based on the Joint Committee's recommendation in favour of amalgamation, which was introduced into Parliament in 1902, never got anywhere. The issue then lapsed until it was suggested again by the Archbishops' Commission of Inquiry into Church Property and Revenues in 1924.

In the post-war period of the 1920s, however, amalgamation seemed a less pressing matter. A division of functions had been worked out under which, after 1919, Queen Anne's Bounty left the augmentation of stipends to the Commissioners, whilst it concentrated on administering a dilapidations scheme and making decisions about sale and purchase of parsonage houses. In 1927, the Bounty was given the task of collecting and administering benefice tithe, and when tithe was finally redeemed in 1936 it became the holder of the redemption money (Government stock worth £53,000,000) for tithe-owning clergy. The collection of first-fruits and tenths was abolished by Church Assembly Measure in 1926. Amalgamation was again suggested by a Church Assembly

1 *P.P.* 1901, Qs. 1099 and 1103.

2 Ibid., Q. 197.

3 Ibid., Qs. 628–31 and 701.

Commission in 1933,[1] but it was not accomplished until after the second World War.

When *The Economist* examined the finances of the Church of England in 1944, the separation of Queen Anne's Bounty and the Ecclesiastical Commission was still a major element in securing the division of powers in the Church and in preserving it from over-centralization and bureaucracy.[2] The subsequent amalgamation of the two and the attempt to make the new organization partially responsible to a representative central authority, by having Church Assembly representatives on the Board, might have been expected to bring about an increased central authority. However, the Monckton Commission, in 1963, found that the Commissioners had maintained their independence, and that not all the Church Assembly representatives elected to the main body of the Church Commissioners were put on the more important, and smaller, Board of Governors; nor were they on the main committees. The central control was still largely exercised by the powerful and isolated three Church Estates Commissioners.[3]

Some positive attempt at decentralization had been made after amalgamation by the Commissioners' policy of making block grants to diocesan stipends funds and allowing the bishops and diocesan boards of finance to direct augmentation.[4] The problems which this posed for diocesan organization will be discussed in a later chapter, but its main function in relation to maintaining the division of powers in the larger organization has been to substitute a limited degree of decentralization for the previous division between Queen Anne's Bounty and the Ecclesiastical Commission.[5]

Although bureaucratization has occurred within the central financial organization of the Church, where there was a need for 'stable, strict, intensive, and calculable administration',[6] because it was the most rational form from a financial point of view, certain restraints have been placed

[1] *Church Assembly Paper* No. 440.

[2] *The Economist*, op. cit., p. 374.

[3] *Monckton Report*, pp. 29 and 41.

[4] Ibid., p. 27.

[5] The part played by Church Assembly and its departments as extra countervailing powers will be discussed later.

[6] Max Weber, op. cit., p. 338.

on the development of a monocratic or oligarchic control. The first restraint has been that exercised as a result of the division of powers even between the financial agencies—Queen Anne's Bounty, Ecclesiastical Commission, dioceses, and Church Assembly. The second restraint is provided by the different types of authority which exist within the organization and which, to some extent, act as a check on each other. Thus, although Weber characterized bureaucratic authority generally as being based on spheres of legal competence (so that he could speak of the Roman Catholic Church as a bureaucratic organization in which the universal episcopate constitutes a universal legal competence in religious matters)[1] in the Church of England there are different sources of legality. It is the differences in sources of legality—whether from Act of Parliament, valid ordination and consecration, or pragmatic/expediential criteria—which provide a major ingredient in the differential ideational backgrounds of the bureaucrats and makes for differences in the character of each of the offices. The effect of these ideational backgrounds and different sources of authority has been discerned in the different characters of Queen Anne's Bounty and the Ecclesiastical Commission. The relatively strong influence of the episcopate in Queen Anne's Bounty was reflected in its paternalistic behavioural characteristics; the civil service influence on the Ecclesiastical Commission appeared in its internal structure, its responsibility to Parliament, and the characteristics of impersonality, formalization, and caution in its policies. The third ideational background and source of authority—that of pragmatism and expedience, which Harrison found to be typical of a denomination with strong democratic values, will be shown to have played some part in shaping the bureaucracy associated with Church Assembly.

[1] Max Weber, op. cit., p. 334.

IV

THE CHANGING SCENE AND DEVELOPMENTS IN THE SECOND HALF OF THE NINETEENTH CENTURY

THE NEED FOR A SYSTEM OF REPRESENTATIVE CHURCH GOVERNMENT

THE development of the Church of England's organization in the period 1850–90 can be seen as a search for an acceptable system of representative assemblies. The pressures to develop such a system came from many directions. Changes in the political power of the different social classes required the Church to seek to enlist middle-class laymen to responsible positions in its organization if it was to influence public opinion in its favour, once it could no longer rely solely on its traditional ties with aristocracy and squires. The process of social differentiation and increasing institutional autonomy likewise deprived the Church of its traditional sources of income and administrative provisions. This brought about a development of autonomous church organization, and, consequently, a demand for representative diocesan and central authorities which could control that organization, and provide a new basis of legitimacy for such developments. However, it will be shown that the growth and structure of the various councils and conferences which appeared between 1850 and 1890 were not determined by any agreed theory in the Church. Rather, they were shaped by the defensive stand which the Church had to make against external attack whilst rent internally by party divisions. In the 1850s the defence was stretched across a wide front; from High Church defence against liberalism in all its forms, to defence against the attacks of the Liberation Society, and the 'aggression' of Roman Catholicism. In the 1880s the direct political threat of disestablishment produced a new defence movement, alerted by the ominous words in Gladstone's address to the Electors of Midlothian on 17 September 1885, about the possibility of a future disestablishment.

In the case of internal conflict, and its effect on the developing organization, the problems stemmed from disagreements over authority. According to Max Weber, the nature of the claim to legitimacy determines the type of authority as well as the mode of social organization of a group. On the basis of this, Paul M. Harrison suggested that, in contrast to the American Baptist Church, in an episcopalian church there might be expected to exist a commonly accepted belief in the 'legality' of patterns of normative rules and the right of those elevated to authority under these rules to issue commands.[1] It was just such agreement on legitimacy which was lacking in the Church of England, however, and the history of its organization in the second half of the nineteenth century is concerned mainly with attempts to secure such a consensus. These attempts will be seen to have developed steadily in the direction of creating more inclusive representative assemblies.

The development of the Ecclesiastical Commission and Queen Anne's Bounty, and the proliferation of voluntary societies, had been required to meet the challenge presented by population increases, urbanization, and the missionary opportunities of the expanding Empire, at a time when older sources of income and administrative provision were being eroded as the State became more secular and denominational equality was approached. On the other hand, the deliberative and legislative functions in the Church, and its policy-making and co-ordinative requirements, were also affected by the process of structural differentiation in the society at large.

A committee which reviewed these developments at the end of the century concluded that:

> The tendency of modern legislation has been uniformly in the direction of so separating ecclesiastical from civil offices and duties, as to destroy the old hypothesis of the relation of the machinery of national government to the Church, to introduce some ambiguity into the status of church officers, and to minimize, almost to the point of

[1] P. M. Harrison, *Authority and Power in the Free Church Tradition*, p. 208.

obliteration, the direct influence of the Church laity, as such, upon the government of Church affairs.[1]

Not only had Parliament ceased to be the representative assembly of the laity of the Church of England, but at the local level, the ecclesiastical parish had ceased to be the civil parish in which the vestry, composed of all householders, undertook both the upkeep of the church and the general administration of the parish. The long-drawn-out Braintree Case, from 1837 to 1853, eventually established that the law could not enforce the payment of church rates if the rate had not been passed by a majority at the vestry meeting. The remedy according to ecclesiastical law was excommunication, but that was practically obsolete, and anyway it was hardly appropriate for Dissenters. The passing of Gladstone's Compulsory Church Rate Abolition Bill, in 1868, abolished compulsory church rate altogether, and the Church was thrown back on the voluntary system, and endowments, for its finances.

Some conservative churchmen had refused to face up to the need for such an adjustment on the Church's part. To a militant, typically traditionalist, church defender like Archdeacon Denison, church rates and a national Church were the same thing: 'Take away the former and you destroy the latter,' he told the Church Congress at York in 1866. But to a fellow High Churchman like J. G. Hubbard M.P., who was an expert on taxation and finance, such a view was fifty years out of date, or, if such grounds were admitted, the National Church had gone long ago.[2]

Hubbard had warned the Church Congress four years before his confrontation with Denison that the only financial system which could satisfy the Church's needs was that of regular giving through the offertory. However, even Hubbard admitted the difficulty and novelty of this in the Established Church. Not only was there the problem of finding a definition of membership, which had never been necessary heretofore, but there were also the problems which this would raise with regard to the clergyman's status and social

[1] Report of the Joint Committee of the Convocation of Canterbury on *The Position of the Laity in the Church*, p. 50.

[2] *Proceedings of Church Congress*, pp. 260–73.

relations. Hubbard mentioned that one clergyman had told him that he dare not ask for money from his rich parishioners because it would create 'an irreparable breach between us and I should lose all my influence.'[1]

VOLUNTARY SOCIETIES

One way of mitigating this was to use voluntary societies as an intermediary for the purpose of fund-raising, and in this period of transition for the Church, these central and regional agencies served just such a function. One of the most perspicacious of speakers on Church organization, Thomas Turner, told the Dublin Church Congress, in 1868, that, although much of the recent improvement in the organization of the Church Establishment was the result of the exercise by the Ecclesiastical Commissioners of the powers which the Legislature had vested in them, without the preparatory labours and continued co-operation of the societies the efforts of the Commissioners would have been well-nigh barren. He remarked that they were the only independent agencies which the Church as a body possessed, and that this was a significant fact at a time when the manifest tendency of events was to throw the Church upon its own resources.[2]

But both on grounds of efficiency, and of legitimate authority and control, the societies left much to be desired. In 1864 in London alone there were nineteen different charities for necessitous clergy and their families, and although these realized between them about £30,000 annually, there were still many examples of humiliating clerical poverty.[3] To one clergyman who had examined the problem there seemed only one answer:

> It seems to me that a grand corporation like the Church of England ought to institute means for the relief of its necessitous clergy as a distinct department of its executive; and not to leave it, as it now does,

[1] *P.C.C.*, Oxford, 1862, p. 97.

[2] *P.C.C.*, Dublin, 1868, pp. 25–6.

[3] See the Paper by the Revd. J. H. Titcomb, 'Associations for Aiding Poor, Enfeebled, and Disabled Clergymen, and the Widows and Children of the Clergy', in *P.C.C.*, pp. 224–9.

either to the irregular and spasmodic efforts of individual beneficence, or to local benevolent societies. . . .[1]

In addition to their inefficiency, their duplication of functions, and the absence of any co-ordinating and policy-making body to decide on priorities, the societies lacked authority, and some High Churchmen denied that they were legitimate organs of the Church. The objections were twofold:

. . . first, that these Societies are voluntary Associations, not emanating from any legitimate ecclesiastical authority. Secondly, that they are not to the extent that they should be, placed under the control and direction of the Bishops of the Church.[2]

The answer given to these objections was that the societies did not obtrude themselves into the posts of the 'regular army' but manned positions and undertook services which the 'army' was unable to occupy and provide for. Also, the bishops exercised control and direction in their positions as presidents or patrons and on management committees.[2] However, although the societies possessed certain advantages when it came to undertaking new work, as the Church became more conscious of its corporateness and sought to develop its own executive, and as formal rational criteria of efficiency were applied to administration generally, the deficiencies of this system of societies were revealed.

The co-existence of so many unconnected, and occasionally rival societies, the number of which is too often recklessly increased by the formation, on slight or inadequate grounds, of separate Associations for objects already provided for, indicates a defect in the organization of the Church; and involves, moreover, a useless expenditure of funds, and a waste of power, which constitute a most serious drawback to the efficiency of the Societies themselves. Who has not at one time or another cherished a vision (who would not rejoice to see accomplished the reality) of the English Church, acting together as one body, and under one administration, having, indeed, its separate departments for this and that description of labour, but all working in concert, and as parts of one harmonious and comprehensive whole?[3]

It was the Evangelicals, however, who supported and

[1] Ibid., p. 225. [2] Turner, op. cit., p. 27. [3] Ibid., p. 28.

directed the majority of societies, and, as the party conflict in the Church became more acute they became increasingly reluctant to give up control of the societies to diocesan boards or bishops. The Evangelicals had long pursued a policy of exerting their influence through the media of societies, and their tenacious adherence to this form of organization was made all the stronger by the memory of their earlier exclusion from the councils of the older church societies. In the 1820s one of their leaders, Charles Simeon, when proposed as a member of the Society for the Promotion of Christian Knowledge, was 'black-balled', and was only admitted subsequently owing to the personal efforts of C. J. Blomfield.[1]

Most of the bishops were hostile to the Evangelical societies in the first decades of the nineteenth century.[2] After a time, however, the society form of organization had gained wider support, but the Oxford Movement's stress on legitimate authority, and the growing emphasis in favour of a distinctive church organization, under the authority of diocesan bishops, brought a new spate of criticism of the society system. Even the older church societies, such as the Society for the Propagation of the Gospel and the S.P.C.K., were attacked by the Tractarians. William Palmer used strong language about the S.P.C.K. at a members' meeting in 1840 and called it a 'congregational society' and a 'joint stock club'. He also castigated the S.P.G. because the bishops were not *ex officio* members of the governing body, but had to be elected. 'What', he asked, 'would be thought of guinea subscribers in the early Church *inviting* the Apostles to become members of their Committee?'[3]

DIOCESAN ORGANIZATION

Samuel Wilberforce, a more moderate High Churchman, was responsible for setting a new pattern of diocesan organization, and even before he became a bishop, as Archdeacon of

[1] *Christian Observer*, July 1863, p. 536; also, Eugene Stock, *The History of the Church Missionary Society*, vol. i, p. 66.

[2] Stock, op. cit., p. 134.

[3] Ibid., p. 389.

Surrey, he advocated the combination of societies in church unions at deanery and diocesan level.[1] The Evangelical bastion, the Church Missionary Society, put out a reply in a circular saying that even on the lowest ground of financial efficiency such a step was undesirable, and besides which it would also flout the legitimate principle that donors should possess the right to determine how their gifts were applied, and that the societies which it was proposed to combine all differed from each other in various respects. The C.M.S. associations were directed by headquarters to maintain themselves intact.[1]

The Tractarians' advocacy of the authority of diocesan bishops and diocesan organization, and the concurrent increase in diocesan administration which was welcomed and fostered by bishops like Samuel Wilberforce, reduced the willingness of some bishops to perform functions at the national level. To those leaders responsible for the Church as a national institution this seemed a dangerous development of the episcopal role, and one which threatened to render untenable the Church's established status.

Later in the century Archbishop Benson was to feel the need for a central cabinet in the Church so acutely that he wrote to the Dean of Windsor: 'I despair of Prelacy—it recks nothing of the nation or Mankind. Diocesan Episcopacy will be reduced to the level of Diocesan Inspectorship.'[2] Benson held Wilberforce responsible for the development of this 'New Type' of bishop. He complained to his friend Westcott: 'Diocesanism is a new force of dissent as virulent as congregationalism, and more.'[3]

CONVOCATION REVIVAL

It did seem at one time as if the revival of Convocation, practically dormant since 1717, might provide the authoritative central policy-making and co-ordinative body for the Church. Even the Evangelicals had thought that the revival of Convocation might prove to be the answer, and in reply

[1] Ibid., p. 383.

[2] A. C. Benson, *The Life of Edward White Benson*, vol. ii, p. 203.

[3] Ibid., p. 697.

to criticisms that the society system lacked legitimacy, the C.M.S. drew up a document, which came to be known as the Appendix to the Thirty-Ninth Report, stating:

> And hence it may be observed that nothing less than the sanction of a duly-assembled Convocation can more fully identify the acts of any Missionary Society within the Church of England with the Church.[1]

The prominent Evangelical, Francis Close of Cheltenham, made the same point in his St. Bride's Sermon, as late as 1841.[2]

After this time, however, the growing power of 'sacerdotalism' (as the Evangelicals termed it) caused the Evangelicals to oppose the revival of Convocation on the grounds that it would limit the power of the State, infringe the Royal Supremacy, and subject the laity to clerical and episcopal domination. The militant Evangelical organ, *The Record*, said that such synods were 'but great machines for enforcing 'unity', by expelling all opinions but one'.[3] Lord Shaftesbury presided at a great meeting in November 1852 to protest against the imminent revival of Convocation and against the confessional. He said that Convocation meant priestly despotism, which would use the confessional as its most potent engine. He was not opposed to the plan, which Gladstone seems to have communicated to him, of including laity in such a synod.[4] But this was not the plan which most High Churchmen were prepared to support.

Some of the Church reformers who had favoured the establishment of the Ecclesiastical Commission in order to give the Church a central executive were also in favour of a mixed clerical and lay synod, in preference to a purely clerical Convocation; this was the view of Archbishop Whately and Bishop Blomfield.[5] In 1832 Blomfield had hoped that something like the Ecclesiastical Commission might possess all the advantages of Convocation without the evils which had been found to result from it under the latter's

[1] Stock, op. cit., p. 398.
[2] Ibid., pp. 387–8.
[3] *The Record*, 14 August 1852.
[4] Stock, op. cit., p. 11.
[5] E. J. Whately, *The Life and Correspondence of Archbishop Whately*, p. 279, note i; and G. Biber, *Bishop Blomfield and His Times*, p. 390.

old constitution.[1] By 1851, however, he had modified his opinion and on 11 July spoke in the House of Lords in favour of Convocation, although he regarded its representation of the parochial clergy as too few. He still regarded it as a hazardous experiment.[2] The change of mind can be explained only in the light of his recent harrowing experiences at the hands of Ritualists and Evangelicals who flouted his authority in the London Diocese. He commented: 'Recent events have made me individually feel strongly the want of such a body. I do not know to whom to have recourse for counsel and advice. . . .'[3]

To other parties in the Church it seemed that the campaign for the revival of Convocation was not unrelated to the High Church campaign against the nomination of the liberal Dr. Hampden to the see of Hereford in 1847, and the attempt in the same year to prevent the Evangelical, G. C. Gorham, from taking up the living of Brampford Speke because the High Church Bishop of Exeter, Phillpotts, thought him doctrinally unsound. The fact that the Judicial Committee of the Privy Council in 1850 reversed the judgement of the Court of Arches and found in favour of Gorham, was enough to cause Manning and a few others to join the Roman Catholic Church. Many of the remaining High Churchmen threw their weight behind a movement to defend the Church against hostile state encroachment, especially as that hostility seemed likely to be intensified by the propaganda of the British Anti-State-Church Association founded in 1844 (it became the Liberation Society in 1853). Church unions were set up in many towns in 1848 for 'defence against aggression'.[4]

The success of these unions in mobilizing opinion in defence of the Church was obviously due to their combination of clergy and laity in united action, and this led some of the High Churchmen involved in the movement for the revival of Convocation to look favourably on the idea of lay representation in such synods. The two senior leaders of the Tractarians, Pusey and Keble, recognized the

[1] A. Blomfield, *A Memoir of Charles James Blomfield, Bishop of London*, pp. 154–5.

[2] Ibid., p. 329.

[3] Biber, op. cit., p. 395.

[4] J. B. Sweet, *A Memoir of the Late Henry Hoare*, p. 61.

importance of the combined action but their immediate concern was not for diocesan synods, nor revival of Convocation, but for the more limited plan for the representation of all the church unions in a central Church Council in London. They were not really keen on any representative system, but it seemed to Pusey that a desperate situation required or allowed a desperate remedy, especially as they felt they could count on scarcely three bishops not to acquiesce in the present state of things unless they were pressed from without. Their conclusion was that in order to be effectual pressure needed to be consolidated.[1]

Henry Hoare, the layman who did most of the organizing in the two years' preparation which led to the founding in 1850 of the Convocation Society devoted solely to the revival of Convocation, suggested to Pusey that laymen might be included in diocesan synods, but Pusey was against even this if it entailed formal representation.[2] Gladstone thought that laymen could be included in Convocation provided a distinction was drawn between the inalienable powers of the Episcopal College and administrative provisions. Pusey said that Gladstone's distinction between admitting laymen to synods, but debarring them from voting on doctrine and discipline, would not hold up.

> In truth, I think that let people guard how they may, both doctrine and discipline, it can only be for a time. The power of the laity is a growing power. To admit them into the Synods, and then exclude them from what is to both parties of most real interest, will, I am persuaded, never hold. . . I look with terror on any admission of laity into synods. It at once invests them with an ecclesiastical office, which will develop itself sooner or later, I believe, to the destruction of the Faith.[3]

His forecast of the difficulty of maintaining the distinction was to be borne out later in the history of the Church Assembly.

The difference of opinion within the High Church ranks caused a division within the London Church Union in 1852. over the question of lay representation in synods. A. J. Beresford Hope persuaded many of the Committee to agree

[1] H. P. Liddon, *Life of Pusey*, vol. iii, p. 342.

[2] Ibid., p. 344.

[3] Quoted in Liddon, op. cit., p. 346.

to such a scheme. Pusey signed an address to him against the Union giving support in that direction.[1] Although Beresford Hope had to accept this position for the London Church Union, it did not lessen his impatience with his High Church colleagues' timidity towards including the laity in a central authority. When Henry Hoare replied to a Church Congress speech in favour of lay representation in Convocation by suggesting that 'harmony and co-operation may be promoted by the simple expedient even of tea-meetings', Beresford Hope told him that he thought the Church Congress had something to do besides talking about tea-meetings and dinners, and that something should be done to settle the important question of the central representation of the church laity.[2]

THE DIFFERENT CENTRAL CHURCH COUNCILS

All the various central church councils which appeared in the second half of the nineteenth century were responses to the same wider process of structural differentiation in English society, since it raised in an acute form the problem of the relation between Church and State. The different aspects of that problem as they affected the functions of legislation, administration, discipline, and communication in the Church, were reflected in the characters of the main central bodies. Convocation revival in 1852, the Church Congresses, begun in 1861, and the Church Institution ('An Association of Clergy and Laity for Defensive and General Purposes'), formed in 1859, all arose in that climate of opinion in the Church which received its emotional charge from the Tractarian reassertion of the Church as a spiritual kingdom resisting encroachment by secular power and liberal thought, and acquired its local embodiment in the church unions and defence associations which grew up after 1848. As central councils, however, the three bodies differed considerably, and although they were to some extent complementary in the functions which they served, the separation of those functions at the centre weakened the comprehensive effectiveness and authority of all three bodies.

[1] Ibid., p. 352.

[2] *P.C.C.*, Cambridge, 1861, pp. 163–4.

Convocation was by far the most important of the three central councils and the only one which possessed an authority legitimated on purely theological grounds. The Church Congress and the Church Institution were usually justified on grounds of their expediency for Church defence: the former developed the character of a forum for constructive discussion of church administration, and the latter, as a propaganda and intelligence unit, set out to improve communication within the Church—channelling information between central and local levels, and consolidating such opinion as facilitated church defence. The advantage which both these bodies possessed over Convocation was their inclusion of the laity.

CHURCH CONGRESS, THE CHURCH INSTITUTION, AND LAY REPRESENTATION

The Church Congress, although lacking theological legitimation, was in many ways the most constructive of the three bodies and most resembled the later Church Assembly in its concern for efficient administration. Like the Church Institution, the Church Congress was a child of the movement which gave rise to local church defence associations in the 1850s. The first Church Congress was summoned by the Cambridge Church Defence Association in 1861, and its purpose was expressed in the invitation:

> We are convinced that a zealous endeavour to stimulate the energies of the Church, and to apply correctives to acknowledged defects of system from within are not less efficient measures of Church Defence than the defeat of destructive attacks from without; and we believe that friendly discussion among Churchmen would greatly aid in devising remedies where needed and in promoting unity of action.[1]

In Convocation, party divisions were occasionally exacerbated by a preoccupation with clergy discipline and the paradox, which appeared in the 1850s, of a laity which demanded discipline in ritual and liberty in dogma, whilst the High Church clergy in Convocation sought the opposite. Church Congress, however, tended to attract those clergy and laity of all parties, who were 'sincerely concerned for

[1] *P.C.C.*, Cambridge, 1861, p. iv.

the promotion of the practical efficiency of the Church of England', and who could agree on one common object, 'the efficient working of the Church for the holy purpose for which she exists'.[1] The co-operation and relative harmony which this concern for practical efficiency and intermediate, or proximate, goals and purposes elicited, was later to be used as an argument in favour of creating the Church Assembly.

The invitation to the first Church Congress, which the Cambridge Church Defence Association sent out, proposed that they should direct their attention to: Church Rates, Increase of the Ministerial Agency of the Church, the Work of the Church in Education, the Sub-division of Dioceses and Increase of the Episcopate, Church Discipline and Church Building Acts, Incomes of the Clergy, Co-operation of Clergy and Laity in Parishes, Rural Deaneries, Archdeaconries and at Diocesan Synods. By concentrating on practical subjects it was hoped to spread harmony and co-operation in place of the party strife that was weakening the Church's defence against external attack. This intention was expressed in the first-ever Church Congress speech which was given by Archdeacon France:

> A few years ago (as you cannot fail to remember) there was apparently no organization whatever among Churchmen for their own protection. . . . It is clear that such a state of things was by no means conducive to the strength of the Church as an Institution: that instead of presenting a united array to any opponent, it absolutely invited attack by its want of harmony and organization.[2]

Despite their ability to promote these ends, both Church Congress and the Church Institution lacked an adequate system of formal representation which would have given their members, lay and clerical (but especially lay), an authority which was based on more than individual personality or social status. Church Congress could be attended by almost anyone, and the Church Institution was little better, although Henry Hoare, its founder, had hoped that it would be part of an overall system of representation in which ruridecanal chapters, co-operating with consulting

[1] *P.C.C.*, Oxford, 1862, p. 161.
[2] *P.C.C.*, Cambridge, 1861, p. 1.

committees of nominated (not elected) laymen, would have unpaid agents in London who would be the means of communication between them and the Church Institution. The Church Institution had itself been formed by the appointment of an Executive Committee by 'lay consultees' meeting in London on 8 July 1859.[1]

The advantage of such a system of representation in High Churchmen's eyes was that it would not infringe the rights of the purely clerical Convocation, whilst at the same time it would involve the laity in church defence. It was apparent that the changes in political power and in the composition of the House of Commons were making the middle classes a force to be reckoned with and that any church defence would need to enlist middle-class laymen, especially as these were the main target of the Liberation Society's propaganda against the Church.

Joseph Napier, who had been Lord Chancellor of Ireland and M.P. for Dublin University, told the Church Congress at Oxford in 1862 that the only way of furthering the Church's influence in the House of Commons was by securing middle-class lay co-operation in the parochial system and in central conferences:

> The clergy can associate with the higher classes; they may visit the humbler; but the *intermediate classes*, on whom so great an amount of political power has devolved, have not been kept in that unbroken connection with the Church which might have given an unlimited security both to Church and State. . . .[2]

Several speakers from the floor supported Napier's call for centralization and lay involvement, and suggested that they should throw all their influence into the Church Institution. Henry Hoare, the chief organizer of the Church Institution, was repeatedly called for by the meeting and he agreed with them that it was with the middle classes that 'the real strength and the real power of this great nation at this moment lies', and that it was up to the middle-class clergy to 'take them by the hand'.[3]

The traditional ties between Church, aristocracy, and

[1] Sweet, op. cit., pp. 423 and 446.
[2] *P.C.C.*, Oxford, 1862 p. 161.
[3] Ibid., pp. 166.

squires, which had given the Church of England its political strength and stability, by the second half of the nineteenth century seemed woefully inadequate in the face of the growing power of the urban middle classes. The various schemes for lay representation were aimed specifically at enlisting the middle-class laity and so influencing public opinion in favour of the Church's interests. In the twentieth century the new schemes which led up to the formation of Church Assembly shifted the emphasis from the middle-class laymen to incorporating working-class laity.

Hoare's complicated schemes for erecting a comprehensive system of councils at ruridecanal, diocesan, and national levels never really provided an adequate basis for a lasting system of representative Church government. His concern was mainly for church defence and he was realistic enough to see that this required lay involvement, but when it came to devising a system of lay representation his regard for High Church principles prevented him from insisting on the principle of election being adopted as its basis.

That the Church Institution never provided an adequate representative body was not surprising in view of the unrealistic system of representation on which it was based. The link between the local and central levels depended on unpaid central agents, or corresponding lay consultees, in London. The way in which such a representative was chosen for the Chesterfield deanery was probably not untypical and explains the limited nature of the scheme. At a deanery meeting at Bolsover Castle, having chosen local consultees to represent the parishes,

> . . . the Chairman said that before they separated they had one thing more to do, viz. to nominate an unpaid central agent, or corresponding lay consultee, in London. A clergyman present having suggested the name of his own son, a solicitor in Old Bond Street, the same was gratefully and unanimously accepted.[1]

The basic division between the various schemes for a central church council was between those who were prepared to base the system of lay representation on election, and those like Henry Hoare who opposed the election of laymen and were only prepared to admit lay consultees of some

[1] Sweet, op. cit., p. 444.

kind. Hoare, because he was the hero of the successful movement to revive Convocation, had great influence in the discussions of the 1850s in which the schemes including lay election suffered a temporary defeat. The various schemes which appeared in this period were collected together by Henry Hoare in his 'Hints on Lay Co-operation'.

The alternatives were: firstly, the introduction of laymen into Convocation. The support for this included some Evangelicals, who said that the exclusion of the laity showed that Convocation was 'an institution totally unsuited to the age, and behind the times'.[1]

The second suggestion made was that there should be a central body of laymen which would sit side by side with Convocation.[2] This plan was implemented in the Houses of Laymen attached to the Convocations later in the century.

A third scheme, advocated by a layman, F. H. Dickinson, was for a national assembly of bishops, clergy, and laymen, which would exist simultaneously with Convocation. It would allow any of the three orders to discuss separately questions specially affecting their interests, and no measure would be adopted without the assent of each order voting separately.[3] This plan most resembled the eventual constitution of the Church Assembly as laid down in the Enabling Act in 1919.

A plan suggested by another layman, G. B. Hughes, in a letter to *The English Churchman*, dated 4 December 1854, aimed at introducing the lay element into Convocation by the selection of two Members of Parliament at each election of diocesan proctors. They would speak and vote in Convocation on all matters not of an exclusively spiritual character.[4] A similar plan, for a meeting of an equal number of members of the Houses of Parliament and of Convocation, was proposed in the Lower House of the Convocation of Canterbury on 26 April 1877.[5]

[1] Revd. J. C. Ryle, in a letter to *The Record*, dated 8 November 1869; quoted in Sweet, op. cit., p. xvi.

[2] Sweet, op. cit., p. 422.

[3] Letter of F. H. Dickinson to the Revd. J. V. Vincent, 6 May 1857; quoted in Henry Hoare, *Hints on Lay Co-operation*, pp. 408–10.

[4] Hoare, op. cit., p. 218.

[5] Speech of Canon Jeffreys, *Chronicle of Canterbury Convocation*, 26 April 1877, p. 121.

A very cautious proposal was that laymen should be allowed to serve on committees of Convocation, but even so Henry Hoare insisted that they should not be allowed to vote.[1] Although Hoare favoured a comprehensive system of representative assemblies he did not envisage that the lay representation throughout should be based on election. His opposition to the election of laymen to a central governing synod was partly on the grounds of the sanctity of the traditional constitution of Convocation, and partly out of a conservative fear of the popular clamour which he associated with elections.

> It is easy to imagine the laity roused to such an energetic interest in Church matters, as should 'develop itself in the form of election placards, stating the controversial merits of the respective candidates, with banners of Broad Church blue, Tractarian red, or Evangelical yellow'. Few would desire this.

He added,

> When the laity are invited, it would of course be a capital mistake to omit the middle class, the men of business; the best among them should be earnestly exhorted to come forward.[2]

A prominent Evangelical, R. B. Seeley, who was the organizer of several Evangelical societies but a staunch upholder of the Establishment, told Hoare that if he wanted 'a working body;—a Convocation, Synod, or Assembly of some kind for the guidance and strengthening of the Church of England', then,

> . . . to create a working governing body, from which laymen are excluded will be quite nugatory. If it is to be merely a talking body, a conference, or conversazione, then people will be careless as to its constitution. But if it is to act and to have power, then the laity will expect to have some voice in its deliberations and decisions.[3]

Hoare's reply showed that his intentions were far more limited:

> You attribute to me a desire for what you call 'a working body; a governing body; a body which is to act; a body having power, not only to deliberate, but also to decide.' If you wish for such a body, it may encourage me to wish for it. But I have nowhere expressed such

[1] Hoare, op. cit., p. 294. [2] Ibid., p. 152. [3] Ibid., pp. 410–11.

a wish; and I certainly should not entertain it without considerable anxiety.[1]

Seeley could only express his disappointment and surprise at Hoare's limited intentions. Like many others he had associated Hoare's name with the revival of Convocation and had not been aware of what seemed to be 'gradual modifications' in Hoare's purposes. Seeley declared:

> For my own part, many circumstances rather increase my desire for some body which might fight the Church's battles. The helplessness of her friends in Parliament, in the matter of Church Rates, and the manner in which her Trustees, the Ecclesiastical Commissioners, are now giving away her property by millions, at the very moment when the Bishop of Exeter rises in Parliament to complain of her poverty,—concur to make me desire some better means than we now have of maintaining the Church's rights.[2]

As far as Hoare was concerned the solution to the lay question would soon be attained by the 8,000 parochial committees which he hoped to see set up. The 'permanent' element which Seeley desired in Church government, Hoare claimed already existed in the House of Bishops, and this could be supplemented by 'voluntary' conferences, which ought not to be despised.[3] Some advocates of a governing assembly with elected lay representatives, such as F. H. Dickinson, were persuaded by Hoare to direct their energies to founding and running the Church Institution, which was itself little more than a voluntary society.

THE CENTRAL CHURCH COMMITTEE

Within a short time of its formation the Church Institution had become simply a London committee for church defence against hostile legislation, and even in that role it was not altogether effective. When Chamberlain launched another, even stronger, attack on the Established Church under the auspices of the 'Radical Programme' in the election of 1885, and a large number of Liberal candidates pledged themselves to Disestablishment, the Church was driven to take new measures of defence and internal reform. Archbishop

[1] Hoare, op. cit., pp. 411–12. [2] Ibid., p. 414. [3] Ibid., pp. 415–16.

Benson encouraged the formation of a Church Parliamentary Committee in the House of Commons in 1893–4. Such a defensive organization in Parliament was not enough unless it could enlist wider public support, and as the Church Institution had lost its earlier national character with the failure of the system of liaison using unpaid agents in London, Benson founded the Central Church Committee in 1894. Its main function once again was to facilitate communication within the Church between central and local levels. Each diocese was to have Church Committees which would work through rural deaneries, and even set up similar committees once again in the parishes. Like the Church Institution, the Central Church Committee elicited widespread support and enthusiasm. Within the first year over 5,000 parishes had committees.[1] In 1896 the Central Church Committee and the Church Institution were amalgamated to form the Central Church Committee for Church Defence and Church Instruction. Very soon, however, the gap between local and national levels was as wide as ever because such voluntary committees lacked regular business and constitutional authority.

REPRESENTATION AT THE DIOCESAN LEVEL

The main problem in the creation of an acceptable and effective central authority was that of securing agreement on a system of representation. Although hostile attack from outside might produce agreement on the need for representative councils in the Church, it did not provide a sound basis on which to erect such a system. The committees and councils which it produced had frail constitutions and depended too much on the initial feelings of enthusiasm and militancy out of which they were created, but which were difficult to sustain. Any viable, and representative, central assembly, needed to appear as the natural apex of a system of representation which comprehended the different levels of organization in the Church. The crucial intermediate level was that of the diocese.

The impetus to form diocesan assemblies had been given

[1] Benson, op. cit., p. 547.

by that same period of church defence that had given rise to the church unions and defence associations, the revival of Convocation, and the Church Institution. High Churchmen especially feared the State's encroachment on the spiritual prerogatives of the Church, and it was the redoubtable High Churchman Bishop Phillpotts who revived the diocesan synod, at Exeter in 1851 (his object being to obtain a synodical condemnation of Gorham's errors).[1] Archdeacon Emery, of Ely, having played the leading role in the founding of the Church Congress in 1861, also turned his attention to diocesan organization. In 1864 he nurtured a system of ruridecanal, archidiaconal, and diocesan conferences in the diocese of Ely, which incorporated lay representatives and so attracted more widespread support than the High Church idea of purely clerical synods.

Although in favour of the principle of lay representation, many Evangelicals feared the development of diocesan organization. The Revd. Dr. Taylor replied to Archdeacon Emery at the Liverpool Church Congress in 1869 that diocesan organization lacked the essential condition of healthful organic action, namely, the 'homogeneousness' of the constituent elements; in every diocese, according to him, there were three antagonistic and mutually destructive schools of thought—Sacramentalists, Evangelicals, and Rationalists. To the Evangelical, not only did diocesan organization seem likely to hasten disestablishment, it would also mean that,

> the Episcopate would become invested with autocratic power, i.e. with the absolute control of the Diocesan Organization. . . . The liberties of the Parochial Clergy would exist but in name; centralization would be the order of the day.[2]

The Evangelical Church Missionary Society's organ, the *Church Missionary Intelligencer*, commented in December 1866 that it was imperative for the Society to retain its independent status and not merge its action in that of church synods because these consisted of men of mixed principles. It felt that it could not identify itself with church synods

[1] F. Warre Cornish, *The English Church in the Nineteenth Century*, p. 312.

[2] *P.C.C.*, Liverpool, pp. 44–6.

because it could not calculate on their actions, for these depended too much on what influence was in the ascendant.[1]

The Church Congress and the diocesan conferences, because of their large lay elements and the practical nature of many of the topics discussed, gradually overcame the fears of at least some Evangelicals. The prominent Evangelical Canon (later Bishop) Ryle advised Evangelicals at the Islington Clerical Meeting in 1872 to attend Church Congresses, and he and two other Evangelicals, Canon Garbett and Canon Hoare, were attacked by the extreme Evangelical paper, *The Rock*, in the same year, as traitors to Evangelicalism because of their attendance.[2]

By 1881 there were diocesan conferences in all but three dioceses, viz. London, Llandaff, and Worcester (although the Bishop of London was about to launch one). The constitutions and operations of the diocesan conferences differed greatly; numbers of members ranged from 150 to 500 and, although the tendency was towards annual meetings, some of the conferences were still either biennial or triennial.[3] The lack of uniformity in diocesan organization was to be a constant limiting factor on any overall rationalization of Church administration.

In 1881, another central council appeared on the scene, this time to serve as the co-ordinating body for the diocesan conferences. The Central Council of Diocesan Conferences and Synods grew out of a meeting, held in 1879, of some leading members of the diocesan conferences who were dissatisfied with the lack of central co-ordination, and the fact that: 'No plan has yet been devised to promote their united consideration of the same subject, or otherwise to enable them to act together on any regular defined system.' They considered that the two independent and coexistent Convocations of Canterbury and York, even if reformed and enlarged in their representation of the clergy, would still

[1] Cf. criticisms of this article and its policy in a speech by the Revd. Charles H. Rice, in *P.C.C.*, Dublin, 1868, p. 38, and the reply by a C.M.S. secretary, the Revd. Maurice F. Day, ibid., p. 44.

[2] Stock, op. cit., vol. iii, pp. 8–9.

[3] See the discussion of the diocesan conferences in the *Proceedings of the First Meeting of the Central Council of Diocesan Conferences and Synods*, London, 7 July 1881, p. 9.

not provide an adequate representative organ for the promotion of 'the greater efficiency of the Church of England' because the laity were excluded. The need for a central council of laity and clergy representing the diocesan conferences seemed all the more necessary in view of the gains which such consultation had produced in the 'successful debates and practical tendencies' of the Church Congresses.[1] Archdeacon Emery, and F. H. Dickinson (who had advocated an elected national assembly before becoming involved with Hoare in the Church Institution), were made honorary secretaries of the new Central Council. However, Dickinson was to be disappointed once more if he still hoped for a strong national assembly. The Central Council never developed any authority and its functions were limited, like the Church Institution, to propaganda and communication.

THE NEED FOR A CENTRAL POLICY-MAKING AND EXECUTIVE AUTHORITY

Emery, who strove so hard to develop a system of mixed clerical and lay councils at different levels in the Church, saw that many of the disciplinary and other troubles which loomed so large in the Church's life at that time were exacerbated by the lack of such organization:

> The whole spiritual body is heaving with life, which, for want of regular healthy organization, results often in rents and sores, in unwholesome excitement and confused action.

Even the traditional authority of the hierarchy was weakened as a result and the bishops were placed in a position of isolation 'not being surrounded and supported by constitutional officers and government' and were weakened and opposed.[2]

Thomas Turner had defended the societies, against the charge that they lacked legitimate authority, by pointing out that they had the bishops as presidents and patrons and on management committees. But he, too, recognized that in this field as elsewhere in the Church 'the influence of the Bishops over the Societies is limited mainly by the amount

[1] *Proceedings of the First Meeting . . .*, London, 7 July 1881, pp. 8–9.

[2] *P.C.C.*, Manchester, 1863, pp. 244–5.

of time which they are able to afford to the management of these undertakings'.[1] Turner's solution to the problem was a farsighted forecast of the Church Assembly:

> The great want of our Church (as it seems to me), a want from which it has long suffered, and which is and will be felt year by year with continually increasing intensity, is that of a General Church Assembly or Convention, which shall comprize, by actual presence or adequate representation, all orders of the Church, Bishops, Clergy and Laity, meeting in Council to deliberate upon and to take steps for carrying out whatever measures are required for promoting the common weal. Whatever else it undertook, the main scope of such an Assembly, in my view of the case, would be, to consider, in a practical point of view, how the work of the Church may be best carried on; to devise means whereby her deficiencies may be supplied, her resources turned to the best account, her influence strengthened, her dominion extended—and where the aid of the legislature is found necessary for any of these purposes—to take the required means for obtaining it.[2]

Without such a system the pressure of business on the Archbishop of Canterbury and the Bishop of London was, by the 1880s, becoming intolerable. They had to bear the brunt of representing the Church at the national level, as the changing role of the diocesan bishops caused them to devote more of their time and attention to their specifically ecclesiastical duties in the dioceses. Archbishop Benson wrote to his friend Westcott:

> I don't think I am mistaken as to the magnitude and increase of duty and labour for the episcopate, but more and more none will enter in (except the Bishop of London, who is overwhelmed) into the *great* field of the Church's work. Everyone is absorbed in his own vineyard and does not look on it as a part. There must be some standing inner council.[3]

Benson was thinking not so much of a Church Assembly as of a Standing Committee (or 'College of Cardinals' as he half-jokingly called it).[4]

An inner council or standing committee, akin to the cabinet system, was the obvious solution to problems of policy-making and executive direction. But such a body

1 *P.C.C.*, Dublin, 1868, p. 27.
2 Ibid., p. 28.
3 Benson, op. cit., p. 126.
4 Ibid., p. 557.

required first the setting up of an authoritative assembly to which it could be attached and from which it would receive its legitimate authority. Although the Upper House of Convocation might possess such an authority in the eyes of some churchmen, there was too much opposition to episcopal autocracy, in Church and State, for it to become a solution favourably regarded by a majority. One parochial clergyman wrote to the Archbishop of Canterbury, Tait, in 1881, to inform him that: 'The autocracy, or quasi-autocracy, of the Bishops, as against the parochial Clergy, is, one fears, resented by many moderate and sober clergymen'.[1]

DIFFERING VIEWS ON THE ROLE AND STATUS OF CONVOCATION

As for Convocation as a whole, in 1868 Thomas Turner had considered claims made for it as an alternative to his own plan for a Church Assembly as the central body for controlling administration and directing the societies. He rejected it on the grounds that the division of power and jurisdiction between York and Canterbury Convocations would 'be fatal to any efficient action of these bodies on behalf of the entire Church', and that the clergy representation was deficient and the laity were not represented at all.[2]

The suggestion of a mixed clerical and lay Church Assembly was too revolutionary for a High Churchman like Archdeacon Denison, who expected the State to support the Established Church. He commented:

> In listening to Mr. Turner's excellent paper I began to be almost afraid that since I had left London the Church had been disestablished, although I had not read of it in either *The Times* newspaper or the *Pall Mall Gazette;* for, if I understood Mr. Turner's paper right, it shewed that he objects to Convocation, because it does not include an admixture of the laity.[3]

But the laity were represented in Parliament as far as Denison was concerned. Like most High Churchmen he still

[1] Revd. John T. Jeffcock, *Convocation Made Fairly Representative: A Remedy for Some of the Church's Present Troubles*, a letter to the Archbishop of Canterbury, 1881, p. 6.

[2] *P.C.C.*, Dublin: 1868, pp. 29–30.

[3] Ibid., p. 45.

placed his hopes for church government in the clerical Convocation. The faults of the societies lay

> . . . in the fact, that the spiritual assemblies of the Church of England have been so long in abeyance that it was necessary for Voluntary Societies to fill up the gap which the silence of these assemblies created.[1]

Central organization might do something to curb the evils in the management and working of the societies, but for Denison the best antidote to 'centralization' (in its derogatory sense) was parochial agency and parochial action.

Although Convocation revival had arisen in a period of concern for church defence, different parties emphasized different aspects of defence. For High Churchmen it meant defence of church doctrine against liberals, Evangelicals, and the secular State. All three enemies were thought to be on the rampage in the middle years of the century, from 1848 to the beginning of the 1850s, as seemed to be demonstrated by the nomination of Dr. Hampden to the see of Hereford, and the Gorham Judgement by the Judicial Committee of the Privy Council. The Roman Catholic Church appeared to be making capital out of the disarray in the Church of England by what came to be known as the Papal Aggression—the restoration of the hierarchy by a Papal brief of 29 September 1850, establishing thirteen sees in England. The Papal Aggression served to unite an even wider movement in the Church of England in favour of revival of Convocation because, it was argued, the Roman Catholics were simply taking advantage of the Church of England's lack of a central authority.

Of all the arguments used to support revival of Convocation and to restore central authority to the Church, only that of the remarkable Tory Richard Oastler was devoted to showing its importance for securing the well-being of the working classes. That was not the role usually cast for Convocation, but it was one which was to play a major part in the later movement to set up the Church Assembly. Although politically far apart from Thomas Arnold, Richard Oastler had a similar vision of the Church's wide responsibilities as a National Church, especially in the protection of

[1] Ibid., pp. 45–6.

the working classes. Oastler's last published work before his death was a lengthy attack on Archbishop Musgrave of York for rejecting a petition for the revival of York Convocation. Like Arnold, Oastler claimed for the Church a role which was to be the main concern of the Life and Liberty Movement in the campaign for a Church Assembly, when he wrote that:

All the great questions of the age, sectionally called social economy, moral economy, political economy, education, poor laws and so on, are each and all directly within the province of Christianity, and consequently, of a National Christian Church.[1]

If Arnold and the Life and Liberty Movement might have found agreement with Oastler's thesis that, 'The office of the Church is to hold the balance in Christian hands between the people and the aristocracy (whether of rank or of gold)',[2] it is doubtful whether they would have shared his confidence in the ability of a purely clerical Convocation to achieve that object. Oastler believed that 'had Convocation preserved its lawful action, the people would have enjoyed a higher state of domestic comfort and of social happiness'.[3] He traced all the nation's political and social evils to the laxity of discipline in the Established Church, and to the refusal of 'the Heads of the Church' to undertake the responsibility of governing it.[4]

In effect, Oastler's diagnosis of the root of the Church's problems, as distinct from his discussion of its most important social consequences, was essentially that of the High Church party: the bishops and archbishops were unable to govern their dioceses and yet refused to 'convoke that assembly which is the only supreme authority in a Christian Apostolic Church', and the result was the subjection of the Church 'to the control and government of councils and commissions foreign to her Christian and Constitutional organization' which 'marred her usefulness, and degraded her in the estimation of the people'.[5]

But the character of Convocation, both as a legacy from an age when it represented the clerical estate in feudal

[1] Richard Oastler, *Convocation: The Church and the People*, a letter to William Walker of the Society for Revival of Convocation, 1860, p. 14.

[2] Ibid., p. 30. [3] Ibid., p. 29. [4] Ibid., p. 28. [5] Ibid., p. 30.

society, and as a result of the revival of an exclusive professional spirit among the clergy by the Oxford Movement, made it an unsatisfactory body for fulfilling the wider role of central policy-making and executive authority. To those liberals who followed Dr. Arnold in believing that 'to revive Christ's Church is to restore its disfranchised members, the laity, to the discharge of their proper duties in it',[1] Convocation was manifestly unsatisfactory. Their view was expressed by Archdeacon Hare when he commented,

> This is the great defect in the constitution of our Convocation; it represents the conscience and will, and expresses the voice, of the clergy not of the Church. This was suited to its original function of imposing taxes on the clergy, but unfits it for being the legislative council of the whole Church.[2]

THE LEADERSHIP OF THE ARCHBISHOPS

The revival of an exclusive professional spirit, as expressed in ritualism, made discipline into a central issue which distracted not only Convocation from other tasks, but also distracted successive Bishops of London and Archbishops of Canterbury. It was the constant warring of the ritualists and their opponents in London Diocese that wore down Bishop Blomfield's earlier opposition to the revival of a purely clerical Convocation, and left him with the hope that it might be able to provide that authority which he had lost. Archbishop Tait was threatened by High Churchmen who were prepared to enter into alliance with the Radical party unless the bishops stopped trying to discipline them. To the High Churchman who wrote to inform him of this, Tait pointed out that:

> Conscientious Radicals may desire to see a small medieval sect take its place amongst other sects, but a Catholic Church such as you are devoted to they would never desire to see flourishing in a prominent and powerful position.[3]

1 Quoted by Archdeacon Hare in his Charge of 1841, 'Privileges Imply Duties' Note (A); see James H. Rigg, *A Comparative View of Church Organizations*, 3rd edn. 1897, pp. 95–6.

2 Archdeacon Hare's Charge, 'The Means of Unity', Note (J); quoted in Rigg, op. cit., p. 96.

3 T. R. Davidson, *Life of Archibald Campbell Tait, Archbishop of Canterbury*, vol. ii, p. 421.

Even Tait's successor at Canterbury, Archbishop Benson, who understood the High Churchmen better than any other archbishop of the period, despaired of this aspect of increased professionalism after attending a High Church service: 'These are things which the old *gentry-clergy* would never have adopted, and they are more Roman in principle than what people foolishly fear.'[1]

Tait, as Bishop of London in succession to Blomfield, from 1856 to 1868, and then as Archbishop of Canterbury until 1883, brought an Arnoldian vision of the partnership of Church and State to the leadership of the Church, which to some extent retarded the development of a central, autonomous Church organization. Although he earned a reputation as 'the laymen's archbishop', he believed that the laity's interests were best safeguarded by Parliament. He told Archdeacon Emery, who presented him with a scheme for diocesan organization, that if the right man could be found to do the work required, then organization was of comparatively little consequence.[2]

Benson, who succeeded Tait as Archbishop in 1883, shared his view of Church and State as coterminous and had 'soaked' himself in the spirit of Arnold, but he had also assimilated a great deal of the High Church tradition.[3] When Tait died and Benson succeeded him, the Evangelical organ, *The Record*, made a remarkably accurate forecast of what his general church policy would be:

> Dr. Benson will push any cause which he wishes to promote, with judgement, and we doubt not with moderation, but he will push it. Under his rule the Church of England, considered as a great Society, will, we believe, gain strength and coherence, and especially independence. Its external aspect will become more obvious, its power of existing as an organization distinct from the State will be confirmed.

Also, it observed, that while Tait and Benson were

> . . . equally desirous that the Church should be national, the one was

[1] Benson, op. cit., p. 244.

[2] Archdeacon Emery's paper on 'The Progress of the English Church in the Last Sixty Years: At Home', in the Supplement to the *34th Annual Report of the Ely Diocesan Conference*, 1897, p. 26.

[3] Benson, op cit., pp. 722 and 765.

willing that the nation should mould the Church, while the other would have the Church mould the nation.[1]

The difference in leadership was to find expression in an unprecedented growth in central organization promoted by the Archbishop. He encouraged the setting up of new organs for church defence inside and out of Parliament; the institution of Houses of Laymen attached to Convocation; the formation of a long-deferred plan for a central Board of Missions; and the establishment of Church House, which was to provide a central headquarters building for various church societies, and later became the central offices of the Church Assembly.

As far as the development of an autonomous, governing body of clergy and laity was concerned, the key difference in the attitudes of Tait and Benson to the laity was expressed by Eugene Stock: 'Tait viewed the laity as Englishmen. Benson viewed them as Churchmen'.[2] This difference in viewpoints was reflected in attitudes towards the proposal that laymen should be incorporated into the Convocation system.

Convocation began to debate again in 1853, and as early as 1857 a resolution was submitted to the Lower House of Canterbury Convocation asking that faithful laymen be admitted. The resolution was rejected on the ground that it would threaten the constitutional position of Convocation. A committee appointed by Convocation recommended that invited laity might be consulted in diocesan synods, but its report was never discussed. In 1870 committees were appointed by York (first) and Canterbury Convocations on the subject of lay co-operation.[3] Their joint recommendations in 1872 were:

That, without for the present deciding the question whether the Laity should deliberate on matters of Faith, Doctrine, and Worship, in all other ecclesiastical matters requiring legislation, either by Canon

[1] *The Record*, 22 December 1882; quoted in Stock, op. cit., vol. iii, p. 270.

[2] Stock, op. cit.

[3] See the *Report of Canterbury Convocation Committee on Lay Co-operation*, pp.3–4, in the *Chronicle of Canterbury Convocation* for 1872, in which there is an account of the Convocation's consideration of the subject of lay co-operation since the revival of Convocation.

or Statute, the co-operation of the laity in accordance with a true principle of representation should be provided for and secured.

That, on any occasion when the Laity are invited formally to co-operate with members of Convocation, it is essential that they debate and vote on equal terms with the Clergy.

That laymen invited to co-operate with members of Convocation should as a rule debate in the same Chamber.

That no action should be taken to promote the enactment of any Canon or Bill until their subject-matter shall have been assented to by the majority of Laymen present, whose votes, in the opinion of this conference, must be taken separately, because of the legal and constitutional position of the Convocations.[1]

It further recommended that the laymen should be equal in numbers to the clergy, and that they should be elected by the laity of the province in diocesan conferences. The two Convocations should hold joint meetings occasionally.[2]

Most of these provisions were to be implemented subsequently and many of them in Benson's primacy, but Archbishop Tait told the Upper House of Canterbury Convocation at the time that such reforms would 'reform the present body off the face of the earth, and constitute another body'. The proposal was for a representative body of clergy and laity, but for Tait, by virtue of the Establishment, the laity had 'a most effectual voice in administration as well as legislation'.[3]

Tait's faith in the Establishment was reflected in his attitude to another reform which was constantly pressed—the need for a larger representation of the parochial clergy in Convocation, to balance the large numbers of *ex officio* members (deans, archdeacons, and canons). His reply to this was to draw attention to the fact that Convocation was always being accused of a tendency to fall into the hands of the High Church party, and that this, in his opinion, was due to the fact that the deans and other 'official' clergy did not attend enough:

I am not sure that many of those official members of Convocation are not better qualified than the parochial Clergy to represent that

[1] Resolutions of the Conference of York and Canterbury Convocation Committees on Lay Co-operation, in *Chronicle of Canterbury Convocation*, 1872, Appendix A.

[2] Ibid.

[3] *C.C.C.*, 5 July 1872, pp. 733–8.

most important element in the Church of England—viz. the laity of the country.

This was because they were appointed by 'the central point of lay influence in the Church of England'. He deprecated any change in the constitution of Convocation 'by placing more power in the hands of the parochial Clergy'.[1]

To many of the parochial clergy and middle-class laymen this traditional, oligarchic government was intolerable and unsatisfactory in a period when conflict raged both within the Church and in its relations with the wider society. Both the parochial clergy and the middle-class laymen desired representation in the Church's government. Canterbury Convocation's composition was to remain a scandal in the eyes of the parochial clergy until it was reformed after the setting up of Church Assembly. In 1881 the Lower House was composed of 85 *ex officio* members (deans and archdeacons), and 23 semi-*ex officio* (proctors for cathedral chapters), with only 46 proctors elected by the parochial clergy. This lack of representation could serve only to fan the flames of theological party strife.

The Revd. John T. Jeffcock, one of the six out of eight archidiaconal proctors in the Lichfield Diocese for whom there were no seats in Convocation, wrote to Archbishop Tait the warning:

> Depend upon it, my Lord Archbishop, presbyters and deacons will think, will devise, will plan. If they cannot do so openly and above board in lawful and recognized assemblies, they will resort to private and party associations, and thus try to force their opinion upon the church and nation. . . . They act as guerillas, having no legal status, no recognized sphere of operation. . . . Give us Representative Constitutional Assemblies, and the *raison d'être* of party societies to a great extent disappears.[2]

CONVOCATION AND LAY REPRESENTATION

It was the High Church parochial clergy who were loudest in their demands for representation in Convocation, as Archbishop Tait perceived. However, the opposite interest was represented by liberal laymen, who likewise

[1] *C.C.C.*, 6 May 1873, pp. 343–4.

[2] Jeffcock, op. cit., p. 7.

demanded a place in the Church's government. Sir Antonio Brady, Archdeacon Emery's father-in-law, and a member of the liberal National Church Reform Union Council, had told the Church Congress in 1870, that: 'The interests of the Laity require consideration as much as those of the Clergy, and how to reconcile these interests is the problem to be solved.' The laymen's claim was for 'a legal and recognized right to a certain measure of control'. If they were denied this the laity had their own threat to match that of the clergy: disestablishment and disendowment would follow and

> . . . the laity would then, as a body, have *too much* power; for all pecuniary support would have to come from them and only the able and energetic, and those who minister to the popular taste, would get a living. To avert such a calamity, let the Church be wise in time, and give every one of her children an interest in the maintenance of the Establishment, by giving them a share in the management of its affairs.[1]

To the middle-class laymen, conscious of their power in other spheres of society, it seemed naïve of clerical committees to lament that they could not secure lay co-operation. To one such as Brady it was clear that 'in slavish subordination to the clergyman, volunteers for church work will never be found'.[2]

To the clergy of the Lower House of Canterbury Convocation who agreed to the proposal to set up a House of Laymen, in 1885, the main function of the House of Laymen would be to influence the House of Commons in the Church's favour.[3] But, as one speaker pointed out, the new proposal was weaker than that recommended, in 1871, by the conference of the Committees of Canterbury and York Convocation on Lay Co-operation. That conference had agreed that the laity should debate and vote on equal terms with the clergy and in the same chamber. Because the new House of Laymen would not be so constituted, it could not expect to possess much authority either in the Church or in

[1] Sir Antonio Brady, *Lay Organization*, a paper read at the Church Congress, Southampton, 1870, and reprinted by the Church of England Laymen's Defence Association, Salford, n.d., pp. 1–2.

[2] Ibid., p. 1.

[3] *C.C.C.*, 13 February 1885, pp. 119–20.

the eyes of the House of Commons.[1] Its status was that of a separate and subordinate debating forum for lay representatives elected by the diocesan conferences; Convocation alone possessed constitutional authority.

Although Archdeacon Emery's painstaking efforts to build up a system of government by encouraging dioceses to hold conferences, and then his achievement of securing their representation on a Central Council of Diocesan Conferences, received passing mention in the successful proposal for a House of Laymen, both that proposal and the debate on it made clear that the Central Council was now redundant. The system which he had promoted was described as a useful ladder by which the Church had come to the stage of a House of Laymen, and, as one speaker put it:

> Such an institution having been founded, the ladder might be no longer required, and, though they would not rudely and ungratefully throw it down, thay might return it to Archdeacon Emery, who had so skilfully framed it and so carefully adjusted it, and ask him to take it away.[2]

Some deep-seated dislike of the Central Council of Diocesan Conferences was not so politely expressed. One speaker in Convocation referred to it as 'that extremely unecclesiastical affair', and Archdeacon Emery protested against it being called a 'mongrel body'.[3] He preferred the principle of mixed assemblies to the system of separate Houses, and was in accord with the earlier proposals of the 1871 Joint Committee Conference. He warned Convocation that the new constitution for the House of Laymen, which excluded the laity from discussing matters of faith and doctrine, would not be enforceable. If there was not to be a new, mixed assembly, then, in his opinion, the Central Council of Diocesan Conferences was a preferable body to a separate House of Laymen; they ought to remain content with that system, rather than commit themselves to a 'dangerous innovation in their constitution'.[4]

The Central Council lacked authority, however, and so,

[1] Ibid., pp. 117–18. [2] Ibid., p. 115.

[3] *C.C.C.*, 4 July 1884, p. 422.

[4] *C.C.C.*, 13 February 1885, pp. 126–7.

despite its inclusion of a lay element, it did not serve to convince Parliament or the laity that the Church's government was sufficiently representative of lay opinion. The General Election of 1885 made it clear to the Church's leaders that, if the Church was to be defended then it was imperative that the laity should appear to be involved in its internal government. Archbishop Benson was an ardent advocate of the scheme for a House of Laymen, and in February 1886 he was able to open the first session of Canterbury House of Laymen. York followed suit in 1892, and then in 1898 provision was made for joint meetings of the two provincial Houses of Laymen.

The basic aim of these schemes was to influence Parliament in favour of legislation proposed by the Church and against hostile legislation desired by the Church's enemies. The High Churchmen who had worked for the revival of Convocation had hoped to obviate the need for parliamentary legislation for the Church by reverting to government by Canon Law. But although on 26 February 1861 Convocation of Canterbury received the royal licence for the revision of a canon, and so raised hopes for this form of delegated legislation, the revised canon never received the royal assent. It was probably partly as a result of this experience that Tait, after he became Archbishop of Canterbury in 1868, preferred to depend on Acts of Parliament.[1]

The Radical Programme of 1885, under the auspices of which Chamberlain raised the issue of religious equality, served to intensify the Church's attempts to organize for defensive purposes, including internal reform. On 12 December 1885 a memorial was presented to Archbishop Benson, signed by the leading members of the Senate of Cambridge University, expressing the belief that 'the Church of England has long suffered serious injury from the postponement of necessary reforms'.[2] Benson had not the same taste or ability for Parliament as his predecessor, Tait, but he accepted the leadership of the movements for defence and reform.

When he opened the House of Laymen the following

[1] See E. W. Kemp, *Counsel and Consent*, The Bampton Lectures, 1960, pp. 190–1.
[2] Benson, op. cit., p. 73.

year he represented it as a means of initiating 'a central organization of lay power'.[1] This was meant to impress on Parliament that the Church's proposals for legislation, or its opposition to hostile legislation, had lay backing. To the same end, in 1894, he encouraged the formation of a Church Parliamentary Committee within Parliament itself, and the Central Church Committee to represent diocesan and parochial committees devoted to church defence.

The positive side of the policy, of securing internal reforms by Act of Parliament, met with little success. Parliament was no longer suited to the purpose of preparing and passing constructive legislation for the Church. In the later movement for the setting up of Church Assembly the case against depending on Parliament alone was often illustrated by the story of how it had taken nine sessions of Parliament to settle the salary of the Archdeacon of Cornwall.[2]

The voluntary status of the Houses of Laymen convinced neither the laity nor Parliament that the lay voice was truly represented in the Church's internal councils. In 1902 a Joint Committee of Canterbury Convocation reported that the Houses of Laymen had 'failed to rouse full enthusiasm for they have no legal status, they have no power to legislate'.[3] This Committee, which had been set up in 1898 by Benson's successor, Archbishop Frederick Temple, and included once again the indomitable Archdeacon Emery, recommended the formation of a National Council of clergy and laity. They were influenced in their recommendations by the coexistence of church councils and establishment in the Churches of Sweden and Scotland (although they did not advocate the appointment of a Minister of Ecclesiastical Affairs as in Sweden).[4] The immediate result was the creation of the Representative Church Council in 1903. The new Council did not supersede Convocation, and it was a purely deliberative body composed basically of the Houses of Convocation and the Houses of Laymen meeting in joint session. But it was this Council which recommended the

[1] Ibid.

[2] F. A. Iremonger, *Life of William Temple*, p. 223.

[3] *1902 Joint Committee Report*, op. cit., p. 54.

[4] Ibid., pp. 63–4.

appointment of the Commission on Church and State in 1913, which in turn produced the basic proposals for the subsequent constitution of the Church Assembly, which came into being in 1919.

SOCIOLOGICAL COMMENTARY

On the whole, it was not the espousal of any theory of organization, theological principle, or political doctrine, which determined the shape of the central church government as it grew up in the second half of the nineteenth century, but rather the conflict of values and interests within the Church, and between the Church and its critics outside. Seldom was there any discussion of a comprehensive system of church government which would both secure representation of interests and legitimate authority, and also co-ordinate and direct the Church's instrumental or administrative agencies. Party conflict within the Church, and the threat of disestablishment from without, were the main forces which mediated the effects of the deeper structural differentiation of English society, and compelled the Church to begin to develop a representative system of government in this period.

It was mainly in the Church Congress that an occasional speaker like Thomas Turner in 1868, or G. A. Spottiswoode in 1894, would consider the comprehensive topic of

> The best means of securing a representation of the Church, at once fuller and more compact, and of bringing the representative and deliberative bodies of the Church into closer connection with her practical work, with special references to the establishment of a closer connection between the above bodies and the Church's work, as carried on by existing organizations.[1]

The problem, as Spottiswoode stated, was the old constitutional one of correlation of deliberative and executive bodies. But most of the discussion centred on the development of satisfactory deliberative and legislative bodies. Spottiswoode was perhaps over-sanguine in thinking that the Church of England could simply copy the Wesleyan

[1] Title of the paper given by G. A. Spottiswoode at the Church Congress, Exeter, 1894, published London and Derby, Bemrose and Sons, n.d., p. 1.

Connection's solution to the problem, which involved allowing the Legal Conference (or Legal Hundred) to transact legislative business, as laid down in the Rules of the Society, whilst a representative mixed assembly met for the rest of the session to transact business from the departments. He suggested that Convocation, the equivalent of the Legal Conference, should meet after a mixed General Assembly and legally promulgate the latter's decisions, and in so doing it would maintain the legal and traditional authority of Convocation and yet make it more efficient and representative, and so able to control the executive.[1] Spottiswoode's mistake was in wrongly equating the Wesleyan Legal Conference and Convocation and forgetting that in the Established Church it was with Parliament that the traditional legal authority rested—a mistake not likely to be made by most Broad Churchmen and Evangelicals.

In the 1830s structural differentiation had not proceeded so far in England that the traditional partnership of Church and State could not be used by a handful of strong leaders successfully to impose instrumental adaptation on the Church through such a device as the Ecclesiastical Commission. In the second half of the nineteenth century, however, this was less of a possibility, as Archbishop Tait's difficulties illustrated. When the traditional partnership of government and shared administration could no longer function adequately, the Church found itself in dispute over the nature and locus of authority. In the absence of agreement the church parties castigated each other's solutions as 'sacerdotal', 'irregular', or 'unecclesiastical'. Meanwhile conflict within and attack from without necessitated the creation of more inclusive, representative assemblies, in which all points of view and interests could be represented. But the problem of legitimating their authority and of bringing them into acceptable relationships with Convocation and Parliament had not been solved by the turn of the century. Between 1850 and 1890, there had been virtually no discussion of the relation of church assemblies to the working classes, nor had much attention been paid to the

[1] Ibid., p. 5.

internal organizational problem of correlating legislative and executive functions. The perceptive contributions of Richard Oastler, Thomas Turner, and G. A. Spottiswoode seem to have made little impact on their contemporaries.

Basically, the discussion had revolved around two other issues: the emergence of a more exclusive, professional spirit among the clergy; and the need for the church to enlist the support of middle-class laymen. The task of reconciling the demands of both these groups, and of guaranteeing them adequate representation in the Church's government, had overshadowed all other issues.

PART TWO

V

CHANGES IN THE CHURCH PARTIES AND THEIR ATTITUDES TO REFORM

A POSITIVE BASIS FOR REFORM

THE central organization that developed in the Church of England in the second half of the nineteenth century was part of the defences thrown into being as the Church reacted to external attack. As such it depended little on any theory of organization, theological system, or political doctrine. By contrast, the period of church reform, which can be dated from the return of a Conservative Government in 1895 to the passing of the Enabling Bill setting up the Church Assembly in 1919, was marked by a positive attempt to remedy that deficiency of theory.

Between the First and Second Readings of Gladstone's Home Rule for Ireland Bill in 1893, Asquith, the Home Secretary, had introduced a Welsh Suspensory Bill to disestablish the Welsh Church. This drew from Lord Randolph Churchill the accusation that the Prime Minister was selling the Welsh Church in order to buy votes for Home Rule.[1] There was much political profit to be gained in terms of Welsh Nonconformist votes for such a policy, whilst for Gladstone it was perfectly consistent with the policy which he had pursued when he disestablished the Irish Church in 1869. Although Gladstone might seek to quieten the fears of the Church of England, by saying that he considered it a special case, many churchmen believed,

[1] Philip Magnus, *Gladstone. A Biography*, 1963 edn., p. 410.

with Queen Victoria, that it was 'the first step towards the disestablishment and disendowment of the Church of England'.[1] In fact Asquith's Bill was subsequently dropped, and the Home Rule Bill was rejected by the House of Lords. Gladstone resigned, to be succeeded by Lord Rosebery in March 1894, and then in June 1895 a Conservative Government under Lord Salisbury took office. This seemed to offer the Church a respite from its feverish organizing for defence, and gave it an opportunity to take stock. In particular it allowed the Church time to change its tactics from negative defence to considering the possibilities for an overall reform such as would commend it to all classes of society.

The Times, in a weighty article on 8 September 1896, set out to encourage the Church to change from a policy of defence to one of reform. It pointed out that the disestablishment threat had faded temporarily and that it was no longer a popular cause with the working classes:

> A campaign against capital, the wild schemes of Socialism, and its wilder dreams of equality of fortune and worldly position which can never be realized so long as Nature makes men unequal in ability and in character, seem more attractive nowadays to the working classes of this as of other countries, and it is at least possible that the cry of disestablishment, if raised by Radical statesmen in search of a policy, may fall flat.

However, *The Times* considered it neither politic nor proper that the national Church should continue to depend too heavily on the support and protection of the Conservative Party. Its advice was: 'Put not your trust in Princes', for even Conservative Members of Parliament were beginning to ask whether the support of the Church was vital to their interests.

At the beginning of the century it had been sufficient for the Church to commend itself to the upper classes for its social utility in preserving order in society, and, for this end, it could secure their co-operation in its reform and extension. By the end of the century it was clear that whilst the Church had helped to preserve social order, by its support of what

[1] Philip Magnus, *Gladstone. A Biography*, 1963 edn., p. 410.

Alasdair MacIntyre[1] has called the 'secondary virtues', such as the pragmatic approach to problems, co-operativeness, tolerance, fair play, and the gift for compromise, it had failed to overcome the deeper and socially divisive effects of the Industrial Revolution. Both urbanization and the increased autonomy of industrial and capitalist economic relations had reduced the Church's capacity to give expression to a common set of primary virtues which would set final goals which all classes could pursue.

The conscientious endeavour of liberal theologians to overcome the problems presented by modern, scientific knowledge, by reducing the distinction between the sacred and the secular, ran the risk of seeming to equate religious values with secular values. The Oxford Movement arose to combat that trend in the Church. Thus C. C. J. Webb in his *Religious Thought in the Oxford Movement*, found 'moralism' to be the ruling idea in the Movement; but it was an assertion of religious values explicitly emphasizing 'as against the liberals, the transcendence by those values of the rational order as represented by secular civilization.'[2] But, as Webb points out, the Oxford Movement's theology was pre-Darwin and Spencer, and so it clung to a static and pre-evolutionary view of the Church, especially in the years after Newman's secession (which had been caused by his adoption of a developmental doctrine). It was only with the publication of the volume of essays, *Lux Mundi*, in 1889, that a large section of the party adopted the evolutionary principle as a ruling idea in its theology. Until this occurred, the Oxford Movement's only interest in church reform was in the prospect of restoring the patterns of some earlier, normative period of church life.

The prevalence of the secondary virtues and their public commendation in English society, according to MacIntyre, had the effect of ruling out any kind of metaphysical exclusivism:

> They are virtues which express an attitude to the world in which the making of cosmic and universal claims for one's own group, as

[1] Alasdair MacIntyre, *Secularization and Moral Change*, The Riddell Memorial Lectures 1964, p. 24.

[2] C. C. J. Webb, *Religious Thought in the Oxford Movement*, p. 153.

against other groups, is no longer possible. Both the economic and social needs that were met by co-operation between classes and the accompanying moral schemes led to a situation in which every attempt to universalize, to give cosmic significance to, the values of a particular group was bound to founder. And so all those attempts made in the late nineteenth century to provide a new religious expression for the life either of one part of the English nation or of the nation as a whole founder too.[1]

MacIntyre discusses three such attempts: the Labour churches; organized Marxism; and the attempt of T. H. Green to produce something that would be a genuine religious expression of the life of the whole English people and would have a supra-class character. It was towards this end that all Green's work was directed, whether through his philosophical teaching of an idealist metaphysic, his work for workers' education, or as a supporter of Settlements in the East End and social welfare in general.[2] And it was towards this end that the authors of *Lux Mundi*, many of whom had been Green's students, directed all their efforts in the same channels. Although the final judgement of this present discussion will be that their attempt to attain this wider goal met with little more success than the attempts which MacIntyre discusses, they will be seen to have played a vital role in the movement for church reform.

THE *LUX MUNDI* GROUP

The genesis of *Lux Mundi* can be traced back to 1875 . . . when a group of young High Church theologians at Oxford, who had been influenced by F. D. Maurice and the idealist philosopher T. H. Green, started going away together from time to time for the purpose of sustained discussion.[3]

The synthesis of Maurice's Christian socialist thought and a modified version of Green's idealist philosophy produced a new grafting upon the stock of the Catholic party in the Church of England. A. M. Ramsey, whilst drawing attention to important modifications to Green's teaching which the *Lux Mundi* group were bound to make by their stress on

[1] Op. cit., p. 25.
[2] Ibid., pp. 27–8.
[3] Alec R. Vidler, *The Church in an Age of Revolution*, pp. 190–1.

redemption, shows how considerable was Green's influence in providing a background for their thought:

> Green's influence was towards a spiritual interpretation of the world; and consequently towards finding the significance of religion within the world itself. . . . If it be held that Green's strength lay less in metaphysics than in social ethics, it is clear that he so presented metaphysics as to make religion and ethics inseparable.[1]

The sub-title of *Lux Mundi* was 'a series of studies in the Religion of the Incarnation' and it was this incarnational theology that 'enabled a genuine contact between supernatural religion and contemporary culture'.[2] More specifically: 'It was an outcome of the *Lux Mundi* appeal to the Logos doctrine that both democracy and socialism were held to be expressions of the working of the divine spirit.'[3] In the same year that they published their volume of theological essays, the same group founded the Christian Social Union, the ultimate aim of which was to 'claim for the Christian Law the ultimate authority to rule social practice'.[4] Three of the group who were most attached to Christian socialist principles were also to prove the most active advocates of church reform. They were Edward Stuart Talbot, Charles Gore, and Henry Scott Holland.[5] In the period from 1895 to 1918 they epitomized the emerging synthesis of three important movements: the new liberal trend in Catholic theology (later to appear in modified form in Evangelicalism), Christian socialism, and the demand for church self-government. This synthesis, partial though it may have been most of the time, will be seen to have

[1] A. M. Ramsey, *From Gore to Temple*, p. 10. [2] Ibid., p. 28.

[3] Ibid., p. 14. Although the content of the 'socialism' varied, it meant usually, in Ramsey's words, 'the repudiation of laissez-faire, and the elimination of gross inequality and injustice by the organizing of society for the common good'.

[4] Quoted in Maurice B. Reckitt, *Maurice to Temple: A Century of the Social Movement in the Church of England*, p. 138.

[5] Edward Stuart Talbot (1844–1934), successively the first Warden of Keble College, Oxford (1870), Vicar of Leeds (1888), Bishop of Rochester (1895), Bishop of Winchester (1905).

Charles Gore (1853–1932), successively first Principal of Pusey House, Oxford (1884), Vicar of Radley (1893), Canon of Westminster (1902), Bishop of Worcester (1902), Bishop of Birmingham (1905), Bishop of Oxford (1911)—resigned in 1919 over the proposed baptismal franchise.

Henry Scott Holland (1847–1918), a Canon of St. Paul's and Regius Professor of Divinity at Oxford.

constituted a remarkable attempt to fulfil that aim of producing something that could be a genuine religious expression of the whole English people, such as would restore a supra-class character to the Church.

The Times, in its article on church reform in 1896, pointed out the political facts of life which would have to be faced if the Church was to be saved from a sect-type exclusivism:

> No one can deny that the Church has been in former days too exclusively the Church of the 'classes', as distinct from the 'masses'. The Church has attracted the gentry, while the strength of Nonconformity has always lain in the middle and lower classes—among the small tradesmen in towns and agricultural labourers in the country. When the first Reform Bill transferred political power from the aristocracy to the middle classes, Nonconformity became a strong political force, and acquired that specially political character with which we are all familiar. Now, however, that political power has been transferred to the working classes, Nonconformity as a purely political force will, perhaps, be less influential than it has been. The working classes are not so largely or so earnestly Nonconformists as the lower middle classes. Many of them are nominally members of the Church of England; many are indifferent to any form of religious organization. And any hostility which they may hereafter show to the Church will be more probably due to a feeling that the Church is identified with capital and privileges—that it is, in fact, the Church of the 'classes' —than to any sectarian jealousy. . . . And it is of the utmost importance that the impression of exclusiveness should be diminished or removed if the national Church is to defend her title in the eyes of democracy.[1]

THE CHURCH REFORM LEAGUE

It was clear to *The Times* that, of the two remedies open to the Church—church defence and church reform—church defence had so far had the advantage of episcopal sanction and parochial organization. The cause of reform was only just beginning to gather strength with the inauguration of the Church Reform League in November, 1895, and it still lacked official support: 'No Bishop or Church dignitary as

[1] Op. cit.

yet lends his name to the League. The need for reform is naturally less apparent to highly-placed and well-paid officials. . . .'[1]

Only E. S. Talbot, by that time a bishop and the youngest on the bench in 1896, had given outright encouragement by authorizing the C.R.L. to publish a sympathetic letter from him. Later the League was to attract more widespread episcopal approval, so that the very weight of episcopal vice-presidents, by the beginning of the First World War, had caused it to sacrifice reforming zeal for respectable gradualism, and caused some of its supporters to form a new 'ginger group'—the Life and Liberty Movement.[2]

The process which took place in reform movements such as the Church Reform League, and to a certain extent in the Life and Liberty Movement, was one which has been observed in other organizations, in which the co-optation of new groups resulted in deflection from the original goals.[3] This goal-deflection effect of co-optation, especially in so far as it involves deflection into more conservative channels, can be explained by the tendency for the co-opted elements to see existing agencies as machines to meet their own problems, or the problems as they conceive them, and this seems to be the case with church administrators no less than with Tennessee Valley farmers.

[1] Op. cit.

[2] The suggestion to form a 'ginger group' was made by H. R. L. Sheppard to William Temple, early in 1917. Sheppard was then Vicar of St. Martin-in-the-Fields, and Temple Rector of St. James's, Piccadilly. See F. A. Iremonger, *William Temple*, London, O.U.P., 1948, p. 219.

Sheppard (1880–1937) had previously worked at Oxford House, Bethnal Green and the Grosvenor Chapel. He had to resign St. Martin's because of ill health in 1926. He was Dean of Canterbury 1929–31, Canon of St. Paul's 1934–5, and then devoted his time to the Peace Pledge Union which he founded in 1936.

Temple (1881–1944), was the son of Archbishop Frederick Temple; Fellow of Queen's College, Oxford (1904), Headmaster of Repton (1910), and later successively Canon of Westminster (1919), Bishop of Manchester (1921), Archbishop of York (1929), Archbishop of Canterbury (1942). Also from 1908 for sixteen years he was President of the Workers' Educational Association.

[3] In the case of the church reform movements the co-optation of highly placed administrators (whether bishops or lay office-holders) was the inverse of that which Philip Selznick observed in his *T.V.A. and the Grassroots* (1949). In the case of the Tennessee Valley Authority it was the co-optation of local, 'grassroots' people into the organization which led to the same pattern of goal-deflection as occurred in the church reform movements.

Although the Church Reform League drew much of its support from those Broad Church clergy and laity who had long favoured some moderate reform, provided it did not lead the Church into greater exclusivism, in its first years it was the more radical *Lux Mundi*-Christian Social Union axis which provided its strongest advocates. So it was that at the big Church Reform League meeting held on 10 May 1897, Talbot took the chair, and Scott Holland and Gore were two of the main speakers. But the Christian Social Union seemed too radical a body to church reformers at this time (although like the Church Reform League itself its radicalism eventually gave way to respectable moderation: between 1889 and 1913, out of 53 episcopal appointments, 16 went to members of the C.S.U.).[1] When the Christian Social Union suggested, in 1898, that it should hold a joint meeting with the Church Reform League, devoted to the subject of parochial church councils, the C.R.L. Council decided that it was 'not wise for the two organizations to act jointly in the matter'.[2] This policy of avoiding a formal alliance with the Christian socialist movement, despite the large contribution which that movement made to the church reform agitation, was to be maintained even in the Life and Liberty Movement, which at times openly recommended socialist policies.

T. H. Green's influence on church reform, as one of the intellectual forces behind the *Lux Mundi* liberal Catholics associated with the Church Reform League, has already been noted; but he also had a more direct connection with church reform as a member of the Council of the National Church Reform Union. This body, although it was overlooked by *The Times* in its account of the church reform movement, was founded in 1870 and was liberal in Arnold's succession. Canon W. H. Freemantle, later Dean of Ripon, was one of those who created the Union for the purpose of furthering church reform through the agency of Parliamentary legislation, after the Ritual Commission of 1868. Its liberalism was reflected in its statement of aim to promote 'a form of Christianity in harmony with progress,

1 Reckitt, op. cit.

2 Church Reform League Council Minutes, 18 July 1898.

liberty and knowledge'.[1] The Council included, in 1880–1, in addition to Green, Antonio Brady, the notable advocate of the lay cause in church government, A. P. Stanley, the Dean of Westminster and Thomas Arnold's biographer and disciple, and Albert Grey, M.P. The principles of the Union were much more in favour of the existing Establishment than those of the Church Reform League. They stated:

(1) A National Church organized upon national endowments can most efficiently provide for the spiritual necessities of this Christian nation, since such an Institution can alone secure religious teaching and worship universally and equally for all classes and in all places.

(2) Amidst divergences of sects and parties there exists a common ground and a common purpose which all communions faithfully admit; and upon this sacred and eternal unity, not upon the jealous distinctions of human interpretation and feeling, the National Church must ultimately take her stand.

(3) The Church of England by law established, endowed throughout the land by the piety of our forefathers, and adapted from time to time to the necessities of each epoch by their wisdom, presents an incomparable organization for the maintenance of religion, and needs but Reform to make it national once more.[1]

To the growing number of clergy influenced by the Oxford Movement's teaching, such a view of the Church seemed to blur the important distinction between the Church and the sects, and between Church and State. The Union's proposals for the abolition of clerical subscription, and the formation of church boards in every parish, were equally unpalatable. It was the Union's support of Albert Grey's Church Board's Bill in 1881, which would have established boards composed of parishioners of any denomination or none, and with no safeguards of the power of the incumbent, which antagonized not only the parochial clergy, but also the bishops and many of its own members.[2] The National Church Reform Union gradually faded from the scene of active agitation for reform.

[1] Statements of its aims are contained in pamphlets entitled 'The People's Interest in the National Church', 'The Church and the People', and 'Why should you support the Church Reform Union', issued by the National Church Reform Union, n.d., Nos. 73402–4 in Pusey House Pamphlets Collection, Oxford.

[2] Cf. Revd. S. J. Hume, *Church Boards. A Letter to Albert Grey M.P.*, 1881.

The Church Reform League's proposals were much more in tune with the changing times and with the feelings of those clergy who held a Catholic doctrine of the Church and yet wished to see it made more effective by self-reform. The pamphlet setting out its aims, entitled *Reform of the Church. The Proposals of the Church Reform League* (1896), began with the first clause of Magna Carta: 'that the English Church be free and have its rights whole and its liberties unimpaired'. It advocated:

(1) Self-government of the Church.—That, saving the supremacy of the Crown, and subject in legislation to the veto of Parliament, the Church should have freedom for self-government by means of reformed Houses of Convocation, which should be thoroughly representative.

(2) Discipline.—That all ministers and church officers be removable by disciplinary process, benefices being made tenable only during the adequate performance of duties.

(3) Patronage.—That all transfers by sale of next presentations and advowsons be made illegal, but where patronage is transferred to a diocesan trust reasonable compensation should be given.

(4) Finance.—That a diocesan trust be established in each diocese to receive and administer diocesan and parochial endowments on lines similar to those of the Ecclesiastical Commission.[1]

The League was to learn that it was upon the success of the first proposal, the attainment of a greater degree of self-government, that the majority of the other reforms depended. The Life and Liberty Movement was begun at the end of the First World War because many reformers had learned this lesson and wanted a new 'ginger group' which would concentrate solely on attaining that primary objective. However, the Church Reform League was able to further the implementation of its proposals on finance before the setting up of the Church Assembly, and in its Annual Report for 1915–16 claimed that the new diocesan system of church finance and the Central Board of Finance, set up in 1914, were obtained largely through its action.

The League could also claim responsibility for suggesting the important collection of essays on church reform, which were published under the title *Essays in Aid of the Reform of*

[1] Quoted in *The Times*, 8 September 1896.

the Church, and edited by Charles Gore, in 1898.[1] In addition to Gore there were several of the League's most prominent spokesmen among the contributors. The proposals which these essays made were to set the lines on which future church reform proceeded, and it was revised and published in 1915 at a strategic moment for launching the final campaign which issued in the formation of the Church Assembly. Nowhere in the book was the synthesis of liberal Catholic theology, social concern, and church reform advocacy more evident than in the essay by T. H. Green's most ardent pupil, Scott Holland, on 'Church and State'. It pleaded for church reforms which would allow the Church of England to present a geniune religious expression of the people which comprehended all classes:

> Every day the blank is felt more acutely. For every day we are learning more and more the vital unity of the human brotherhood: and, with that, comes inevitably the sense of awe, of solemnity, of dignity, which belongs to this deep social communion. Every day we feel the burden of its responsibilities to be heavier, the demands for sacrificial surrender of individual to corporate interests to be more urgent. The will has to nerve itself to a harder task: the passion of love is summoned to a nobler exercise. As the tension sharpens, the cry for the underlying strength of religious sanctions and religious succours grows more intense. The heart of the nation pulses to a more mystic music. Secularism, with its narrowness, its hardness, its rigidities, is dying fast out of the land. The people desire to come together under the breath of a larger inspiration. They would, if they might, clasp hands together and swear the great oath which binds them to live and die in the might of a companionship which is deep as life and stronger than death. And, while the secular movement is thus straining to touch the spiritual, the same impulse, working in a counter-direction, has drawn the spiritual down towards the secular.[2]

Having given an idealistic description of the potential spiritual unity which lay below the divisions that marred the surface of the nation's life, Scott Holland went on to press the claims of the Church of England to give

> ... some form to which the vast majority can afford to rally—some historical body to which the State can appeal to give its national feeling some sort of national expression.[3]

[1] C.R.L. Council Minutes, 10 May 1897.

[2] Gore(ed), op. cit., p. 117.

[3] Ibid., p. 123.

The difference between this claim as it had been made in the past by High Churchmen, and its fresh presentation in the church reform movement by liberal Catholics with Christian socialist leanings, was also pointed out:

> Old thoughts these; old pleas. Yes! But they were once only associated with old lost causes, with impossible ideals, with fossilized Toryism, with medieval ecclesiasticism, with high and dry Anglicanism. Their present significance lies in this—that they are coming back to us from the opposite quarter. Democracy, as it ceases to be merely a section of the working community, and becomes the spirit of the entire body, exhibits its natural craving to emphasize the deeper issues of national life, to emphasize the spiritual solemnity of the national task.... Can the Church of England fulfil the part required?... Only if she can reform herself.[1]

Prior to the new reform movement, for the Catholic party in the Church of England church reform had been 'hardly worth considering, because it involved, as things stood, unmitigated Erastianism'.[2] This was the ground of their opposition to the Ecclesiastical Commission, and in more recent years to the National Church Reform Union. The only alternative had seemed to be through the way of disestablishment. But the temporary respite from external attack provided by Conservative government between 1895 and 1905 gave them hope of being able to secure some power of self-government, whilst at the same time maintaining the Establishment. It was to this end that the church reform movement directed its efforts between 1895 and the passing of the Enabling Bill, 1919. The concentrated lobbying and propaganda of the Church Reform League effectively sowed the seed for the eventual success of the reform movement, although it required the founding of two new pressure groups—the Church Self-Government Association[2] and the Life and Liberty Movement in 1917—before the battle was finally won.

In its early years, the Church Reform League had difficulty in attracting the public support of the bishops (although

[1] Gore(ed) op. cit. pp. 123–4.

[2] This Group, formed by Viscount Wolmer, M.P., in 1916–17, concentrated on extracting promises of support for the Enabling Bill from Parliamentary prospective candidates.

one critic had the impression that, by 1898, most of the bishops had expressed approval or goodwill, and that a quarter of the rural deans had joined). The difficulty of the bishops' position at this stage was expressed in a letter to Dr. T. C. Fry, its chairman, by Randall Davidson, the Bishop of Winchester:

> What you tell me as to the wish entertained for the co-operation of the Bishops in the work of the Church Reform League is interesting and encouraging. Hitherto, a Bishop who has tried to move in Church reform has been apt, I think, to find himself between two fires. Many reformers seem to regard Bishops as *ipso facto* (or *ex-officio*) old fogies, whose adhesion may do the cause of genuine reform more harm than good; while those who are satisfied with things as they are, not unnaturally resent the defection of a Bishop from their cause. To my mind, as I think you know, Church reform of a rather thorough-going sort seems absolutely essential if the Church is to do her true work in modern England.[1]

It was perhaps the pessimistic view of the effects of episcopal sponsorship which led the Life and Liberty Movement to exclude bishops from its Council, although otherwise it was eager to have their public support. The fact that Life and Liberty was able to count on the support of some of the bishops was very much due to the prior work of the Church Reform League as it sowed the seed of church reform in diocesan conferences and Church Congresses. In 1897, only two years after the formation of the League, thirteen diocesan conferences passed resolutions supporting its first principle.[2] It also secured discussion and support for its principles at the Church Congresses at Shrewsbury in 1896, and at Nottingham in the following year. The League's lobbying extended to important politicians such as A. J. Balfour, the Leader of the House of Commons, and on 11 April 1899 he came out strongly in favour of self-government for the Church, in a House of Commons speech.[3] Church committees on reform invariably included members of the League. The most important of these, the

[1] Letter dated Farnham Castle, 4 January 1897, in C.R.L. Papers, Church House, Westminster.

[2] C.R.L. Annual Report, May 1898.

[3] The lobbying is reported in C.R.L. Minutes, 7 December 1898.

Archbishops' Committee on Church and State, which was appointed in 1914 and made the main proposals which became embodied in the Church Assembly, had as its chairman a vice-president of the Church Reform League, the Earl of Selborne. Political weight was given to the committee by the inclusion of Arthur Balfour.

ATTITUDES OF THE CHURCH PARTIES TO THE REFORM MOVEMENT

The developments in the reform movement which began in 1895 were not universally welcomed. One of its most constant critics throughout the whole period was Herbert Hensley Henson.[1] Henson was a Low Churchman, with liberal leanings in theology, and a strong attachment to the Establishment (until the rejection of the Revised Prayer Book by the House of Commons in 1927–8). In a paper on church reform which he gave in 1898, Henson commented: 'The reforming agitation now in progress includes three distinct elements; which may be designated severally, the clerical, the democratic, and the practical.'[2] He observed that the cry for self-government had powerfully affected the imagination of the 'Catholic' clergy, and that they would reject with abhorrence the reforms for which they clamoured if the agent of those reforms was Parliament. He then went on to denounce the Church Reform League for covering up the problems which the combination of Catholic theology and democratic theory would present in church reform, especially in deciding on the church franchise:

> The democratic reformers are oppressed by the problem of the franchise. Their political theory requires that it shall be low—their religious creed restricts it within the narrowest limits. For purposes of agitation they shirk the question; but when agitation gives place to the actual work of legislation, it must be faced. The Church Reform League has issued 'an appeal to individual Churchmen', in which this disingenuous and irrational policy is openly avowed.[3]

[1] Herbert Hensley Henson (1863–1947) became Bishop of Hereford in 1918, and then Bishop of Durham (1920–39.

[2] H. Hensley Henson, *Cross-Bench Views of Current Church Questions*, p. 11.

[3] Ibid., p. 15.

In the view of Henson, and of many Broad Churchmen, self-government, especially if accompanied by a franchise qualification such as confirmation or communion status, rather than simply baptism, would reduce the Church of England to a denomination. This franchise issue and the fear of becoming a denomination were to persist in creating difficulties for the reform movement. Although the Selborne Committee reported, in 1916, in favour of a confirmation franchise, this was subsequently dropped in favour of the wider baptismal franchise. The issue caused some heart-searching in the Life and Liberty Movement, which eventually came down in favour of baptism, and in so doing led to its estrangement from Charles Gore, who resigned his bishopric partly over this issue.

What was remarkable was that the church reform movement had been able to attract such a coalition of supporters from different theological parties. The most important and influential group in that coalition had been the liberal Catholics, of whom Gore was the chief. It is interesting to speculate whether, if matters had come to a head sooner and Gore had withdrawn his support from the reform movement in its early days, the whole coalition might not have collapsed. In those early days there were not a few Anglo-Catholics who resented the effects which the liberal Catholics were having on the party. They bemoaned the loss of the old conservative leadership which Canon Liddon's death in 1890 had brought about. As one of them lamented:

> Subsequently the leadership of the party, to all intents and purposes, was put into commission—a body of Canons and Socialistic clergymen; almost all untrammelled Liberals, except with a little useful Gladstonian baggage, some of them being quite ready to throw unacceptable dogmas to the Radical wolves.[1]

The attitude of this conservative wing of the party to church reform was fearful and largely negative:

> Let not the *Convocatio Cleri*, perhaps unique in Christendom, be destroyed or fundamentally altered. Let the 'House of Laymen', save for 'the serving of table' and the practical labour of spiritual

[1] Revd. Frederick George Lee, *The Ecclesiastical Situation in 1899 from a Tractarian Standpoint*, p. 32.

accountants, be terminated; there being quite enough talk amongst Church people in general without it.[1]

In so far as there was an official leader of the Catholic party it was Lord Halifax, who throughout the period of reform was President of the English Church Union. His coolness towards the movement for a Church Assembly was noted by his biographer.[2] Halifax himself wrote that:

> Machinery for expediting measures the Church is agreed upon through Parliament is one thing—schemes for creating a legislative body of the Church are another—and I cannot help feeling how dangerous the latter may be, especially at the present moment. There is a readiness to change everything everywhere abroad, which suggests the need of caution. The Church is not a Democracy. . . .[3]

The English Church Union, however, eventually came out in favour of the scheme for a Church Assembly, although the special committee which it set up to advise it, wanted the omission of the proposal for compulsory parochial church councils, and objected to the suggestion that the Convocations' powers should eventually pass to the Church Assembly.

It was not only within the Catholic party that liberalism was breaking down old barriers and disposing men brought up in a rigid tradition to co-operate with those of a different party persuasion. Some Evangelicals, like the liberal Catholics earlier, turned their attention, at the beginning of the twentieth century, to the problem of developing a theology and a church policy which would come to grips with the problems presented to the Church by a changing society. That barometer of Evangelical thinking, the Islington Clerical Meeting, devoted its attention in January 1901 to the theme *The Old Century and the New—Experiences of the Past, and Lessons for the Future*.[4] The most significant paper for the Evangelical policy towards future church reform was that given by the Bishop of Coventry entitled 'Effectiveness of Organization'. In his paper, the

[1] Revd. Frederick George Lee, *The Ecclesiastical Situation in 1899 from a Tractarian Standpoint*, p. 50.

[2] J. G. Lockhart, *Charles Lindley Viscount Halifax, Part 2, 1885–1934*, p. 252.

[3] Quoted in *The Church Union Gazette*, January, 1919.

[4] Published in a collection of papers under that title in 1901.

Bishop dared to impugn the all-sufficiency of voluntary societies as the only form of extra-parochial organization which Evangelicals could trust: 'In so far as they have formed bonds between Churchmen of different parishes and dioceses where there was no machinery, they have helped build up the body of Christ.' But, he added, 'We need a power—a strong outside power to co-ordinate the claims and spheres of the Societies which the last century has bequeathed to us.' The Houses of Convocation were little more than 'a medieval waggon in an age of railways and tramcars'. He concluded that if the Evangelicals accepted that the Church of England had a corporate life, then 'we must feel that one of the first tasks of the twentieth century must be to find an outlet, a channel of some sort or other, for that corporate life'.[1]

Theologically a more liberal type of Evangelicalism had already begun to emerge from the newer Evangelical theological colleges—Wycliffe Hall, Oxford, and Ridley Hall, Cambridge (founded respectively in 1877 and 1881). It was in 1905 that the movement took on an organized form on the determination of three Ridley men working in the Liverpool Diocese: A. J. Tait, Principal of St. Aiden's College, Birkenhead (later Canon of Peterborough), C. Lisle Carr, Vicar of Blundellsands (later Bishop of Hereford), and Guy Warman, Vicar of Birkenhead (later Bishop of Manchester). For eighteen years this important movement, which came to be known as the Anglican Evangelical Group Movement, remained a private, almost secret, organization.[2]

Although this liberal Evangelicalism was to work within the Evangelical party, as liberal Catholicism had worked within the Catholic party, to gain acceptance for a scheme of church reform which entailed a certain degree of compromise of party principles, the two groups were in many respects very dissimilar. If the liberal Catholics provided the intellectual and theoretical content of the reform movement, the liberal Evangelicals provided much of the administrative ability that would be necessary to work the new

[1] Ibid., p. 57.

[2] Cf. Leonard Elliott-Binns, 'Evangelicalism and the Twentieth Century', in G. L. H. Harvey (ed.), *The Church and the Twentieth Century*, pp. 347–90.

church organization. Socially and intellectually the two groups were also very different; whereas the *Lux Mundi* group were Oxford fellows and had attended the best public schools, the Anglican Evangelical Group Movement on the whole had a different complexion:

> Socially it was a symptom of the rise of the middle classes to power in the Church as well as in the State. Among its protagonists there were no Gores, or Lyttletons, or Talbots, not even the Ashleys and Waldegraves of the older Evangelicalism. They were for the most part sons of the counting-house and the factory rather than the parsonage, and their outlook on life was swayed by no clerical antecedents. Educationally they were the product of the big day-schools of the country; . . . Thus their social and clerical influence was small. So was it intellectually, for there was among them not a single fellow of a college. . . .

And yet they worked themselves up through the church hierarchy until a substantial number of them occupied higher posts.

> Energy indeed was the leading trait of this group of men, that and efficiency and adroit finance. In fact they brought into the Church the methods, and even the ideals, of the business world from which most of them had sprung.[1]

Some of the Group were to play an important part in bringing Evangelical support to the church reform movement, and at least three of them, T. Guy Rogers, Guy Warman, and Edward Woods (later Bishop of Lichfield), were prominent on the Council of the Life and Liberty Movement. Woods even succeeded Temple as Chairman, after Temple became Bishop of Manchester in 1921. He had greater hopes for the Church Assembly than some of the other liberal Evangelicals, but even he seems to have lost his ardour after sitting in the Assembly for some time. His biographer, Oliver Tomkins (now the Bishop of Bristol), comments that

> . . . for one who had played so great a part in promoting the Enabling Act, he treated the Assembly in cavalier fashion, writing his interminable diaries and letters on his knee or slipping off to take innumerable weddings and christenings.

[1] Leonard Elliott-Binns, 'Evangelicalism and the Twentieth Century', in G.L.H. Harvey (ed.), *The Church and the Twentieth Century*, pp. 66–7.

He seems to have preferred the pageantry of the House of Lords, which he valued as a pleasant club, and the Athenaeum, where he 'revelled in the opportunities they provided for hobnobbing with the great'.[1]

It is doubtful if the liberal Evangelicals had any comprehensive theory of what the reformed Church's structure and role should be in theological and socio-philosophical terms to match those of the liberal Catholics. But their presence in the reform movement reduced the opposition from the Evangelical party to that which the conservative Evangelicals would inevitably produce towards any movement which had support from the Catholic party. The liberal Catholics' influence was much more extensive. On the one hand it steadily overcame early opposition in the Catholic party by virtue of its inclusion in its numbers of the party's most intellectually able men. On the other hand, the socialist leanings of the liberal Catholics, and their involvement in workers' education and support for the Settlements in the East End, brought them into contact with working class leaders.[2] It was this involvement, and the social philosophy and theology which gave it an ultimate justification, that brought about a certain, although limited, success in the reform movement's efforts to attract the working classes to its cause.

THE REFORM MOVEMENT, SOCIALISM, AND THE WORKING CLASSES

Charles Gore, at the Pan-Anglican Congress in 1908, had called the Church to penitence for not acting as the champion of the oppressed and weak, and 'for having been so often on the wrong side'. He concluded, 'We must identify ourselves, because we are Christians, with the positive ethical ideal of

[1] Oliver Tomkins, *The Life of Edward Woods, Bishop of Lichfield*, p. 132.

[2] The connection with the Settlements was especially strong on the Life and Liberty Movement Council. Sheppard had been Head of Oxford House, Bethnal Green, 1909–11, and was succeeded by F. A. Iremonger (until 1916) who, along with Sheppard and William Temple, formed the inner triumvirate of Life and Liberty. Douglas Eyre, the Head of Oxford House at the time of Life and Liberty, was an important member of the latter's Council, treasurer of the Church Self-Government Association, and on the inner councils of the Church Reform League.

socialistic thought.'[1] In the same year William Temple, as a young Fellow of Queen's College, Oxford, was writing in *The Economic Review* that 'the alternative stands before us—Socialism or Heresy; we are involved in one or the other'.[2] The Christian Social Union, which Gore had founded, included Scott Holland and R. H. Tawney among its members. Tawney was to serve on the Council of the Life and Liberty Movement under the chairmanship of his life-long friend, William Temple, himself a branch chairman of C.S.U. Scott Holland, who died in March 1918, was not able to play a very active part in Life and Liberty, although he gave it unfailing support in his periodical *The Commonwealth*. Life and Liberty also benefited from the Christian socialist connections of the church reformers by being able to attract on to its Council 'distinguished working men' (as they were usually called) such as Albert Mansbridge, with whom Temple was associated in running the Workers' Educational Association, and E. W. Kemp.[3] There were also trade union officials on the Council like Fred Hughes, of the National Union of Clerks, and Miss E. Willson, of the Independent National Union Boot and Shoe Women Workers.

Despite the socialist leanings of some of the most prominent members of the church reform movement, both the Church Reform League and the Life and Liberty Movement avoided any formal association with socialist groups. The sympathies of the leaders of Life and Liberty were unmistakable, however. One Life and Liberty pamphlet quoted with pride a complimentary remark about the Enabling Bill which Sidney Webb had made in a Fabian Lecture on 14 November 1919.[4] Its most outspoken statement appeared in the Life and Liberty leaflet on *The Social Message of the Church*, which appeared to advocate socialist principles. It announced:

> The principles of a Christian Social Gospel should be *Co-operation*, *Fellowship*, and *Mutual Service*. The implications of our existing social system are *Competition*, *Profits*, and *Self-Interest*.

[1] Quoted in Roger Lloyd, *The Church of England in the Twentieth Century*, vol. i, p. 85.

[2] Quoted in Reckitt, op. cit., p. 15.

[3] Temple was President of W.E.A.

[4] Life and Liberty Pamphlet, no. 19, p. 15.

Among the causes of the Church's failure was, 'A domination of *class patronage* and *control* within the Church.' It asked for social policies which followed the principles of 'joint control' and 'co-ownership', reduction of indirect taxation and more direct taxation, reorganization of agriculture and education, the creation of a Ministry of Health, better housing, and a reduction in maximum working hours.[1]

But even this did not go far enough for some Christian socialists, who felt that unless Life and Liberty condemned the Church's attachment to material riches, such as those held by the Ecclesiastical Commissioners and enjoyed by the bishops, and openly allied itself with the Labour Party, it would never win the working classes. Thus the Revd. Percy Dearmer wrote from India to his mother-in-law in answer to a letter from her concerning Life and Liberty, in February 1918:

> I know little of the 'Life and Liberty' business, and am probably all wrong in my ideas. But (1) I don't think the Church is worthy to arrange her own affairs. The State keeps her from doing much harm, and making herself a mere sect, which the clergy want her to be. The only chance of the Church of England surviving what is going to come, is for the People to save her from herself. If only the Labour Party would take a little interest in her! (2) I feel profoundly that God will never bless any Church Reform movement that does not begin by repudiating the worldliness of the Church. These movements crop up —the Church Reform League is nearly 20 years old: they propose everything—except to give up money: and nothing is therefore ever done. We cling to our wicked abuses, our sinecures and 'prizes', because the only clergy with any power grow fat on them, and the others hope to one day. If all the useless dignitaries and all the overpaid bishops—or a quarter of them—would come out tomorrow and lay their emoluments at the Apostles' feet (even to the extent that Annanias and Sapphira did) there would be no more difficulty about getting 'Liberty', and we might even get a little 'Life'. But we shall never persuade the powers that we deserve self-government, and we shall never persuade the masses of the people that we stand for Christianity—until we show that we are terribly in earnest; that religion means sacrifice, and does not mean a milch-cow.[2]

[1] Life and Liberty Leaflet (G).
[2] Nan Dearmer, *The Life of Percy Dearmer*, p. 213.

The suggestion of Life and Liberty allying itself with the Labour Party was never taken up, and on the Labour Party's side there must have been a great deal of puzzlement as to how it should regard this movement. On the one hand the chairman of the Life and Liberty Movement, Temple, caused consternation in Convocation by announcing in 1918 that he had joined the Labour Party; whilst on the other hand, Fr. Paul Bull, another Christian socialist and an Anglican, had written to Arthur Henderson offering to support the Labour Party if it would place disestablishment on its official programme.[1] Fr. Bull wrote to the *Church Times* on 7 June 1918, urging other churchmen to follow suit and informing them that a sub-committee of the Labour Party was considering the matter.

The true situation, as *The Times* had predicted in 1896, was probably that as political power was transferred to the working classes, not only would Nonconformity (which it associated with the middle classes) become less influential as a political force, but organized Christianity as a whole would decline in political influence, because however much was done by the Church to remove reproach, the gulf was already too great, and the masses were so indifferent to any form of religious organization that a real marriage would prove impossible. Further evidence of the accuracy of this analysis was provided by the difficulties which the Church experienced in securing the interest and participation of the working classes in its developing representative assemblies and administrative organs. Despite all well-meaning efforts in this direction, the growth of this organization seemed to work in the opposite direction by providing more positions and influence for upper- and middle-class laymen.

This was to be the experience of the Church Assembly, and it had already been evident in the Representative Church Council, and in the Central Board of Finance, and its associated diocesan finance boards, which had been established in 1914 on the recommendation of the Archbishops' Committee on Church Finance, which reported in 1911. The Committee's report made it plain that one of its

[1] See Temple's speech in *Chronicle of Canterbury Convocation*, 1 May 1918, p. 351; Fr. Bull's letter appeared in the *Church Times*, 7 June 1918.

chief concerns was that the new church administration should involve the laity and give them back a sense of responsibility, which they had lost as a result of endowment, and church rates in the earlier period. It envisaged that at parochial, diocesan, and central levels, the finance boards would derive their authority from, and be responsible to, representative councils. At the central level the obvious candidate for controlling the Central Board of Finance was the Representative Church Council (composed of the two provincial Convocations and their associated Houses of Laymen), and the committee's report assumed this. However, the bishops had no liking for the Representative Church Council, and on 2 February 1914 the Archbishop of Canterbury wrote to the Committee informing them:

> I have had a full talk with the Archbishop of York about the Central Board of Finance, and have also had the opportunity of a general discussion with a good many other Bishops. I find among them no difference of opinion as to the course we ought to follow. We must not let the Representative Church Council become an executive body which itself elects committees and is responsible for what they do. They have no machinery for such modes of action and the membership of the Representative Church Council is so varied that it is not reasonable to regard each individual vote among its members as of equal value. We believe in the representative character of the Central Board being secured by its consisting chiefly of delegates from the various Diocesan Boards. Of course it would then have to choose its own Executive Committee. There would be a nominated element as well, but we are convinced that this is the right principle.[1]

This plan threatened to dilute the representative principle so much that some members of the Committee wanted to defy the bishops, but they were outvoted 11 to 3, as the minutes reveal.[1] In the following year the Central Board of Finance's Annual Report shows that of the thirty-six diocesan boards of finance formed by that time, thirteen had a bishop (archbishop in the case of York) as chairman, another two had a knight, five had a titled chairman, and three had laymen bearing military officer rank. The diocesan boards of finance, and so too the Central Board of Finance, were even less representative of the class structure of

[1] Archbishops' Committee on Church Finance, Minutes for 14 February 1914.

English society than the Representative Church Council. At least some people still believed that the Representative Church Council was meant to be representative in that sense, and the Second Annual Report of the Central Board of Finance (1916) announced that an anonymous donation of £100 had been handed to the Board to pay the expenses of

> . . . a genuine working man representative of the York House of Laymen, the diocese to which Bradford or Leeds is situated to have a first claim, afterwards any other diocese in the Northern Province.[1]

Evidently the donor was not too optimistic about the chances of finding many such specimens! In 1917, however, the Annual Report proudly published a letter from a 'manual worker' in the Rhondda Valley, who had written to thank them for sending him the Annual Report, and asking them to send any other publications they might have issued 'since the first Report of the Pensions Committee'. He wrote:

> I shall be only too glad to have any reports sent out by the Board, and will send the money by return for them.
>
> I write as a working man, very anxious to do my whole duty in this respect and meet my obligations; but my chief difficulty lies in not knowing what is expected of me.[2]

Nothing brought out more clearly the growing influence of middle-class laymen in running the business of the Church than the manner in which a national appeal for £5,000,000 for the Central Church Fund was launched in 1918. The decision to launch the appeal arose from the Central Board of Finance's experience of the impossibility of getting the richer dioceses to accept an assessment from the Central Board of what they could afford to contribute to the Central Fund for the purpose of aiding the poorer dioceses.[3] The manner in which the appeal was made can be attributed to a too close observance of the policy advocated by the Central Board's new full-time Secretary, Canon F. Partridge, in his book *The Soul of Wealth*, when he counselled the Church to make the fullest use of business-

[1] Central Board of Finance Annual Report, 1916, p. 9.
[2] Ibid., 1917, pp. 17–18.
[3] Ibid., pp. 13–14.

men. The appeal was nothing if not business-like. One of its advertisements, which appeared in *The English Church Review*, November 1918, proclaimed:

> The Church of England Central Fund is the most profitable investment that the nation through its citizens—whether Churchmen or not—can make. The dividends will be paid in the cure of social mischiefs, the growth of better and more efficient citizenship, the birth of better ideals, the stabilization of the social order.

Another, in *Truth*, 18 November 1918, claimed: 'Apart from its spiritual importance, the upkeep of the Church's social and educational activities is in the most commercial sense a productive investment.'

Such reasoning had been acceptable when it came from a Lord Liverpool in 1818, or a Blomfield in the 1830s, but the efforts of Gore, Scott Holland, and the other Christian socialists, had persuaded many churchmen that the Church must learn a new language if it was to commend itself to the wider society. Although Scott Holland had died in March 1918, exactly one year later his periodical, *The Commonwealth*, asked the question which he would have put: What would be the effect of such advertisements on the working man? 'He seizes upon the unfortunate expressions contained in some of the appeals, "the stabilization of society"'. All the good work would be undone, especially that of the military chaplains who had led the men to think that the Church shared their aspirations. Now 'the working class will have read the appeal to the rich to support the Church as a bulwark of the existing social order'. It added,

> It is felt by some that the Church is simply trying to get its hands into the pockets of wage-earners, while wages are kept up by the Wages Temporary Regulation Act, which operates for six months from last December.[1]

The Church Socialist League sent a manifesto to the Archbishop of Canterbury stating:

> We can only describe it as utterly deplorable that the Church should thus be made to appeal to the nation for support in the capacity, first and foremost, of the obedient watchdog of the bourgeoisie.[1]

The *Church Times* on 7 February 1919 published a reply

[1] *The Commonwealth*, March 1919, vol. xxiv, p. 279.

to the criticisms which seemed to emanate from somebody associated with the Central Fund Committee, although it was signed 'Z'. It claimed that although the advertisements might not appeal to the Christian Socialist League

> They do appeal to the committee, consisting almost entirely of businessmen, which is responsible for the Central Fund, and if the Church wants the help of its laymen it must take them on their own terms.

After all, it pointed out, they were meeting their responsibilities 'in a business-like way and by business-like methods'.

SUMMARY

The confluence of the two streams of Christian socialism and church reform can be traced back to the year 1889, and the appearance on the scene of *Lux Mundi* and the Christian Social Union; it began to make itself felt within the Church Reform League, and flowed together most strongly in the Life and Liberty Movement. With the founding of the Church Assembly, however, the alliance ended, partly because of developments and divisions within the Christian socialist movement, but more particularly because of the nature of the Assembly and its business. One of the founders of the Life and Liberty Movement, F. A. Iremonger, in his biography of William Temple, gave a conclusion on the relation between the Movement and its creation, the Church Assembly, which would have been echoed by many of his colleagues:

> Generally, it may be said that at the outset there was a sharp and fateful struggle between two groups in the National Church Assembly who differed widely in their conception of its policy and its purpose and may be called, roughly, the legalists and the moralists. The struggle was a brief one. The legalists—of whom Sir Lewis Dibdin, the trusted advisor of Randall Davidson, will be remembered as the leader—were soon in control; the voice of the Assembly is now the voice of the administrator, not of the prophet; and so long as its constitution and time-table remain unrevised (so that, for instance, few of the laity outside the more or less leisured classes can spare the time to attend the sessions) its present tone and temper will persist.[1]

[1] Iremonger, op. cit., p. 281.

In the light of this analysis it is ironical that one Member of Parliament who spoke on the Second Reading of the Enabling Bill on 7 November 1919 should have expressed the view that: 'As far as I can understand the political principles embodied in this constitution, they are purely Bolshevist. . . .' He refrained from suggesting that the Archbishop of Canterbury had been in consultation with Lenin, only adding:

> But the fact that the organization proposed by the Archbishop of Canterbury is precisely the same organization as has been adopted by Lenin is attributable to the desire of both to secure the same end. . . . The real principle at the root of Bolshevism is a desire to combine a democratic form with autocratic effects, and that is what has taken place in this constitution.[1]

Despite the incongruity in the juxtaposition of the names of Lenin and the Archbishop of Canterbury, in retrospect some of those who had worked for more democracy in the Church might have been inclined to agree with him if they shared Iremonger's disillusionment.

The church reform movement had failed to achieve its most ambitious goal—a new religious expression of the life of the whole English people with a supra-class character. The result was much more limited and localized within the area of church administration. It had taken the Church of England a little further along the road towards a denominational form of organization, by increasing its autonomy as an institution and its administrative efficiency. As Iremonger generously conceded:

> A case can be made out for the contention that the Assembly was never intended to provide a platform for the prophet . . . and if it be granted that the object of the Assembly is to reorganize the administration and finances of the Church, its members deserve credit for many useful reforms which it might have taken two generations to effect under the old system of passing church Bills through Parliament. The power in the Church remains exactly where it was before, but at least it has a constitutional sanction in the hands of the bishops, archdeacons, and elder statesmen, who now direct the procedure and control the policy of the National Assembly of the Church of England.[2]

[1] Major Barnes, M.P., *Hansard*, Fifth Series, vol. cxx, col. 1835.
[2] Iremonger, op. cit.

VI

THE MOVEMENTS LEADING UP TO THE ENABLING ACT, 1919

THE LIFE AND LIBERTY MOVEMENT AND THE COALITION OF REFORM FORCES

THE church reform campaign entered a new and more dynamic phase during the First World War. The character of that campaign, and the part played in it by the Life and Liberty Movement, from its formation in 1917 until the passing of the Church of England Assembly (Powers) Act—the 'Enabling Act'—in December 1919, provides an insight into the course of ecclesiastical politics. It also illustrates the vicissitudes which beset attempts to apply theory to structure in church organization, and the respective parts played by pressure groups and by administrative exigency in determining the outcome of such endeavours.

The Life and Liberty Movement was formed specifically to play the part of a pressure group. It announced its intention in its first public utterance, a letter published in *The Times* on 20 June 1917, in which it stated:

> Amid the ruins of the old world, the new world is already being born. In the ideas of reconstruction now being formed there is hope of a new and better era. The Church has felt, and to some extent imparted, the new impulse in the National Mission. It has in altogether new ways realized its responsibilities and its impotence at the present time to discharge them. . . . A vigorous forward movement just now may revive waning enthusiasm and hopes, retain for the service of the Church the eager souls who now doubtfully watch it, and, by combining these together, exert such pressure on the official bodies as may result in real reform. . . . Those who are promoting this movement are convinced that we must win for the Church full power to control its own life, even at the cost, if necessary, of disestablishment and of whatever consequences that may possibly involve.[1]

[1] The letter was signed by William Temple, who was described as Chairman; A. P. Charles, F. A. Iremonger, and H. R. L. Sheppard, who were described as

There were four factors which built up the pressure for reform and provided the impetus for the Life and Liberty Movement. Related to three of these factors was the general factor of the alienation of the working classes from the Church, as had been suggested earlier by the social surveys of Charles Booth and the personal experience of the Christian socialists.[1] During the War, the seriousness of this situation was discovered by the large number of clergymen who served as chaplains, and so mixed with a class of men they might never have got to know in ordinary circumstances.[2] The National Mission, which the Church of England launched in 1916, brought home the extent to which the Church had been failing to make an impact on the nation. This lesson, and the changes which were needed to redress the deficiency, were spelled out by the five Committees of Inquiry which followed the Mission. Their reports, published in 1918, dealt with: *The Teaching Office of the Church*; *The Worship of the Church*; *The Evangelistic Work of the Church*; *The Administrative Reform of the Church*; and *Christianity and Industrial Problems*. The third precipitating factor was the existence of the Report of the Archbishops' Committee on

Hon. Secretaries; and five others, namely, Louise Creighton, A. A. David, A. Mansbridge, J. B. Seaton, and A. L. Smith.

1 Charles Booth, 'Religious Influences' series of the *Life and Labour of the People of London*, London, 1902–3. One comment of Booth's which may have fired the church reformers with the desire to address themselves to the workers as a 'class', was his remark that: 'The great section of the population, which passes by the name of the working classes, lying socially between the lower middle class and the "poor", remains, as a whole, outside of all the religious bodies, whether organized as churches or as missions; and as those of them who do join any church become almost indistinguishable from the class with which they then mix, the change that has really come about is not so much *of* as *out* of the class to which they belonged' (vol. vii, p. 399).

The situation was made more serious by the fact that, over the last two decades of the nineteenth century, the Church of England had been losing members at a far higher rate than the Nonconformist churches, and that loss had been fairly uniform throughout all classes. The figures were given by R. Mudie-Smith (ed.), *The Religious Life of London*, 1904, pp. 280–1.

2 More than 7,000 Church of England clergy offered themselves for service during the War, and 3,060 of these were commissioned. The figures are given in R. T. Davidson, *The Testing of a Nation*. The *Church Times* said on 28 March 1918 that the chaplains had gained much: 'They have found that the English workingman is a much finer and stronger type than cultured well-to-do folk had ever imagined, and they have had to deal with battalions which are a microcosm of the nation.' See also the book of essays by seventeen temporary Church of England chaplains on active service in France and Flanders, F. B. Macnutt (ed.), *The Church in the Furnace*.

Church and State (the Selborne Committee), whose proposals for the establishment of a new central council or assembly had not been taken up since they were presented in 1916.[1] Finally there was the experience of church administrators of the impossibility of securing church legislation from Parliament, and the concomitant need to increase the Church's own capacity for governing itself and for controlling its administrative agencies.[2]

The chaplains' experience of the gulf which existed between the Church and the working man in uniform filtered back to the Church at home during the War. William Temple received a letter from the chaplains of the Seventh Division in France urging him on after publication of the Life and Liberty letter to *The Times* of 20 June:

> No matter what type or party we belonged to of old, we are now all haunted by the fear that the Home Church cannot see, and will not rise up to meet, the needs which have shocked each of us on entering, as minister of Christ, this huge intermingling of all sorts and conditions of our countrymen.[3]

The pessimism of some chaplains even extended to doubts as to the seriousness and sincerity of the movements for reform. One of them, Charles E. Raven, wrote an article

[1] This Committee had been set up as the result of a motion moved by Sir A. Cripps (later Lord Parmoor, a leading figure in the Church Assembly, and father of Stafford Cripps) in the Representative Church Council: 'That there is in principle no inconsistency between a national recognition of religion and the spiritual independence of the Church; and this Council requests the Archbishops of Canterbury and York to consider the advisability of appointing a committee to inquire what changes are advisable in order to secure in the relations of Church and State a fuller expression of the spiritual independence of the Church as well as the national recognition of religion.' It was passed with one (unnamed) dissentient (*Report of Proceedings of the Representative Church Council*, for 3 July and 4 July 1913).

[2] Since 1880 the Church had introduced 22 Bills to end the scandals in the sale of livings, 21 of these had to be dropped; of 40 Bills to create new bishoprics, suffragan bishoprics, and archdeaconries, 30 had to be dropped; of 32 Bills introduced to deal with the ritual question, only one was ever debated. The story was the same with regard to Bills to deal with other church matters; Parliament had neither the time nor the inclination to attend to them. The figures are given by Viscount Wolmer, M.P., *The Failure of the House of Commons in Ecclesiastical Legislation*, Church Self-Government Papers, No. 10, 1919.

[3] Unpublished letter, dated 1 July 1917, in the possession of Lambeth Palace Library (hereafter abbreviated as Unpub. Lam. MSS.).

for *The Challenge*, of which Temple was the editor, in which he observed,

> All these reports and committees and movements—one doesn't know what lies behind them. Are they the expression of a genuine purpose and a widespread desire for change? Or are they simply 'feelers' put forward by a few picked men without serious hope of action for a generation or two?[1]

Raven suggested that the chaplains should band themselves together 'and refuse, if need be, to take any part in organized traditional religious life unless certain things which are now just topics for debate are carried out'.[1]

Temple, although Chairman of the Life and Liberty Movement, was known to have a close relationship with the Archbishop of Canterbury, Davidson, who was cautious about the expediency of undertaking reforms during the War or immediately after it. In the long term it was Temple's statesmanship and flair for tactics, especially in dealing with the Archbishop, that was to bring the movement its success, but in the early days his methods seemed somewhat detached and calculating compared with those of some of his more impatient associates. In his first letter to the Archbishop about the Movement, Temple suggested that his own role might be that of mediator.

> I suppose the group that Dick Sheppard has got around him are people who are really keen on what the Church stands for, and want to be keen on the Church. But the War and the Mission have brought them to boiling-point. It is a psychological necessity that they should explode. To ask them to wait six months may be right, but is requiring about a miracle.[2]

As for his own feelings, Temple said that he did not sympathize very much with the others, but he could understand them. He added,

> I wonder if there could be any harm in a meeting with this resolution: That this meeting pledges itself to do all in its power to support the authorities in the Church in any well considered and thorough plan of action whereby the Church may be made more effective as a spiritual force and moral witness.[2]

[1] *The Challenge*, 29 November 1918.

[2] Unpub. Lam. MSS., Letter, Temple–Davidson, 4 February 1917.

The Archbishop replied through his chaplain that he would have no objection to such a meeting, although it must not appear that he himself was associated with it.[1] Meanwhile, Temple had been in consultation with Charles Gore and they had agreed that a 'forward move' was necessary. But he still saw his own role as that of mediator. He told Davidson:

> I should certainly desire to keep it absolutely loyal to the Church and the Church authorities; and so I think there is some point in some of my sort going in, because I feel sure that a move of this sort is going to be begun, and if people like myself keep out of it, it will become much more dissentient as a result.[2]

Once again the Archbishop replied that he would not dream of dissuading Temple, even though he had 'not the least idea what a "forward movement" in these general terms covered'.[3]

He was soon to find out. The Life and Liberty Movement held its first public meeting at the Queen's Hall, 16 July 1917, and the resolution passed was much more unfavourable to the Archbishop than the one which Temple had suggested. It insisted:

> That whereas the present conditions under which the Church lives and works constitute an intolerable hindrance to its spiritual activity, this meeting instructs the Council, as a first step, to approach the Archbishops, in order to urge upon them that they should ascertain without delay, and make known to the Church at large, whether and on what terms Parliament is prepared to give freedom to the Church in the sense of full power to manage its own life, that so it may the better fulfil its duty to God and to the nation and its mission to the world.[4]

The Archbishop became rather annoyed with the unfavourable light which this 'ginger group' threw on his own leadership, despite Temple's earlier assurances. He could not object to their specific proposals for reform, because most of them had already been made by his own Committee on Church and State, which he had welcomed along with most

[1] Unpub. Lam. MSS., Letter, Davidson–Temple, 7 February 1917.

[2] Ibid., Letter, Temple–Davidson, 14 February 1917.

[3] Ibid., Letter, Davidson–Temple, 17 February 1917.

[4] *The Challenge*, 20 July 1917.

of the other bishops at a special Bishops' Meeting in May 1917.[1] However, he told Temple that whilst he could not object to his speech at the Queen's Hall meeting, except on the 'possibilities of the present hour in Parliament', he did object to his giving the impression of the bishops as

> Lucretian divinities, or say like the eighteenth century Archbishops (Cornwallis or Moore) bewigged and besleeved, who might doubtless pass placid Resolutions in Convocation but had no thought of putting them into action.[2]

Davidson also brought to bear his strongest weapon—his own unrivalled knowledge and skill with regard to Parliamentary statesmanship on the Church's behalf. At a time when the nation was 'at death-grips with the Germans', he asked Temple,

> Could I really insist on an interview at Downing Street, which generally means calling the Prime Minister out from a Cabinet meeting to speak standing up in the ante-room, and ask him what conditions of Church life he would regard as the right ones for the future?[2]

Archbishop Davidson's style of leadership had been formed by his experience as chaplain to Archbishop Tait.[3] It assumed a close partnership between Church and State and within those terms of reference it could boast the traditional virtues of statesmanship. In the new circumstances, however, it often appeared negative or autocratic, especially as the Church's changing relations with the State had the internal corollary that an increased burden was placed on the Archbishop of Canterbury. Temple had published a pamphlet setting out the aims of Life and Liberty in which he drew attention to the unsatisfactory situation whereby the Archbishop, without a Cabinet or G.H.Q. staff, was the sole pivot of the church system.[4]

[1] G. K. A. Bell, *Randall Davidson*, vol. ii, p. 960.

[2] Letter dated 17 July 1917; quoted in Bell, op. cit., pp. 962–3.

[3] Tait was Archbishop from 1868 to 1882, and Davidson, besides being his chaplain, was also his son-in-law and biographer.

[4] W. Temple, *Life and Liberty*, 1917. F. A. Iremonger had also suggested the idea of a G.H.Q. staff to Davidson, only to have it rejected, as he disclosed later in a sermon published under the title *On the Need for a G.H.Q. for the Church of England*, 1945. Although Davidson does seem to have flirted with the idea of copying Lloyd George's War Cabinet; see his correspondence with Temple, 1–4 June 1918, Unpub. Lam. MSS.

Randall Davidson insisted on bearing that burden, but in so doing it made him impatient with any interference or attempt to deflect him from the course which he was trying to follow. On the issue of implementing the Church and State Committee's proposals, he had judged that wartime and the immediate post-war period were inopportune times for the Church to submit proposals to Parliament, even assuming that agreement could be reached between the church parties. Although the Bishops' Meeting had given a general welcome to the Selborne Committee's proposals, Davidson knew that even there deep divisions existed between such strong figures as Bishop Gore, a keen supporter of confirmation as the qualification for church electors, and, on the other hand, Bishop Knox of Manchester, and Hensley Henson, when he became Bishop of Hereford in 1918, who opposed any narrowing down of the Church's membership. And outside the Bishops' Meeting there were more extreme parties. All these circumstances had an effect on Davidson's leadership, as described by Roger Lloyd:

> It was the tragedy of Dr. Davidson's life, and especially during the first war, that he could never turn the negative, and, in the circumstances, considerable achievement of avoiding schism into that positive unity of creative fellowship with a scale of values which puts first things first. He tried hard but the parties in the Church, and primarily, alas! the extreme Anglo-Catholics, would never let him.[1]

It was the great achievement of the Life and Liberty Movement that it managed, for a short period, to ally members of different parties into a pressure group with one first priority the passing of an Enabling Bill to give the Church of England a measure of self-government. The life history of the Movement shows that it changed its character to some extent in the interests of preserving its unity and maintaining a sufficiently wide coalition. The original group which Dick Sheppard gathered around him, and whom Temple described as being near to 'boiling-point', gradually gave way under Temple's leadership to a more weighty and wider cross-section of moderate reformers. This was revealed by the inclusion among the signatories of the first

[1] Roger Lloyd, *The Church of England in the Twentieth Century*, vol. i, p. 237.

letter to *The Times* of such respected names as Louise Creighton, widow of the late Bishop of London, Mandell Creighton; A. A. David, Headmaster of Rugby; A. Mansbridge, Secretary of the Workers' Educational Association; J. B. Seaton, Principal of Cuddesdon Theological College; and A. L. Smith, Master of Balliol College. However, some of the first Life and Liberty leaflets still reflected the passionate reformist opinions of the original 'ginger group'. This was especially evident in Leaflet (G), on *The Social Message of the Church*, which denounced competition, profits, and self-interest in society, and advocated joint control and co-ownership. The socialist language which it used to condemn the 'domination of *class patronage* and *control* within the Church' and the fact that 'our Church appointments are made, our Church assemblies are manned almost exclusively, by men of one class', this was strange language indeed to some of the new members.

The complexion of the Movement was further changed in 1918, when it attracted into its membership and on to its committees a number of influential laymen, many of them businessmen, who subscribed generously to the funds and persuaded their friends to join. According to Iremonger,

> Several had had business experience during the war which left them more than a little uneasy about the general tone of public life and affairs, and were ready to take an active part in any corporate effort to emphasize the fundamental decencies of social and commercial life. Most of them held no very high doctrine of the Church or, at least on their first attachment to the Movement, of its divine mission; but they saw in it an institution which above all others should provide a rallying-point for men and women of 'an honest heart', with a certain traditional authority to proclaim the high principles from which the country seemed at that time to be falling.[1]

At the first public meeting of Life and Liberty, however, a convinced opponent like Hensley Henson could still ridicule its unrepresentative composition. The Archbishop of Canterbury could have been excused if he had dismissed the importance of the Movement after receiving a description of the meeting from Henson. He described them as,

> The academic, the feminist, the Socialist, the clericalist—these are

[1] F. A. Iremonger, *William Temple*, pp. 252–3.

not the constituents of an ecclesiastical policy which is likely to be tolerant, or wide, or just, or large.[1]

Although Temple was to reach a section of the working class with the message of Life and Liberty, by the simple expedient of combining his lecture tours for that Movement with his tours on behalf of the W.E.A., the first Queen's Hall audience had not that advantage. Hensley Henson commented that it was

> . . . three-parts composed of women, and the remaining part was mainly made up of youngish parsons. Socially I conjectured that the meeting consisted of upper middle-class people, who form the congregations of West-End churches. There was no trace of the working classes perceptible.[1]

But even Henson later came to realize the singular achievement of Life and Liberty in attracting and holding together all the diverse strands of the church reform cause. The achievement was made possible by the sacrifice of radicalism and the stipulation of a single aim—that of securing an Enabling Act along the broad lines laid down by the Archbishops' Committee on Church and State in 1916, subject to the modifications made by the 'Grand' Committee of the Representative Church Council, which reported in 1918. Thus Life and Liberty was able to overcome a split which had been evident throughout most of the nineteenth century between those churchmen who had a responsibility for the general administration of the Church and so sought only such instrumental reforms as would increase efficiency, and on the other hand, those churchmen whose main concern was to stress the autonomy of the Church and its values, and to heighten the sense of churchmanship (or self-consciousness of the organization). The spread of liberalism, especially within the Catholic party, and the confluence of that stream with the formerly separate streams of Christian social witness and church reform, has already been noted. However, the Church Reform League, which was the main reform organization prior to the First World War, had never tested the strength of the desire for

[1] Unpub. Lam. MSS., Letter, Henson–Davidson, 17 July 1917; and quoted in Bell, op. cit., vol. ii, pp. 963–4.

reform among the different church parties by submitting detailed legislative proposals. Party strife over other issues was as strong as ever and loomed far larger in the Church's life than the concern for reform, until the War. The Church Reform League's Annual Report for 1918–19 revealed that its membership was still under 5,000, despite a recent expansion.

Nor had the extent of the League's own determination to secure reforms been tested. It had never suggested, as did the Life and Liberty Movement, that the demand for reform should be pressed home 'even at the cost, if necessary, of disestablishment'. Although as time went on Life and Liberty found it prudent to play down this commitment, nevertheless it served to show that the new Movement meant business.

Despite Henson's tendency to see all movements for increased self-government as movements for disestablishment, he was the one contemporary commentator who could analyse the separate forces involved in the process by which the 'autonomist' and 'instrumentalist' groups came together in the successful reform movement.

The war had interrupted an energetic agitation for ecclesiastical autonomy in which were combined two movements different in origin and temper, but drawn together by a common dislike of the existing Establishment. The one movement was religious, desiring Disestablishment on the ground of religious principle; the other was political, desiring it on the ground of practical efficiency. The secularizing of the nation by the triumph of democracy destroyed the necessary postulate of the Establishment in the view of the first: the difficulty of carrying measures of ecclesiastical reform through the House of Commons which was overburdened with its secular work, destroyed the practical value of the Establishment in the view of the last. It is apparent that while the combination of the two movements would notably increase the power of the autonomist agitation, it was not in itself capable of permanent maintenance.

The war had brought into prominence a considerable number of the younger clergy, who had gained in the course of their military service a dislike of the restrictions imposed by normal ecclesiastical discipline. . . . They formed the backbone of the 'Life and Liberty Movement' which was organized to 'force the pace' of the agitation for autonomy. The casuistic facility and untiring eloquence of

William Temple, the infectious enthusiasm of 'Dick' Sheppard, the adroitness and audacity of Lord Hugh Cecil and Lord Wolmer, with the 'Church Lads Brigade' in the House of Commons, formed a powerful combination.[1]

The combination of forces did not always remain in step. In 1918 *The Challenge* newspaper, edited by Temple, devoted two leading articles to the Central Church Fund, for which an appeal had been launched in that year. It said that, whilst it recognized that such a growth of central administration was necessary if the Church was to become a corporate entity, it advised that contributions should be made to the Central Fund only on the condition that it became a committee of the Church Assembly when it was formed. It added, 'That Assembly will hold real power only in the way in which other assemblies obtain it, and that is by control of the purse.' After lamenting again the lack of a general headquarters staff responsible to a representative assembly, to replace the Archbishop of Canterbury as the 'one pivot about which the whole system revolves', it said that the same criticism applied to the Central Board of Finance and the diocesan boards, which were 'not calculated to promote a general confidence such as is obtained by really responsible administration'. The remedy was for churchmen to concentrate on the prime objective of obtaining a Church Assembly, and 'churchmen should support the Central Fund not yet with money but with promises' to be fulfilled after self-government and the reform of abuses.[2]

Not surprisingly the businessmen running the Central Fund felt this to be a stab in the back from a quarter which previously they had regarded as an ally in their common cause of making the Church more efficient. The Chairman of the Service Candidates Committee wrote to *The Challenge* to protest, and said that there were hundreds of ordination candidates being demobilized who would be dependent on the Central Fund, and if *The Challenge*'s advice was followed they would be destitute.[3] *The Challenge* stuck to its guns and replied that 'the advance of Church Self-Government

[1] H. Hensley Henson, *Retrospect of an Unimportant Life*, vol. i, p. 206.
[2] *The Challenge*, 13 and 20 December 1918.
[3] Op. cit., 27 December 1918.

should precede the claims of the Fund'.[1] The Chairman of the Propaganda Committee of the Central Fund then answered bitterly that the Fund had issued half a million leaflets in which it commended the Life and Liberty Movement, but he added that the Central Fund itself could establish the machinery necessary for reforming abuses if only it was given enough money.[2] At this point a conciliator appeared on the scene in the figure of Lord Wolmer, who was leading the Parliamentary forces in favour of church reform. He pointed out that the establishment of new finance organs was one of the surest ways of helping to bring into being representative assemblies:

> Just as the adoption of the Report of the original Archbishops' Committee on Church Finance by the several dioceses gave birth to thousands of Parochial Church Councils and to the representative system of Church Finance in every diocese, so the corollary of the creation of the Central Fund is the creation of a Church Assembly.[3]

Sheffield Diocesan Conference was reported to have acted on *The Challenge*'s advice and to have passed a resolution supporting the Central Fund on the condition that the administration of central funds was reformed. The Vicar of Sheffield, H. Gresford Jones, wrote to *The Challenge* to underline that condition and to point out that the most important facet here was the Ecclesiastical Commission and its 'large surplus of £650,000 annually'. He asked whether it was right that the Church should have two central funds, or should not both endowments and voluntary contributions be placed under one Central Board of Finance, constitutionally representative of the whole Church.[4] Life and Liberty, as it grew more moderate in its endeavours to attract the widest possible support, including those with administrative responsibilities, avoided grasping this nettle. It was only after the Enabling Act was safely through that it issued a new leaflet, *Administrative reform. A Guide to Study and Discussion* (1920), by F. A. Iremonger, which suggested that one of the questions which might be discussed was whether the Ecclesiastical Commission and Queen Anne's Bounty might be made more representative by the election

[1] Op. cit., 3 January 1919.
[2] Op. cit., 10 January 1919.
[3] Op. cit., 24 January 1919.
[4] Op. cit., 7 February 1919.

of lay representatives, and whether both bodies should be united and brought under the control of the Church Assembly. It was the failure to bring these bodies effectively under the control of Church Assembly which limited the amount of executive power which accrued to that Assembly, as *The Challenge* had predicted in its comment on the 'control of the purse'.

The most important figure at the Ecclesiastical Commissioners' office during the reform period was Sir Lewis Tonna Dibdin. He was the outstanding ecclesiastical lawyer and administrator in the Church of England, and as First Church Estates Commissioner (1905–30) and an active governor and chairman of committees at Queen Anne's Bounty, he had an unparalleled knowledge of church business. Archbishop Benson had relied greatly on him and when Archbishop Davidson was at Lambeth Dibdin advised him almost daily.[1] As late as 8 June 1919, after the Enabling Bill had been submitted to Parliament, Dibdin was plotting with one of the main opponents, Lord Haldane. In a letter to Haldane he reminded him that in 1904 there was an idea of passing a Bill to enable Provisional Orders to be made for certain church purposes. The Bill was drafted but never introduced. The idea was that a Secretary of State, on the recommendation of the Ecclesiastical Commission, would make the Provisional Orders.

Dibdin admitted that such a plan would not do in 1919, but he suggested that something on similar lines might be done. An Ecclesiastical Committee in Parliament could be set up, and a Secretary of State acting on the advice of that committee could, on the recommendation of the two Archbishops, make Provisional Orders for carrying into effect all sorts of administrative, legislative, and legal changes.[2] The idea appears to have been intended to preserve an oligarchic form of government along the lines of the traditional Church and State partnership. Dibdin gave the Archbishop to understand, through G. K. A. Bell, the Archbishop's Chaplain, that the main idea was that the Archbishops would be the natural spokesmen for the Church with regard

[1] *D.N.B.*

[2] Unpub. Lam. MSS., copy of letter, Dibdin–Haldane, 8 June 1919.

to any particular legislative measure, although there would be some clause to ensure that when the Archbishops approached the Secretary of State they would have church opinion behind them. Apparently he did not consider this last provision would present any difficulties. Lord Haldane was quite prepared to sponsor such a proposal in the House of Lords, despite the fact that previously he had spoken against church self-government. He told Dibdin, however, that as he was looked upon as a leader by the extreme Radical peers such as Lord Sheffield, and they would view him as a 'snake in the grass' if he appeared too generous to the Church, it would have to appear that his generosity came by compromise or compulsion.[1]

Dibdin represented one type of 'instrumentalist' reformer upon whom the pressure of opinion marshalled by the Life and Liberty Movement made little impression. He held high office and responsibility in the Church, and he wanted to improve its efficiency, but he was less interested in democratic theories of church government. When the Church Assembly began to transact business, it was this type of churchman, with his technical knowledge of law, legislative procedures, and church finance, who was found to be indispensable. Archbishop Davidson, because he had borne official responsibility in the Church for so long, tended to take the same line of following whatever course was instrumentally efficient and most expedient. It was for these reasons that, under pressure from the forces marshalled by the Life and Liberty Movement, he steered through the Enabling Bill, even though he did not share their high hopes for its effects. Even after he had introduced the Enabling Bill in the House of Lords, he was well disposed to Dibdin's alternative plan when it was suggested to him in June 1919. However, he told Dibdin that having introduced the Bill he would have to stand by it for the present, only adding,

> . . . but I am never a man to turn a deaf ear to reasonable proposals of amendment if these are supported by adequate argument or are more expedient for adoption than my own proposals.[2]

[1] Memorandum, dated 24 June 1919, prepared by Bell, the Archbishop's Chaplain, and based on his discussions with Dibdin. Unpub. Lam. MSS.

[2] Unpub. Lam. MSS. letter, Davidson–Dibdin, 13 June 1919.

This was consistent with the speech which he had made when recommending the Enabling Bill, as drawn up by the 'Grand' Committee, in the Representative Church Council, on 27 February 1919. The main reason he gave for supporting the scheme was the inability of Parliament to find time for church business. He did not believe the work of the Church was hampered by any intolerable hindrance (as Life and Liberty supporters said):

> We find ourselves prevented from doing it better by things which it is in our power to get removed. Therefore we want to get them removed, not necessarily to satisfy any large or far-reaching theory, but for the practical doing better of the work with which we are entrusted as administrators for the sake of all.[1]

The Life and Liberty Movement's success in attracting the support of different church parties was purchased at the high price of sacrificing some cherished hopes. One such hope was that working men would be substantially represented in the new Assembly. The Selborne Committee had recommended that diocesan conferences should have a definite proportion of working-class representatives, so that some of these would then be elected on to the new Assembly. This proposal was the work of those members of the Committee who were later to serve in the Life and Liberty Movement (as Appendix IX to the Report makes clear). In particular it was the suggestion of H. E. Kemp, the Committee's 'expert' on the working classes, who, along with Albert Mansbridge who gave the proposal his general approval, was to occupy a similar position on the Life and Liberty Council. Kemp's memorandum on the subject gives a valuable insight into the considerations which influenced the church reform movement in its thinking about the working classes. He submitted to the Committee that,

> It is futile to close one's eyes to the fact that the greater solidarity of workers is making it possible for them to force their claims upon any government, and it is probably not an exaggeration to say that never in the world's history has it been more necessary than at present to enlist the active sympathies of the great mass of people on the side

[1] Quoted in G. K. A. Bell, *Randall Davidson*, vol. i, p. 969.

of religion and order, if the recognized standards of civilization are to be maintained and improved upon.[1]

Kemp maintained that the new scheme of church finance based on diocesan and central finance boards, and the wider issues of corporate church life, would only attract the interest of the workers if they were represented in the central councils of the Church by some of their own class.

Class-consciousness is a very real sentiment, and the workers will not be satisfied with any administration in which they have not a voice; mere selection by the authorities of the Church of apparently suitable advisers will not meet the needs of the case. What is needed both in Church and State is not that brilliant or fortunate individuals may be lifted into another class, but that the working classes may be recognized through their representatives as an active thinking part of the corporate whole, and this can be done only through some form of election.[2]

The Selborne Committee was small in numbers; it began with twenty-four members when it was appointed in 1914, and its Report had twenty-one signatories (one member had died, and two resigned on account of military duties). The future Life and Liberty Movement was substantially represented, although they were not on the Archbishop's own list of suggested names.[3] One name which the Archbishop did strongly urge on the chairman, the Earl of Selborne, was that of Sir Lewis Dibdin. It was he who expressed dissatisfaction with the proposal for working-class representatives, in a memorandum in which he stated, 'I deprecate class representation altogether. . . .'[4] He made it

[1] *Report of the Archbishops' Committee on Church and State*, 1916, pp. 256–7, Appendix IX, 'Memorandum on the Church in its Relation to Lay Feeling as Evinced amongst the Working Classes, Students, etc.'

[2] Ibid., p. 258. Kemp's comments clearly echo those quoted previously as made by Charles Booth about working-class churchgoers being lifted out of their class. His prescription likewise seems to be based on that given by Booth, who had observed that the only parishes which had had some partial success with the working classes 'base the degree of success they can claim on the adoption of democratic methods' (Booth, op. cit., p. 47).

[3] The Archbishop's suggestions appear in his letter to the Earl of Selborne, 30 October 1913, Unpub. Lam. MSS. The one exception was Douglas Eyre, whom the Archbishop recommended on the advice of Bishop Gore.

[4] Sir Lewis Dibdin's Memorandum in the *Report of the Archbishops' Committee on Church and State*, 1916, p. 68.

clear that he only reluctantly acquiesced to it as a temporary measure. This opinion was to be more strongly represented on the 'Grand' Committee of the Representative Church Council, which had seventy members, and the proposal for working-class representatives was dropped.

The fact that the Life and Liberty Movement acquiesced in the dropping of that proposal may have been due to the changed complexion of the Movement, but it was also connected with a countervailing concession which the Movement had made. Originally it had been inclined to support the Selborne Committee's recommendation that the franchise qualification should be confirmation, which was in keeping with the strong theological influence of the Catholic party in the reform movement. But this offended many Broad Churchmen whose support was indispensable.

The liberal Churchmen's Union published a memorandum in its organ *The Modern Churchman*, in January 1918, which claimed that the confirmation franchise would exclude millions of Church of England members, and added,

> Nor should it be forgotten that confirmation is to some extent a class distinction. For the children of well-to-do Churchmen are confirmed almost as a matter of course, whereas among the wage-earners confirmation is exceptional.

The Challenge, under Temple's editorship, was usually a faithful barometer of Life and Liberty policy. On 13 July 1917 it had come down firmly in favour of the confirmation franchise. But on 28 September it noted:

> We are told by many that the Baptismal basis is gaining ground, and it may be so; indeed, there must be great difficulty in securing that any large body of the working classes shall be brought in on a more stringent basis.

On 2 November it announced that the Life and Liberty Council now favoured the baptismal franchise. But the decision almost lost the Movement the support of that section of the Catholic party which had been one of its main strengths. One of the leaders of that group, the

Revd. Francis Underhill, a member of the Life and Liberty Council, wrote to Temple:

> It seems to me that the Committee's proposals would do much to stop progress in a Catholic direction by giving too much power to an ultra-conservative laity. Now Catholic progress in the Church of England is the object of my life and doings—hence these expostulations.[1]

The effect on others of that group, especially Charles Gore, was described by Henson:

> The latent discord within the autonomist camp was disclosed when . . . the agitation had so far succeeded, that its proposals had to be submitted to Parliament. Then the question of the franchise within the self-governing Church could not be avoided, and the contention between those who took with Gore their stand on Catholic 'principle' in requiring Confirmation as the basis, and those who with the majority of the Representative Church Council were prepared to conciliate the 'national' feeling of Parliament by accepting Baptism, was so sharp, that Gore 'shook off the dust off his feet', resigned his bishopric, and declined further concern with the Life and Liberty Movement.[2]

Another group who became disaffected were those who had hoped for some more radical developments. One such was Miss Maude Royden, who had made a name for herself as 'one of the strongest and most influential personalities of all the religious leaders and teachers of the day'.[3] As one of the main speakers at the first Life and Liberty Meeting in the Queen's Hall she had made a powerful impact with her call to all those who had worked in other great democratic movements, 'such as the Labour Movement or the Women's Movement, to come into the Church and bring their enthusiasm and devotion to an even greater cause'.[4] She maintained that the Life and Liberty Movement was not a mere demand for legislative reform, but for freedom in spirit as well as in organization. Unfortunately Miss Royden anticipated that freedom by preaching and baptizing at the City Temple, a Nonconformist stronghold. When

[1] Unpub. Lam. MSS., Temple papers, letter, Underhill–Temple, 16 October 1918.
[2] Henson, op. cit., vol. i, p. 210.
[3] Iremonger, op. cit., p. 236.
[4] Reported in *The Challenge*, 20 July 1917.

she subsequently came to attend the Life and Liberty Council conference at Cuddesdon Theological College, on 1 October 1917, a fellow member of the Council, J. B. Seaton, refused, as Principal of the College, to allow her to sleep under its roof. To the embarrassment of Temple and some of the other members of the Council, she was driven to resign. According to Iremonger, who was at the Conference, the whole incident came as a severe shock to the more revolutionary members of the Council, who realized how far removed they were from the 'official' approach to church problems.[1]

Liberal churchmen claimed to see in these developments further success for the Catholic group in Life and Liberty, despite the decision in favour of the baptismal franchise. The editor of *The Modern Churchman* thought that Temple might lose control and that the Catholic party's policy would prevail.

> Its policy is Disestablishment; combined with bureaucratic centralization especially in the matter of finance; followed by bloodless administration. . . . The Life and Liberty Movement seems blind to this policy, if indeed some of its adherents do not sympathise with it. Mr. Temple may feel that he is strong enough to control these elements. Frankly we doubt whether he is. We imagine that he parted most unwillingly with Miss Maude Royden, but he was forced to do so by the Catholic section of the Life and Liberty Movement. It seemed to us also that the Baptism Franchise was in some degree forced on the Life and Liberty Movement. . . .[2]

Despite all the obstacles William Temple continued resolutely in the task for which he had resigned his comfortable living at St. James's, Piccadilly, steering the Life and Liberty Movement and holding together its mixed membership. There are no statistics available as to how many members it attracted into its Fellowship, but at times it seemed optimistic that it was in reach of its target of 100,000. At first there was some jealousy between it and the other two reform organizations, the Church Reform League and the Church Self-Government Association—

[1] Iremonger, op. cit., pp. 237–8.
[2] *The Modern Churchman*, vol. vii, no. 12, March 1918, p. 628.

mainly on the part of the older C.R.L.[1] Very soon, however, by the beginning of 1918 they had set up a joint co-ordinating committee, and arrived at some rough division of functions. The Church Self-Government Association had been created by Lord Wolmer, who led the group of church reformers in the House of Commons. It became active in 1917 in pursuing the suffragettes' technique of obtaining pledges of support from Parliamentary candidates, and it concentrated its efforts mainly in this direction. Its Executive was made up largely of members of the Life and Liberty Council. The Church Reform League continued its work of educating churchmen with regard to the scope for reform in the Church's organization. The success of their joint efforts came with the enactment of the Enabling Bill on 23 December 1919.

Both supporters and opponents admitted that credit for success lay mainly with the Life and Liberty Movement and with the leadership of William Temple. But even supporters of long standing expressed some disillusionment. *The Challenge*, under its new editor, declared on 6 June 1919,

> The Enabling Bill is the topic of the hour, and the general verdict of Churchmen and Churchwomen appears to be that it is better than nothing. It is a far cry from such a phrase to the fine enthusiasms engendered at the initial stages of the Life and Liberty Movement. Obviously the Bill is a singularly skilful and adroit compromise. But like all compromises which are intended to avoid offending anyone, it runs the risk of giving pleasure to no one.

DIFFERING VERDICTS AS TO WHAT HAD BEEN ACHIEVED

Constitutionally the Enabling Act was significant for the extent to which it delegated legislative power to an autonomous Church Assembly. Important amendments to the original Bill had been made by Parliament which ensured that the measures which Church Assembly submitted to it would have to receive positive Parliamentary approval before they became law. A further change had been the

[1] Church Reform League *Quarterly Chronicle*, 18 July 1917, p. 187.

substitution of an Ecclesiastical Committee of Parliament for the proposed Committee of the Privy Council, for the purpose of examining such measures before they were submitted to Parliament. Despite these provisions, however, the chief increment which the Church received from the Enabling Act was its delegated legislative power. Views as to its possible wider effects on the Church's financial and administrative system, and on its moral witness, varied enormously.

Archbishop Davidson had said when he introduced the Bill into the House of Lords, 'I find a little difficulty in making my own all the hopes and ambitions which have found eloquent expression in the fine body of men and women who advocated it.'[1]

It was church leaders like Davidson, however, who were responsible for working the new machinery at the national level. In the parishes the leadership depended on the clergy and churchwardens working in partnership, and here too hopes varied. The Life and Liberty office received a postcard from a churchwarden ('Lt. Col. R.A. retd.'), who stated, 'I understand that now the Enabling Bill is through we can get rid of our parson. Please send full particulars by return. I write as a member of the Fellowship'.[1]

Opinions varied also as to what the new system connoted in terms of ideal types of religious organization. Hensley Henson regarded it as the reduction of the Church to the status of one denomination among many.[2] In the Catholic party opinion was divided. The extremists remained indifferent to structural reform. Thus the Revd. Francis G. Belton criticized Francis Underhill for even using the term 'Church of England' in advocating reform, because the term 'connotes a national and separatist body. . . in fact a sect'.[3] For moderate Catholics the reform lessened the Erastian stigma which dependence on the State for its government had brought on the Church; but against this had to be set the defeat which they had suffered when the

[1] Quoted in Iremonger, op. cit., p. 275.

[2] See his letter to *The Times*, 15 December 1919, entitled, 'Church and State—a Bill passed an ideal destroyed'. The ideal was that of a National Church.

[3] F. G. Belton in *The English Church Review*, January 1918.

baptismal franchise was accepted. To them the compromise structure was almost as far away as ever from the ideal. Another Catholic, Athelstan Riley, bemoaned the failure to translate theory into structure, and told Temple that at the Day of Judgement the people who would be held responsible to the 'great Head of the Church' would be the bishops and not the National Assembly.[1] Temple was more sanguine about the results of his endeavours, and replied that he was not satisfied that 'because the Church was a monarchy it was best administered by a feudal hierarchy'.[1] In those terms the result was not unlike that political reform of 1832 which had been one of the begetters of the modern church reform movement. But this was a judgement on a completely different dimension to that of dichotomous ideal types on which Henson and the Catholic party stood opposed. Henson distinguished denomination (or sect) from church on the same ground as had Max Weber: that the former was exclusive in terms of some selective principle, whilst the latter was inclusive.[2] He maintained that the narrowing down of the Church's membership either by setting a confirmation franchise, or even by limiting the franchise to baptised members, whose inclusion on the new parish electoral rolls involved making a declaration that they were not members of any other religious body, was to reduce the Church to a denomination. The Catholic party argued from the opposite direction, that the inclusion of members who were not fully qualified by baptism *and confirmation*, was to sacrifice an essential church principle. Thus Dr. Kidd, in his letter to the clergy of Oxford Diocese, when standing for a proctorship in Convocation, in 1918, affirmed:

> If it be said, in order to keep the Church 'national and not sectarian', that Baptism without Confirmation is sufficient, then I reply, *inter alia*, that a local Church does not become a sect by ceasing to be co-extensive with the nation. A sect is a body of Christians which has departed from the Faith, or the Order, of the Catholic Church.[3]

[1] Report of a meeting of the English Church Union at Church House, Westminster, at which Temple was the guest speaker, in *The Church Union Gazette*, January 1921.

[2] Max Weber, *The Protestant Ethic and the Spirit of Capitalism.*

[3] *The English Church Review*, January 1918.

What was 'compromise' of a principle to one party was not compromise to the other, and their value-laden distinctions between denomination (or sect) and church, simply reflected the mixture of values and principles which had co-existed in the national Church.

PART THREE

VII

THE CHURCH ASSEMBLY AND ITS ORGANIZATION

THE FORMATIVE YEARS

THE new Church Assembly, which met for the first time on 30 June 1920, was largely composed of members of the old Representative Church Council; it included the 38 bishops and 251 clergy who made up the two provincial Convocations, and 357 laity elected by the lay members of the diocesan conferences.[1] Despite the compromises which had been made in determining its final composition and powers, it was the object of both high hopes and deep fears in its early years. Later on it was to be regarded with indifference by many and disillusion by a few, so that in the mid-1950s another era of commissions and debates on the best form of government for the Church was ushered in, and will one day constitute another chapter in a story which, in the 1920s, seemed almost complete. In its first years, however, there was a fierce struggle over the exercise of its legislative, deliberative, and executive functions.

Sociologically this was typical of the dynamics of an organization which consisted of a combination of several principles, some of which were mutually incompatible. The controversy prior to the setting up of the new organization based on the Church Assembly provided an empirical case

1 With the subsequent reform of Convocation to include more elected representatives of the parochial clergy the numbers grew, so that in 1964 the total membership of the Church Assembly was 739, made up as follows. House of Bishops 43, House of Clergy 350, House of Laity 346.

of the sociological observation that severe strains might occur within a social system without practice coming into conflict with formal beliefs: inconsistencies can arise within the belief system itself.[1] The dynamics of organization involve constant adjustment of conflicting principles, and of older and new elements.[2] This dialectic between rival principles was intensified by the structural innovation to which the Church Assembly gave rise in the Church of England's organization. To various groups within the Church such innovation represented a potential threat to either their interests or their ideals, and they were anxious to limit and control it. The first piece of business transacted by the Assembly mirrored that apprehension. The Marquess of Salisbury (no doubt with the prior approval of the archbishops) moved that a Standing Committee that should have only 11 members be appointed, so that it could work 'more quickly than a relatively large one'. An amendment was immediately carried that the number should be increased to 20 in order to make it more representative of different schools of opinion.[3] Like the Assembly itself, the Standing Committee had to come quickly to terms with the organized church parties and their demand for representation. A member who resigned from the Standing Committee over twenty years later complained about the tradition of choosing members for party reasons rather than for their personal qualifications, which weakened its efficiency.[4]

The secretary of the main Catholic party organization, the English Church Union, claimed that the Catholics had been taken unawares by the extent of the innovation in the structure of church government which the Assembly represented. He told his members:

> If we had realized the possible implications and consequences of this revolution in Church government which has taken place we should

[1] Cf. Marion J. Levy, *The Structure of Society*, pp. 178–9; and P. M. Harrison, *Authority and Power in the Free Church Tradition*, p. 10.

[2] This dialectic between principles of organization can be regarded as equivalent to role conflict in personality theory. Cf. R. G. Francis and Robert C. Stone, *Service and Procedure in Bureaucracy*, p. 153.

[3] *Proceedings of Church Assembly* (hereafter—*P.C.A.*), vol. i, 1920, p. 9.

[4] Statement made to the Church Assembly by Mr. George Goyder on 3 November 1964, quoted in the *Church Times*, 6 November 1964.

have been at some pains to secure also some valuable modifications of the scheme before it actually took shape.[1]

He told Catholics that they must organize, although in the Assembly itself something had already been done. At a meeting of Church Assembly Catholics on 15 November 1920 Lord Phillimore had been chosen as their 'Leader' in the Assembly, along with an influential 'Watching Committee' and a 'Convener'. The Secretary remarked that,

> These arrangements give some guarantee that the ideals of the Anglo-Catholic Party and the Catholic principles for which it stands will not be allowed to be ignored or over-ridden in the Assembly.[1]

The E.C.U. and the Federation of Catholic Priests also set up joint committees to select candidates and to canvass in elections to diocesan conferences and the Assembly.[2] The Evangelical party organization, the Church Association, followed suit.[3]

This policy was condemned by many of the bishops who dreaded the effects of further party conflict. The E.C.U. Secretary expressed surprise at the condemnation, which he suspected had been made as a result of a joint decision by the bishops.[3] The policy was defended in an article in the *Daily Telegraph*, on 25 March 1922, on the grounds that, 'Whether we like it or not, the Church is committed to representative assemblies having a quasi-Parliamentary constitution and organized on semi-political lines'.

Viscount Wolmer, who had been one of the architects of the Church Assembly's constitution, had justified its quasi-parliamentary character on the grounds that there was no reason why the Church, when dealing with non-spiritual matters, should not work through democratic channels in the present age, just as it had worked through monarchic or oligarchic channels in past ages.[4] What he did not anticipate was the point of view which maintained that parties were an essential element in any democratic institution.

1 *The Church Union Gazette*, December 1920.

2 Ibid., March 1921, and January 1922.

3 Ibid., April 1922.

4 Viscount Wolmer, 'The Church Assembly and the Clergy', in F. Partridge (ed.), *The Church Assembly and the Church*, p. 60.

The creation of the Church Assembly had been made possible by a compromise which made a distinction between spiritual and non-spiritual matters, and sought to limit the Assembly's functions to the latter sphere. In this sphere, models and principles of organization could be applied which did not touch on theological doctrines of authority, and so Catholics could excuse their concessions to secular principles of organization. For them the important limitation of the Assembly's powers was laid down in Clause 14 of its constitution. This stipulated that any measure touching doctrine or the Church's rites had to be accepted or rejected in the terms proposed by the House of Bishops; that it did not belong to the functions of Church Assembly to define doctrine; and that nothing in the constitution should be deemed to diminish or derogate from the powers belonging to the Convocations, or the bishops.

The bishops' powers were safeguarded in Church Assembly by the provision that when a vote by separate Houses was called for it was necessary for all three Houses—Bishops, Clergy, and Laity—to be in favour of a motion if it was to pass. The small House of Bishops could always exercise a veto. But in the diocesan conferences, which were an integral part of the system of representative government, it looked as though they might lose some of their powers. In the debate on the regulation of diocesan conferences on 8 February 1922 the Bishop of Norwich put the bishops' objection to the original scheme, which would have omitted any veto power for the bishop in his diocesan conference. His amendment sought to preserve the bishop's power to exercise a veto. 'After all,' he said, 'the government of the Church is episcopal and not congregational. . . .'[1] The Dean of Manchester, who had served on the Life and Liberty Council, said in reply that the amendment would 'negative the whole idea of self-government of the Church which the Assembly was called in being to create'.[2] Viscount Wolmer took a different line, and said that when he and the Dean were fighting together for self-government, he certainly understood that bishops were part of the Church.[3] The

[1] *P.C.A.*, vol. iii, 1, 1922, p. 37. [2] Ibid., p. 38.
[3] Ibid., p. 40.

Catholic party's interpretation of self-government was put by a speaker who informed the Dean that self-government, which had been a legitimate demand at the time, referred not to government of the Church by democracy, but to the government of the Church independent of the State.[1] The amendment was accepted overwhelmingly by the bishops and clergy, but it failed to secure a majority in the House of Laity. The amendment was therefore negatived and should have lapsed, but instead a compromise was arrived at whereby the assent of the bishop was still required, although the bishop, clergy, and laity would be allowed to vote as separate Houses in the diocesan conference, and their respective votes would be recorded.[2]

Many of the clergy outside the episcopal ranks, and especially the High Church clergy, looked to the exclusively clerical Convocations as the guardians either of clerical interests, or of ultimate governing authority in the Church. The Archbishops' Committee on Church and State, which drew up the original scheme for the Church Assembly, in 1916, had envisaged that the Convocations would naturally fade away after the Assembly came into being. But this suggestion was eventually dropped in order to recruit wide support for the Enabling Bill, and Clause 14 in the Assembly's constitution explicitly upheld the undiminished authority of Convocation. Nevertheless, the Convocations began to feel themselves to be in danger when the Assembly began to transact business, and a Convocation committee was hastily set up to consider its relations with the Assembly. Its report in 1922 expressed the warning that,

> There has consequently arisen some danger that the inherent authority of the older bodies in the constitution of the Church may be overshadowed; and on occasion the proceedings of the Assembly have appeared to trench upon the spiritual authority of the Convocations.[3]

It noted that the Assembly had started on its career with considerable enthusiasm and that it had been called into

[1] Ibid., pp. 40–1.

[2] Ibid., p. 44.

[3] Report of the Committee on the Relations between Convocation and the National Assembly, no. 546, in *Chronicle of Canterbury Convocation*, vol. iv, no. 3, 1922.

being by men of influence and the laity as a whole thought this was their chance at last. It added,

There is a danger not so much lest the National Assembly should assume supreme power in the affairs of the Church to the detriment of the spiritual authority of its synods as that such power should pass to it by default.[1]

A much more strongly worded minority report by an E.C.U. member on the Committee, Canon E. G. Wood, said,

I cannot accept the view that the Assembly has any authority either spiritual or temporal. . . . The provincial synods are by the common law of the whole Church the bodies which are representative of the whole hierarchy of the Church to which, and to which alone, belong, as of Divine right, the ruling of the Church to the complete exclusion of the laity and of any democratic notions of the constitution of the Church.[1]

In the subsequent debate on the report in the Lower House of Canterbury Convocation, Canon Kidd, who moved the resolution on the report, said that the Press was referring to the Assembly as the ultimate legislating authority. He added that the Assembly's only authority was based on the representative principle, whereas in Convocation authority was not derived from below but from above, although it was not easy for the outside populace to understand that. He quoted a personal promise of the Archbishop in the National Assembly that 'no vital matter touching the special business of the spirituality shall be concluded without reference to the Convocations', but Canon Kidd warned that they had still to be on the watch.[2]

One of the few speakers who could not see any cause for alarm was the Archdeacon of Winchester, who seemed to think that the outside populace was not alone in not being able to understand the distinction between authority from above or below. He said it left the impression

. . . that Convocation might expect, and rightly expect, the guidance of the Holy Spirit in its deliberations, but that in regard to the National Assembly it was a somewhat doubtful matter.[3]

[1] *Chronicle of Canterbury Convocation*, vol. iv, no. 3, 1922.
[2] Ibid., p. 459.
[3] Ibid., p. 461.

He did not accept the explanation of the previous speaker that,

> The vesture of the members of Convocation was an outward and visible sign that they were assembled in synod. When they were in the National Assembly they were not there synodically, and therefore they did not contribute to the spiritual authority of the National Assembly by their presence then and there.[1]

The liberal Evangelicals regarded this as substituting for the logic of efficiency that of magic. As one of them commented:

> The future relations of the historic Convocations of Canterbury and York to the National Assembly do not create for us an intricate or a harassing problem. The Spirit of God will show us in time the line of progress which makes for sound and efficient government. It is not possible to argue that the same people meeting for the same purpose and seeking the guidance of the same Spirit are more in touch with God when they are constituted as members of one body rather than of another. Can we seriously believe that the Bishops are more inspired when they sit in the Upper House of Convocation, than when they sit in the National Assembly or in their periodical private meetings? Can anyone believe that 'something happens' to the clergy when they sit in Convocation which gives their decisions more authority than when they sit in one of the three Houses in the National Assembly? Such beliefs can only exist in the twilight where magic supplants reason.[2]

Not only did the Assembly fail to convince many of the clergy that it could be reconciled with their ideals of authority in church government, it also failed to convince them that it had their best interests at heart. In its first years, the Assembly devoted itself to clearing arrears of administrative reform, and many of the measures which achieved this seemed to bear hard on the clergy, from whom compulsory premiums for pensions and dilapidations were extracted. *Crockford's Clerical Directory*, which invariably defended the clergy's interests, reckoned that those clergy who would be affected by the Pensions Measure and the

[1] Ibid.
[2] T. Guy Rogers (ed.), *Liberal Evangelicalism*, pp. 48–9.

Pensions Authority established in 1926, had opposed it almost unanimously (and those who supported it were bishops, clergy over 56 years of age, and laity). It said that the Pension Authority's system of having contributions deducted at the source was regarded as a gratuitous insult by the clergy, because it implied that they were employed by the Assembly and that the Ecclesiastical Commissioners and Queen Anne's Bounty owned the funds which they administered, rather than holding endowments in trust for the clergy. It claimed that its abolition would go far towards reviving goodwill towards the Assembly among the clergy.[1] A constant fear of the clergy was that they would be reduced to salaried employees of the central organization. The loss of ancient sources of revenue at the local level, and the increasing centralization of church finance, which continued unabated during the first two decades of the Assembly's life, caused the clergy to regard with suspicion any further bureaucratic encroachment on their independence.

The failure to enlist the clergy as the vital connecting link in the chain of communication between the Assembly and the parishes had serious consequences in preventing the development of an informed and sympathetic support for the Assembly in the Church at large. Studies of organization functioning stress the importance of the personal link in communication processes, which cannot be considered as simply a functional alternative to formal, written transmission of information.[2]

Within five years of the first meeting of Church Assembly *Crockford's Clerical Directory* was remarking that,

> 'Dean's Yard' (which may be adopted as a convenient term for the various functionaries of the Church Assembly, on the analogy of 'the Vatican' or 'Whitehall') has never fully understood how much the Assembly depends upon the rank and file of the parochial clergy.

[1] Preface for 1930, in *Crockford Prefaces: The Editor Looks Back*, pp. 91–2.

[2] As Amitai Etzioni has observed: 'Communication studies demonstrate the low effectiveness of formal communication not supported by informal leaders, and the importance of positive affective interpersonal relations between the priest and parishioner. . . . In short, the attainment of culture goals such as the creation, application or transmission of values requires the development of identification with the organizational representatives' (A. Etzioni, *A Comparative Analysis of Complex Organizations*, p. 83).

Apart from those parishes with representatives in the Assembly,

> In the remaining 13,000-odd hardly anyone will realise that the Assembly exists unless the parson speaks and writes about it, and much will depend upon his estimate of its value. . . . Dean's Yard will be wise to recognize that whatever it does it cannot afford to alienate them.[1]

The lay representatives in the Assembly did not always help matters. One of the prominent members of the House of Laity, speaking in the debate on a Benefices (Ecclesiastical Duties) Measure, said that he ought to be able to change an unsatisfactory incumbent as easily as he could change an unsatisfactory doctor, solicitor, or cook. It was not surprising that Crockford waxed indignant and said that as long as such speeches were made 'Dean's Yard' should not affect surprise 'if the conviction that "The Assembly is the Enemy" continues to gain ground amongst the rank and file of the parochial clergy'.[2]

The Assembly could not even derive much authority from the 'power of the purse' as *The Challenge* had recommended when the Central Church Fund had seemed set to become the new financial power. The promoters of the Central Church Fund had hoped to raise £5,000,000, but in fact it never raised more than one-quarter of a million pounds. The Church Assembly took over the Fund along with the Central Board of Finance, but it found that it had to rely for its income on funds contributed by the dioceses, which in turn depended on the parishes to contribute to the diocesan funds. In this way the Assembly was deprived of any large, autonomous fund, and so it was dependent ultimately on the parishes, and in particular, on the goodwill of the incumbent of each parish (as Crockford was not slow to point out).[3] The dioceses constantly failed to meet their quotas and so the Central Board of Finance was always kept short of funds.[4] This failure to develop a strong central fund

[1] *Crockford*, op. cit., p. 41.

[2] Ibid., pp. 145–6.

[3] Ibid., pp. 49–50.

[4] *Report of the Commission to Enquire into the Expenses of the Assembly and Its Organization*, C.A. 910, 1949.

was due partly to the distrust of the clergy, but also to a widespread fear of developing a monocratic, central bureaucracy.

Because the Assembly did not create its own financial organization, but inherited the Central Board of Finance and the Central Church Fund, its own organization was affected by the already fixed character and public image of these two entities. An account of the development of the Central Board of Finance and the Central Church Fund will provide some understanding of one of the main ingredients which determined the character and image of the Church Assembly's administration.

The Central Board of Finance was the result of the Archbishops' Committee on Church and State which reported in 1911. On its recommendation the Central Advisory Council of Training for the Ministry was founded in 1912, and the Central Board of Finance was brought into existence in 1914. Previously each diocese had had its own plans for financing its work, but under the new system they were brought into relation with the Central Board of Finance, so that in 1920 out of 140 members on the Board, 100 were the direct representatives of the diocesan boards of finance, and the remaining 40 were either nominated by the archbishops or co-opted by the Board. The Board was too large and met too infrequently to be an effective policy-making and co-ordinating body, and the dioceses' reluctance to contribute funds to it was a further cause of weakness. An attempt to persuade the dioceses to contribute to the Central Fund on a scale fixed by the Board was pronounced a failure in the Annual Report in 1917, and it was decided to launch a wide national appeal for the Central Church Fund.[1]

The archbishops had intended to raise a special Candidates Fund (for ordinands) and they were against the idea of the Central Board of Finance of having a more general appeal. This led to a conflict with the inner core of businessmen on the Central Board's Executive Council, who felt that as the hierarchy had called them in to use their expert knowledge on the Church's behalf, it ought not to dismiss

[1] *Annual Report of the Central Board of Finance*, 1917, pp. 13–14.

their plans so lightly. The Honorary Secretary of the Central Board of Finance, Canon Bullock-Webster, remonstrated with the Archbishop of Canterbury, and complained to him,

> I think this decision came rather as a shock to the Council because, rightly or wrongly, the members believed that as business men they were really able to give some help and advice of value and weight on this important issue.[1]

The Bishop of St. Albans, who was the member of the hierarchy most closely involved in the Board's work, was furious with the Archbishop of York, who had brought the message to the Executive Council, purporting to represent the bishops' opposition to the proposed general appeal. He sent the Archbishop of Canterbury an account of the Board's attempts to involve 'laymen of quality' in that part of the Church's work where they could use their talents, and added that the rebuttal was 'straining episcopal authority almost to a breaking point'.[2] Archbishop Davidson simply assumed that the Bishop must have 'lost grip', and he told the Archbishop of York that he was saddened by St. Albans' 'lack of balance'.[3]

The matter was not allowed to rest there, however, either by the Bishop of St. Albans or the powerful lay group on the Central Board of Finance. On 28 November 1917 the Bishop circulated a private and confidential document to all the diocesan bishops, disclaiming all responsibility for the message which the Archbishop of York had delivered to the Executive Council, and dissenting from the decision which it claimed to represent. He stressed the responsibility of the Central Board of Finance and the need for its business experts to be behind any appeal. He used the language of business to oppose the exercise of an over-riding episcopal authority in such matters, stating,

> I submit that it is contrary to all rules of sound finance that a message should be sent to the Central Board of Finance from the

[1] Unpub. Lam. MSS. Letter, Bullock–Webster–Davidson, 15 November 1917.
[2] Ibid., Letter, Bp. of St. Albans–Davidson, 17 November 1917.
[3] Ibid., Letter, Davidson–Archbishop Lang, 21 November 1917.

Bishops without a distinct recognition of the responsibility of the collecting Board.[1]

This was the first major confrontation between the rival principles of authority which became institutionalized in the Church Assembly organization. The institutionalization process involved a constant dialectic between the different principles of organization in the Church, and especially as this was made manifest in the distinction between the rational–pragmatic authority of the lay administrators and the traditional authority of the bishops. (It was formally institutionalized in the practice of making bishops chairmen of the councils, boards, and committees, although the effective operation of their departments was in the hands of the full-time secretaries.) This first confrontation served to establish the authority of lay expertise in the Central Board of Finance, but it also aroused suspicions and fears which ensured that its powers would remain limited, especially in the sphere of policy-making.

The businessmen had the better of this first confrontation, although the archbishops continued to place obstacles in their way by finding fault with the 'Statement of Needs' which they drew up to launch their appeal for the Central Church Fund. The archbishops' reluctance to allow their names to be associated with it was to receive a certain amount of justification in view of the unfavourable reception which it received from many churchmen, and from the Christian socialists in particular.[2] The sub-committee which compiled the 'Statement of Needs' was composed mainly of aristocrats and businessmen, and they based the appeal on the assumption that,

> The new conditions in the life and circumstances of the people of England which the war has occasioned require that the forces of organized religion should be utilised more than ever before for the stabilisation of society, for the inspiration of the future, and for the general welfare of the nation.[3]

[1] Unpub. Lam. MSS., Memorial from the Bishop of St. Albans.

[2] The Christian Socialist League sent a manifesto of protest to the Archbishop; quoted in *The Commonwealth*, March 1919.

[3] Quoted from the draft copy of the 'Statement of Needs' for the Central Church Fund, in Archbishop Davidson's papers at Lambeth Palace Library. The Sub-Committee which drew up the 'Statement of needs' consisted of Earl Brassey

It was the reference to the 'stabilisation of society' which infuriated the Christian socialists. The objection of the archbishops was on different grounds, however. They objected to references in the original statement which implied that a strong central organization was going to be set up to administer and control church affairs.

In the original statement submitted to the archbishops and the Bishops Meeting, the sub-committee stated that the poorer dioceses required supplementation from central resources, which could only be met by central administration and control, and the first step would be to establish a central organization on sound lines.[1] In a private memorandum on the administration of the Central Fund the sub-committee further stated that the Central Board of Finance could not make policy decisions because it met too infrequently, whilst the Executive Council did not carry sufficient weight. It added, 'Some additional organization is obviously needed and this can be only in the form of Administrative Committees'. It wanted all the voluntary societies merged into these committees and financed out of the Central Board of Finance budget.[2]

Archbishop Davidson was alarmed at this suggestion, and wrote to Earl Brassey, the chairman of the sub-committee, that, 'We must avoid the appearance of suggesting that a central organizing committee is going to take over the control of Church affairs'.[3] Brassey replied that he and his sub-committee could not support the appeal unless the funds were administered by a strong central administration on a 'business-like basis'.[4] The secretary of the Organization Committee, which had set up the sub-committee, had great difficulty in persuading the archbishops to sign the appeal which the sub-committee had drawn up.[5] Archbishop

(chairman), the Marquess of Salisbury, the Earl of Selborne, the Bishop of London, the Bishop of Southwark, Earl Beauchamp, Lord Joicey, the Hon. H. B. Portman, Viscount Wolmer, Major the Hon. E. Wood, M.P., Colonel A. Griffith Boscawen, M.P., Mr. B. H. Burton, Mr. G. A. Bryson, and Colonel Ames.

1 *Statement of Needs*, op. cit.

2 Unpub. Lam. MSS., Private Memorandum on the Administration of the Central Church Fund.

3 Ibid., Letter, Davidson–Brassey, 20 July 1918.

4 Ibid., Letter, Brassey–Davidson, 23 July 1918.

5 Ibid., Letter, Partridge–Davidson, 21 August 1918.

Davidson told him that if they had known they would have to sign they would have insisted on drafting the appeal themselves.[1] The archbishops feared that they would be held responsible for the mistakes of others, and that, whatever authority the expertise of the businessmen might carry, 'Yet if the letter goes out in our names all the responsibility for such machinery will not unreasonably be made to devolve upon us Archbishops'.[1] Davidson suggested that if they did sign they should add: 'we are leaving in the hands of the Central Committee full freedom as to modes of management, etc.'.[1]

In the absence of a constitutional authority, such as the Church Assembly was intended to supply, any development in the central organization of the Church, especially if it was in the hands of determined laymen, was viewed with some anxiety by the archbishops and bishops. They feared that, justly or unjustly, they would be held responsible for its administration. The Convocations did not exercise any executive powers, and so the archbishops and bishops were the repository of whatever autonomous, traditional authority existed in the Church. But that authority was vulnerable, and it was not so well legitimated in the eyes of the different church parties that they could not discount it when it suited them. The Catholic party were likely to brand it as Erastian and the Evangelicals as Romanist, if it was exercised contrary to their wishes, whilst to some Broad Church clergy and to some laymen its very existence as a separate power in a democratic age was an anachronism. These divisions affected all thinking about central administration. Sir Trustram Eve, the chairman of the Organization Committee responsible for the Central Fund, informed Archbishop Davidson that the Evangelical Bishop of Manchester had told him privately that, with regard to the Central Fund, he thought the diocese and the parish should be the only units of action.

> The Bishop is evidently frightened of future Archbishops being Popes! In the Meeting of Bishops no doubt you will hear this fear of a Pope with a Central Fund behind him put forward. . . . *All* laymen

[1] Unpub. Lam. MSS., Letter, Davidson–Partridge, 23 August 1918.

are splendidly in favour of a Central Fund but some parsons and a few Bishops are timid—they fear loss of power.[1]

The secretary of the Organization Committee, Prebendary Partridge, wrote to reassure the Archbishop with regard to the administration of the Central Church Fund, and said that most of them realized that it must be placed under the Church Assembly when it was formed. He added, however, that, 'Unfortunately there is still a small coterie of people who are anxious to make the Central Board of Finance autocratic and independent'.[2] Davidson's solution in the interim period before the Church Assembly came into being was to put men in the leadership of the Central Board of Finance who would keep it responsible, and so counteract the coterie who desired independence and autocracy. An opportunity was provided by the death of the chairman of the Central Board of Finance, Lord Barnard. Davidson wrote to Lord Salisbury on 2 January 1919, asking him to consider taking on the chairmanship. He referred to the friction between the powerful Central Church Fund group under Lord Brassey, Partridge, and Sir Trustram Eve, and the Central Board of Finance group headed by the vice-chairman, Mr. Evelyn Hubbard. He said the friction had been allowed to develop partly because of the absence of a strong chairman—Barnard having declined in his latter days.[3] The position was not filled, however, until a month later, when it was accepted by another of the Archbishop's trusted advisers, the Earl of Selborne. Davidson also secured the co-optation of his closest adviser, Sir Lewis Dibdin, on to the Executive Council. In proposing Dibdin to the secretary of the Central Board of Finance, the Archbishop remarked that his policy with regard to the Board was to keep its activities within a limited sphere, and in particular not to allow it to become involved in the augmentation of clergy stipends. He knew that Dibdin, who

1 Ibid., Letter, Trustram Eve–Davidson, 20 October 1918. The Bishop of Coventry also wrote to the Archbishop to complain about the use by the Central Board of Finance of the 'power of the purse to enforce their decisions' and to say that there was a fear of 'papal centralization' (Unpub. Lam. MSS., Letter, Bp. of Coventry–Davidson, 21 March 1919).

2 Ibid., Letter, Partridge–Davidson, 23 December 1918.

3 Ibid., Letter, Davidson–Lord Salisbury, 2 January 1919.

he described as the chief man at the Ecclesiastical Commission, which was responsible for clergy stipends, would maintain that policy.[1] But there was still a section of the Central Board of Finance which wished to extend its powers and to strengthen its control by an inner core of nominated members. Lord Brassey urged the Archbishop that the Board's powers should be extended, especially in relation to clergy maintenance, and that there should be more nominated members on the Executive Council, to overcome the obstruction presented by the large number of diocesan representatives.[2]

The allocation of grants for the maintenance of the clergy was one way of gaining clergy support for the Central Board, and in 1919 that view prevailed and it was allowed to allocate £120,000 to diocesan boards for clergy stipends. The system of having to depend on the raising of diocesan quotas for its funds allowed the Central Board little room for expansion, however, and in 1922 it was unable to make a grant to the clergy because the dioceses had not met their quotas. In 1925, the Annual Report of the Central Board of Finance was concerned that the Board and the Assembly were losing the support of the clergy because of its failure to contribute to their maintenance. It sought to excuse itself by saying,

> The Church Assembly has been criticised as having little regard for the welfare of the clergy because since 1922 it has not administered money for this purpose. It will be understood by those who have read this Report that the money is collected through the Parochial Quota and that it is a mere matter of convenience whether it be dispersed by the Diocesan Board of Finance in each diocese or from the centre by the Central Board of Finance.[3]

But not many clergy bothered to read the Annual Report, and even had they done so, they would still have had a natural tendency to resent the fact that, unlike the Ecclesiastical Commissioners, this Central Fund of the Church made no direct contribution to raising their incomes. These

1 Unpub. Lam. MSS., Letter, Davidson–Partridge, 7 February 1919.
2 Ibid., Letter, Davidson–Brassey, 15 February 1919.
3 *Annual Report of the Central Board of Finance*, 1925, p. 27.

material considerations led them to judge even more harshly the faintest hint of 'bureaucracy' in its workings, or in those other departments which were associated with it in the Church Assembly administration.

The Central Board of Finance was beset with criticisms of its bureaucracy from the first. In 1919 it looked forward to being taken under the wing of the Church Assembly as an answer to its problems.

> The authority of the National Assembly will affect profoundly all these problems and relationships. Its character will neutralize any tendency to bureaucracy in method, and may be expected to preserve the human touch, and eliminate the deadening effect of over-centralization.[1]

In 1920, it was still denying the charge that its affairs had tended to fall into the hands of 'a small coterie of Churchmen resident in London'.[2] Suspicion that it was falling into the hands of a small group of business experts was voiced in the debate on the report of a committee to consider the relationship between the Church Assembly and the Central Board of Finance, at the second session of the Assembly, in November 1920.

The committee had proposed that the Board should be composed of the two archbishops, thirty members elected by the Assembly from its own ranks, five nominated by the archbishops, and five co-opted by the Board. An amendment was submitted that there should be added one representative from each diocesan board of finance. The mover of the amendment, Prebendary Hay, said that without direct representation of the diocesan boards of finance it would fall into the hands of a body of men living in London, and might become a sort of extension of the Ecclesiastical Commissioners. The dioceses were not, he thought, 'willing to surrender to a small body of London experts the control of central Church finances', and also he feared that without direct representation of the dioceses there would be little central finance to control.[3]

The Earl of Selborne replied that the question they had

[1] Ibid., 1919, p. 18. [2] Ibid., 1920, p. 12.
[3] *P.C.A.*, vol. i, 1920, p. 82.

to decide was whether the Assembly represented the Church or not. If it accepted Prebendary Hay's amendment that another body should join in electing almost an equal number of representatives to the Central Board, they would run the risk of parting with the control of their finances.[1] A compromise was eventually agreed to whereby the representatives of each diocese in the Assembly chose one of their number to serve on the Board. Whether or not it was Prebendary Hay's prediction coming true, or perhaps clergy disenchantment with the Central Board of Finance and the Assembly, it was a fact that the Assembly's budget fairly steadily declined during the first years of its existence.[2]

A Commission of Enquiry into the Property and Revenues of the Church, which was set up by the Assembly in 1921, and reported in 1924, thought that the Assembly's need for a large central fund would only be met if the Ecclesiastical Commissioners' increased funds were regarded as the central fund of the Church and not narrowly confined to providing a living wage for the clergy.

> Unless the hands of the Commissioners are set free and their funds made available for other purposes, it will not, in our opinion, be possible for the Assembly to deal successfully with the large central problems which confront it, and for which financial assistance is urgently required.[3]

Among those who gave evidence to the Commission were the Secretary and Financial Adviser to the Ecclesiastical Commissioners, S. E. Downing, and the Secretary and Treasurer of Queen Anne's Bounty, W. R. Le Fanu. Downing was against using the Ecclesiastical Commission's funds for other purposes, even though it might be a temptation to try to make the Church efficient at once rather than to wait 20 years or more. But this use was not feasible from a financial point of view in his opinion. He thought that the existing state of central and diocesan finances offered no hope that the needs of the parochial clergy would be met unless the Commissioners applied the whole of their

[1] *P.C.A.*, vol. i, 1920, p. 84.

[2] Cf. *Annual Reports of the Central Board of Finance*, 1922–8.

[3] *Report of the Commission of Enquiry into the Property and Revenues of the Church*, p. 25.

resources to that end.[1] Le Fanu's opinion was that ultimately the Church should have one central body controlling all its finances, and this should be combined with a greater degree of decentralization in which the diocesan boards would take on most of the work. But he added that this could not happen until the diocesan boards were stronger and employed efficient salaried officials.[2] After the Second World War, the Church Commissioners eventually made a concession to decentralization by adopting a method of making some of their money available by way of block grants to dioceses, which could distribute this at their discretion to the clergy, and to dilapidations, subject only to general rules to ensure some conformity. But even this policy alarmed some clergy. The Archdeacon of Lincoln expressed fears in an article in *The Times*, entitled 'The Diocese Dominant: Parochial Clergy Becoming Salaried Staff'.[3] *Crockford's Clerical Directory*, as early as 1927, felt it necessary to explain that,

> The Church is the Church *of England*, whereof the several dioceses are constituent parts. It is not an agglomeration of virtually independent and self-contained administrative areas. A very eminent prelate of a former generation once declared that diocesanism was the most virulent form of congregationalism. We suspect that he would be still more strongly of that opinion if he were alive now.[4]

The Central Board of Finance was extremely sensitive about its reputation for centralization even before it was taken over by the Church Assembly, and one of its first acts after that takeover was to set up a Special (Diocesan) Relationship Committee, which examined the charge and reported in 1921. It hastened to affirm that ideally much of the administration of money contributed to the Central Church Fund should be on a diocesan basis, but it went on to assert that the old system of church finance was a failure. It concluded that the idea that recent developments in church finance involved over-centralization was mistaken, they were merely engaged in a process of rationalization to produce greater efficiency:

> There is much machinery but no effective machine. The parts of

[1] Ibid., p. 16.
[2] Ibid., p. 33.
[3] *The Times*, 19 June 1957.
[4] *Crockford*, op. cit., p. 69.

that machine which ought to be [a] well-constructed and well-fitted engine have never been assembled. They lie scattered, *disjecta membra*, on the surface of the Church in a state of disorganization, and from them it is hopeless to expect the production of that power which alone will make the engine capable of continual and effective work.[1]

A similar interpretation of its proposals for the Church Assembly administration was to be made by a Committee on Central Funds in 1956. Both committees regarded their proposals as directed towards rationalization, but to critics of bureaucracy in the Church the language and logic of both were the same. In fact the committees thought their proposals would eliminate precisely those dysfunctions of organization which are held to constitute 'bureaucracy' in the vulgar sense: slowness, ponderousness, routine, complication of procedures, and maladapted response of organization to the needs it is supposed to satisfy.[2] To church critics of bureaucracy, the only language and logic appropriate to discussions of church organization were those which derived from the personal relationships of the face-to-face group, or else employed traditional symbols such as the 'Body of Christ' and the 'shepherd and his flock'. The fact that the Church Assembly administration was described in different terms evoked in them feelings of pessimism and fatalism about the onward march of bureaucracy. Within five years of the inception of the Church Assembly the Bishop of Exeter was writing in *The Church Assembly News*:

I think some of us are asking whether a movement, which was good in its inception, has not overrun the line of wisdom, and whether the latest developments are not robbing the locality of some of their interest and rightful powers, and endangering the new life of the Church by creating a bureaucratic government—bureaucracy is the certain result of an exaggerated centralization of government.[3]

[1] *Report of the Special (Diocesan) Relationship Committee*, N.A.F. 1, Central Board of Finance, 1921, p. 25.

[2] Michel Crozier, *The Bureaucratic Phenomenon*, p. 3. Alvin W. Gouldner has remarked that 'the metaphysical pathos of much of the modern theory of group organization is that of pessimism and fatalism'. He added that, 'Nowhere does the fatalism of the theory of organization become more articulate than in the efforts to account for the development of bureaucratic behaviour' (A. W. Gouldner, 'Metaphysical Pathos and the Theory of Bureaucracy', *American Political Science Review*, vol. xlix, 1955, pp. 496–507 (p. 498).

[3] 'Centralization and Decentralization', two articles in *The Church Assembly News*, vol. i, nos. 4 and 5, April–May, 1924; quotation from the April issue.

The bureaucratic features which the Bishop of Exeter listed included: harshness of government or 'red-tapism', which he described as 'an effort to govern different people in different conditions by one rule'; incapacity for experimentation ('history has always credited bureaucratic government with an almost paralytic impotence to accommodate itself to changes that a changing world demands'); extravagance; rigidity; and lack of enterprise.[1] To those who worked in the Church Assembly offices, with their small staff and declining budget, such fears seemed totally unwarranted. The Secretary of the Central Board of Finance replied to the Bishop of Exeter in the following month's issue of *The Church Assembly News:*

> The Church of England in this, as in other matters, has maintained a practical and sensible path between the precipice of autocratic centralization on the one hand, and the abyss of unco-ordinated differentiation on the other. You may argue that the typical Englishman has been created by the Church of England or that the Church of England has been created by the typical Englishman, but in either event the Church of England has avoided alike the Roman autocracy in organism and the Protestant isolation of unit.[2]

The Church of England's attempt to maintain a *via media* in organization involved a constant dialectic between conflicting principles of organization and a division of powers which had to be paid for by sacrificing a certain amount of consistency and efficiency. The bureaucratic mode was only one of the principles operative in the organization and it was constantly in conflict with other principles. The fact that the organization was developing some of the structural characteristics of bureaucracy, such as centralization and standardization of financial provisions, did not justify the critics' assumption that the structural and behavioural components of the 'ideal type' bureaucracy would develop together as if they were harmonious parts of a whole.[3] As

[1] Op. cit., May issue.

[2] *The Church Assembly News*, vol. i, no. 6, June 1924.

[3] A criticism of empirical studies of bureaucracy which make this assumption was delivered by Ferrel Heady, 'Bureaucratic Theory and Comparative Administration', *Administrative Science Quarterly*, vol. iii, no. 4, March 1959, pp. 509–25.

has been observed of the modifications to bureaucracy which occur in other organizations:

> If the dynamics of any organization consists of constant adjustment of conflicting principles and of older and new elements, such an adjustment process should also be operative in organizations containing a bureaucratic mode.[1]

The development of the Church Assembly's organization was a process of constant adjustment, but it was adjustment without the benefit of any overall policy. The conflict of principles soon manifested itself in the early discussions of what should be the main functions of the Church Assembly. The Bishop of London informed the Assembly, in 1921, that it had not yet touched the imagination of the people of England, and unless they had something which would really touch the social and moral condition of the country they would fail as a National Assembly. He proposed that a Church Assembly department should be set up, called the Social Service Committee, which would deal with moral and industrial problems.[2] Lord Hugh Cecil opposed the idea, and professed to be alarmed by the Bishop's concern that the Assembly ought to touch the heart of the people; it should confine itself to legislation and finance.[3] Although the department suggested by the Bishop of London was subsequently created, it was the point of view expressed by Lord Cecil which tended to prevail in practice. This disappointed those who had provided the original inspiration and enthusiasm of the Life and Liberty Movement, but to those who wished to limit the Assembly's authority it was a satisfactory development. *Crockford's Clerical Directory* said, in 1935, that criticism of the Assembly for confining itself to the legislative function for which it was created was unmerited. It added:

[1] Francis and Stone, op cit., p. 152.

[2] *P.C.A.*, vol. ii, no. 3, 1921, p. 87.

[3] Ibid., p. 91. He was supported by another layman who gave as an instance of the danger of churchmen making statements on economics or politics, the recent statement of a church dignitary that rents, royalties, and dividends were contrary to the will of God. The speaker thought such a statement absurd when they remembered that these items constituted the chief sources of income of the Ecclesiastical Commissioners, and therefore every single one of the bishops was living in open sin, if the dignitary's statement was correct (ibid., p. 98).

This had been described as The Triumph of the Legalists. We do not know what title the critics claim for themselves. We can understand that there are some people who would like to induce the Assembly to endorse their favourite social, economic, or political theories.[1]

During the first ten years of its existence, the Assembly's character was firmly fixed as primarily a legislative body. The Assembly held three sessions a year, lasting for less than five days each, and on average three days of each session were devoted to legislation. By 1930 forty measures had been placed on the statute book, a few others had been rejected or withdrawn, whilst a number of others had been considered at length but were not finally complete. In this respect, therefore, the Church's organization was developing the first prerequisite laid down by Max Weber for a legal authority with a bureaucratic administrative staff: the laying down of a body of law which would govern the corporate group within the limits laid down by legal precepts and following principles capable of a generalized rational formulation.[2] But the further feature of bureaucratic organization, the centralized system of offices responsible for the administrative process of applying the rules to particular cases, did not appear to the same extent during that period; nor was there a large, specialized staff, recruited for a lifetime's career in the central administration. Most of the administration of the new rules could be carried out by existing agencies such as the bishops and their officers, diocesan committees, church courts, or the Ecclesiastical Commissioners and Queen Anne's Bounty.

The eventual growth in the Church Assembly departments came not as a result of deliberate policy decisions, but by accretion and improvisation. The accretion was in the form of adhesion of extraneous bodies such as the voluntary societies. Although the strongly partisan missionary societies resisted all suggestions that they should surrender their autonomy to a central Board of Missions,[3] many of the voluntary

[1] Op. cit., p. 166.

[2] Max Weber, *Theory of Social and Economic Organization*, p. 330.

[3] In 1919 the proposal of the Central Board of Missions (a purely advisory body set up in 1884) that it should have a central missionary fund, was rejected by the societies (*Church Times*, 28 February 1919).

societies were only too pleased to be absorbed in to the Church Assembly organization and its budget. The Central Board of Finance sometimes expressed a desire to eliminate their 'spasmodic and ill-considered appeals to sentiment' in favour of 'a properly organized method of proportionate giving based upon definite principle.'[1] During the campaign for the Enabling Bill similar criticisms had been levelled against the societies in *The Challenge*. One letter on 'The Church G.H.Q.' said that of the fifty-two societies with offices in Church House, Westminster, most were extremely small and closed their offices for weeks on end during the summer. The offices were said to be dirty, gloomy, and badly furnished. The correspondent, who signed himself 'Bill Enabling', added that 'The whole place savours of the Victorian Age and lacks the spirit of progress, liberty, and freedom, which the Enabling Bill seeks to bring to the Church'.[2] Another correspondent asked, 'Is there nothing that can be done to. . . transform this monument of antiquity into a modern and well-equipped head office of the Church?'[3]

The Church Assembly administration's character was fashioned by the councils, boards, and societies which it absorbed. In addition to the Central Advisory Council of Training for the Ministry, which was mainly answerable to the bishops, there was the Central Board of Finance, whose character has been described, and then there were the older societies which were absorbed, like the Central Church Committee for Defence and Instruction and the Queen Victoria Clergy Fund in 1923. The societies often brought with them their own constitutions, staff, and methods of work. The total staff of all ranks employed by the Assembly grew from 40 in 1920 (of whom 14 were in the Central Board of Finance), to 60 in 1925, and 86 in 1930.[4] There was then a period of relative stability until after the Second World War when budget, staff, and departments began slowly to increase again.

1 *Annual Report of the Central Board of Finance*, 1920, pp. 20–1.

2 *The Challenge*, 19 December 1919.

3 Ibid., 2 January 1920.

4 Figures derived from salary lists in the Church Assembly archives, Church House, Westminster.

LOOKING BACK—FACTS AND THEORIES ABOUT BUREAUCRATIZATION

The nature of the process by which the organization developed, and the circumstances in which it occurred, meant that it acquired some of the structural and behavioural characteristics of bureaucracy but not others. An investigation carried out by the Organization and Methods Division of the Treasury into the Church Assembly departments, in 1954–5, found that the departments were small, highly autonomous, and each governed by its own constitution. Three partial exceptions were the Church Assembly Secretariat, the Central Board of Finance, and the Church Information Board, which each provided a more general service: the Secretariat, which had a total staff of six, served the Church Assembly and the Standing Committee; the Central Board of Finance, with a staff of 21 (plus 7 temporary staff on statistics), administered the central funds, controlled the budget, and provided financial and establishment services; the Church Information Board, with a staff of 12, provided publicity and publication services. Two bodies, the Central Advisory Council of Training for the Ministry (12 staff), and the Council on Foreign Relations (7 staff based on Lambeth Palace), reported directly to the bishops and the Archbishop of Canterbury respectively. The remaining 12 departments were all small, and because of their constitutions, history, or location, worked separately and as self-contained units. The report commented, 'One of the consequences is that it is difficult to set up a proper division of labour between grades of staff'.[1] Thus the organization lacked one of the chief characteristics of a bureaucracy—a clearly defined hierarchy of offices each with a definite sphere of competence.[2]

The investigation found that the general co-ordination of activities in the organization was inadequate, and the departments did not even circulate their minutes and reports to each other—which to the O. and M. investigators was

[1] *Report of the Organization and Methods Division of the Treasury on the Organization and Procedures of the Church Assembly Departments*, July 1955, unpublished document in Church Assembly archives.

[2] Max Weber, op. cit., p. 333.

a minimum requirement. Inter-departmental transfers of staff were also rare. The investigators' concern about the bureaucratic dysfunction of excessive departmentalization in the structure of the organization was paralleled by a criticism of the behavioural consequence that too much time was spent in keeping records of movements of papers. The report pointed out, 'These records are purely defensive in character, i.e. they do not contribute to the despatch of business'.[1] The report stressed, however, that on the whole the organization was understaffed, and some of the older staff were overworked and underpaid.

The total staff in 1954 was 102. By 1966, it had risen to 183, but this was still small compared with a staff of 472 at the Church Commissioners' office (in 1963).[2] Nor was there the same quasi-civil service career structure in the Church Assembly offices as there was at the Church Commissioners' office. A bureaucratic administrative staff is usually characterized by a defined hierarchy of offices for which candidates are selected on the basis of technical qualifications, and the office should constitute a career in which there is promotion according to seniority or achievement; payment should be by fixed salaries with pension rights.[3] The Church Assembly offices received their character less from the civil service, after the fashion of the Church Commissioners, as from the voluntary societies which they inherited. The chief officer, the Secretary of the Church Assembly, refused to accept any payment for the first two years of its existence, and only after that did he ask to be put on half-pay. Although a rudimentary hierarchy developed, during most of its history the organization had only two main grades: Grade 1 staff were the full-time secretaries to the various councils and boards, and Grade 2 were clerical and manual staff.

In May 1966, out of a total staff of 183, there were 65

[1] *O. and M. Report*, op. cit., p. 4.

[2] Information on the Church Assembly staff was derived from written information supplied by the Central Board of Finance, Standing Committee Minutes, and interviews with Sir John Guillum Scott (the Secretary of Church Assembly) and other members of the staff. Details of the Church Commissioners' office derive from their Annual Reports; Archdeacon Guy Mayfield, *Like Nothing on Earth*, p. 100; and the *Monckton Report*, 1963.

[3] Max Weber, op. cit., pp. 333–4.

Grade 1 staff, of whom approximately one-third were clergymen who sometimes had no specialized training other than for their traditional clerical role. Their appointments were not for life but for short, fixed terms of three or five years (although these were sometimes renewed). Throughout this higher grade there was a general lack of permanence and continuity, and no career structure comparable to that of the civil service and the Church Commissioners' staff. (There was no interchange of staff between the Church Assembly and the Church Commissioners.) The lay members of the Grade 1 staff tended to serve almost twice as long as the ordained members: in 1966, the average length of service since first appointment, was 3·6 years for clergy, and 6·8 years for lay members. The Committee on Central Funds, which reported in 1956, observed that

> Church administration cannot be a life career for more than a very small number of persons. It represents, for most of the Church's lay employees, either a diversion in mid-life from a career which was planned to take another course, or an interlude in the main work of a lifetime.[1]

By virtue of its more specialized business, and the greater need for continuity in its execution, the Central Board of Finance was not only the largest department, but also had a much higher average length of service for its Grade 1 staff (10·6 years). It might have been expected that it would exercise a certain degree of control over the policies of the other departments as a result of its superior position in possessing the most detailed knowledge about the working of the whole organization, and through its control over finance. The Committee on Central Funds found that unofficially the Central Board of Finance helped the spending departments to prepare the estimates they themselves submitted to the Board. In some cases the Board's staff had done the whole work of preparing departmental estimates, obtaining where possible the agreement of the departmental

1 *Report of the Committee on Central Funds*, C.A. 1181, 1956, p. 57. This contrasts with Karl Mannheim's description of a bureaucratic staff as being dependent on 'legalist punctilio, predictable promotion, seniority claims, merit rating, tenure, security, routine, and precedent' (Mannheim, *Freedom, Power and Democratic Planning*, p. 147).

secretaries, before submitting them to the Budget Sub-Committee.[1] But this only amounted to control in the weakest departments. Where there was disagreement between the Central Board of Finance and a spending department, the only provision for resolving it was for the Central Board of Finance to exclude the portion of the estimate in question from the budget, and to make a report on it during the budget debate in the Assembly. This was too extreme a procedure and had never once been used.[2] If a department insisted on including an estimate, then the Central Board had to acquiesce.

A fundamental weakness in the conduct of the Church Assembly's financial business was the partial separation of policy from finance. The reasons for this separation were explained by the Committee on Central Funds:

> This separation may reflect merely the independent origins of the bodies which from time to time have been assimilated to the status of boards or councils of the Assembly; but it may also reflect the notion that policy and finance can and should be separated.[3]

The Central Board of Finance, when it was taken over by the Church Assembly, certainly believed that such a separation was in accord with the theory of government which had given the Church this quasi-Parliament. Due to its experience of being held responsible for over-centralization and extravagance, it was relieved to be able to pass that responsibility to a formal policy-making body. The Annual Report in 1921 emphasized the change:

> In no way is the difference between the management of the affairs of the Board more marked than in the control which is now exercised in questions of policy by the National Assembly. . . . This is as it should be, but it may be remarked that any tendency to extravagance is to be found in the Assembly itself and not in the Board of Finance, which already has to attempt to restrain the tendency to vote monies without due consideration of the implications of such votes.[4]

The existence of this theory of the separation of powers in the Church of England tends to bear out in one respect

[1] *Report of the Committee on Central Funds*, p. 83.
[2] Ibid., p. 17.
[3] Ibid., p. 16.
[4] *Annual Report of the Central Board of Finance*, 1921, p. 15.

the observation made by James Gustafson in contrasting American denominations and European state churches, that,

> While American churches are shaped like other voluntary associations, the political and administrative structures of some European churches resemble state bureaucracies. In these it is still assumed (if it is not the case) that policy and administrative functions are sharply distinguished, and that the latter is simply a matter of execution of policy.[1]

In state bureaucracies, however, the link between administration and the policy-making body is provided by the ministerial cabinet. In some state churches, such as those in Sweden and Denmark, this provision is extended to the church by way of the Ministry of Ecclesiastical Affairs in Sweden, and the Ministry for Church Affairs in Denmark (although these churches have also developed a certain measure of self-government).[2] In the Church of England the State maintained only a final veto over church legislation; in administration the Church Assembly's control was limited by the large size of the Assembly and the infrequency of its meetings. Internal disagreement in the Church over the question of authority as it related to the Church Assembly hindered the development of a strong Standing Committee which could act as a church cabinet. The *ad hoc* growth of the Church Assembly's administration made it even more essential to secure central co-ordination and control, but the Standing Committee had developed only limited powers and functions, and the large number of administrative departments had no representation on it. The departments were more or less autonomous and were adopted or created by the Assembly without any comprehensive planning. It was admitted that the manner in which the Assembly's limited resources was divided between them did not reflect a conscious and considered judgement of their relative importance and there was no body short of the Assembly itself capable of co-ordinating and directing their activities.[3]

1 James M. Gustafson, *Treasure in Earthen Vessels: The Church as a Human Community*, pp. 40–1.

2 Cf. L. S. Hunter, *Scandinavian Churches*.

3 *Report of the Committee on Central Funds*, p. 14.

The Report of the Committee on Central Funds was introduced into the Church Assembly in November 1956 by the Chairwoman of the Committee, Mrs. M. B. Ridley. She began by recalling how she had been taken to a Life and Liberty Movement meeting when she was a child to hear William Temple and Dick Sheppard speak, and she could still remember being thrilled by the spirit of crusade. She thought that they should recall the high hopes and enthusiasm which led to the Enabling Act, especially as many of them now felt the Assembly had reached an unsatisfactory stage in its life.

Although a lot of necessary reforms had been accomplished through the passing of measures, the Assembly did not know where it was going, and the whole thing seemed a bit cumbersome and out of hand. And, as Mrs. Ridley observed, if they had their doubts, it was not surprising that the majority of church people, who were ignorant about the work of the Assembly, regarded it with suspicion and disquiet.[1]

According to the Committee on Central Funds there were three main faults in the organization. The first was that the Assembly was too big to make decisions on policy. The second failing was that policy and finance had been too much separated. The Central Board of Finance had often been faced with the choice of giving advice to councils or to the Assembly which was in fact advice on policy, or else letting the Assembly and the departments go their own way. Since the Central Board did not claim to be a suitable or competent body to determine policy, it had often taken the line of least resistance. The third failing was that the work was done in too many closed compartments. The various central departments had limited terms of reference and over the years this led to gaps not being filled. Since there was no body whose business it was to give continuous thought to overall policy, and guidance, the instinctive reaction of the Assembly had been to fill each gap with another central council, with a consequent increase in the budget. Thus the main failings of the organization were summed up as lack of control and guidance on policy,

[1] *P.C.A.*, vol. xxxvi, no. 3, 1956, pp. 377–8.

separation of policy from finance, and lack of flexibility. The report concluded:

> What is required at the centre to meet the needs of the present day is not an authoritarian bureaucracy, but an organization existing for the mutual advantage of the dioceses, adequately controlled, and sufficiently flexible to be capable of easy and rapid adjustment.
>
> Flexibility is achieved partly by effective control and partly by giving the subordinate bodies general directions rather than detailed terms of reference.
>
> In anything so large as the Assembly effective control can only be exercised through a body upon which the Assembly and its chief Councils are represented, which is able to give detailed consideration to, and to judge any proposal in the light of, the general needs and resources of the Church.
>
> Finance is something integral with policy and cannot be dissociated from it.[1]

The logic of rationalization was maintained in the Committee's specific proposals that the departments should be reduced to four main departments, headed by highly qualified and well-paid full-time secretaries. The Standing Committee should become the body to consider policy in relation to finance, and to advise the departments and the Assembly; it would contain the four chairman of the departments, along with the chairman and vice-chairman of the Central Board of Finance.[1]

Although the proposals may have been appropriate for securing greater efficiency in the Church Assembly organization they almost ignored the conflicts over principles and interests which had done so much to shape that organization and to limit its powers. To many of the clergy, the principles and methods of formal rationality threatened to subvert the primacy of religious values in the organization, and to undermine their own authority. Consequently, the parochial clergy had never provided the vital link in communication between the central organization and the parishes. *Crockford's Clerical Directory*, in 1934, said that the clergy could not be expected to disseminate information about the

[1] *Report of the Committee on Central Funds*, pp. 15–17; summarized by Mrs. Ridley, *P.C.A.*, vol. xxxvi, no. 3, 1956, p. 380.

central organization, and they would violate their ordination pledges

> . . . if they sacrificed real pastoral work to perfecting the machinery of the Church, and bartered spiritual influence for the kind of efficiency which is recorded in statistical returns.[1]

The Committee on Central Funds' proposals did little to ensure the representation of different interest groups and to lessen the conviction among certain sections of the parochial clergy that the Assembly was the enemy. The Parochial Clergy Association (the nearest thing to a trades union or professional association of the clergy) kept up a constant criticism of the Assembly. A typical comment was that of a member of the Association's executive, who stated that,

> Measure after Measure both passed and proposed in the Church Assembly, all without exception, threaten the independence of the Parochial Clergy. There is no doubt whatever that the majority of bishops and laity are keen in their desire to limit the freedom of the Parochial Clergy, so that they can get control over them. By such means the laity could exercise economic control, and episcopacy would quickly change again into prelacy.[2]

The logic of rationalization had a limited success in the amalgamation of the Ecclesiastical Commission and Queen Anne's Bounty into the one body of the Church Commissioners in 1948, but the occasional suggestion that it should be taken a stage further by the amalgamation of the Church Commissioners and the Central Board of Finance was resisted. The clergy resisted it on the usual grounds that it would increase bureaucracy and reduce their independence. The Archdeacon of Stafford expressed one of their fears in the debate on the report of the Commission on the Administration of the Church Commissioners for England (published in 1963):

> If the Commissioners were abolished and the Central Board took over, it would only be a matter of time before a Measure came before the Assembly to alter the terms of the trust, and before long funds

[1] *Crockford*, op. cit., pp. 148–9.

[2] Revd. W. Grimwood in *Parson and Parish* (journal of the Parochial Clergy Association), no. lxvii, July 1965, p. 10.

specifically given for the benefit of the clergy would become part of the general funds of the Church.[1]

It was the long-standing dislike and fear of bureaucracy that dominated all discussions of the Church Assembly organization. The tone of the debate on the report of the Committee on Central Funds was set by the Bishop of Chichester, who said that the Church of England was in danger of being organized too much as a business firm. He thought that there had been too much of the 'Americanization' process in the Committee's discussions. Mrs. Ridley had said she hoped the pioneers of the Life and Liberty Movement, William Temple and Dick Sheppard, would approve this climax to the labours they set on foot. The Bishop of Chichester said that it was no secret that Dick Sheppard, soon after the establishment of the Church Assembly, professed disappointment with its operation, and his disappointment was mainly on the ground that it was being over-organized and was over-concerned with machinery.[2] The debate never broke away from the dilemma of bureaucracy and anti-bureaucracy, and most of the proposals were rejected. The Archbishop of Canterbury predicted that eventually such developments would have to come about,[3] and since that time, bit by bit, the process of rationalization has been taking place, but not without opposition from critics who believe that the end result will be monocratic bureaucracy.

1 *P.C.A.*, vol. xliii, no. 3, 1963, p. 586. For this reason they were prepared to put up with the various faults of the Church Commissioners as described in the debate, such as that of appearing to be a 'pseudo-Government department', 'a honeycomb of watertight departments', 'impersonal', 'sealed off from the rest of the Church' (ibid., pp. 575–5).

2 *P.C.A.*, vol. xxxvi, no. 3, 1956, pp. 393–6. This invocation of the names of Temple and Sheppard is typical of the struggle to determine the character of an organization. Selznick commented on this struggle, that, 'Laudatory references to a set of individuals as the "fathers" of the organization's policy and outlook may help to define the accepted antecedents of the group, as a result, a whole series of doctrinal commitments are inferred from those antecedents, though not necessarily formally included in the program of objectives of the organization' (Selznick, *T.V.A. and the Grass-roots*, pp. 181–5).

3 *P.C.A.*, vol. xxxvii, no. 2, 1957, p. 300.

VIII

SOCIOLOGICAL CONCLUSIONS

ADAPTATION AND PRESERVATION

THE organizational response of the Church of England to social change has been viewed as part of a process of differentiation of institutional domains within the social structure, in which the Church, like other institutions, gained increasing autonomy and had to develop its separate administrative and governmental organization. At the same time that organization had to be capable of relating itself to other differentiated institutions, and so it adopted many of the common operational criteria of formal rationality.

The analysis of this process has favoured an approach that has been found fruitful in other studies of institutional adaptation:

> The study of institutions is in some ways comparable to the clinical study of personality. It requires a genetic and developmental approach, an emphasis on historical origins and growth stages. There is a need to see the enterprise as a whole and to see how it is transformed as new ways of dealing with a changing environment evolve. As in the case of personality, effective diagnosis depends upon locating the special problems that go along with a particular character structure; and we can understand character better when we see it as the product of self-preserving efforts to deal with inner impulses and external demands. In both personality and institutions 'self-preservation' means more than bare organic or material survival. Self-preservation has to do with the maintenance of basic identity, with the integrity of a personal or institutional 'self'.
>
> Our problem is to discover the characteristic ways in which *types* of institutions respond to *types* of circumstances.[1]

The proposition that, throughout the process of organizational change, there would be an overall tendency to seek to evaluate the possible effects of such changes on the institution's basic identity, provided the main hypothesis

[1] Philip Selznick, *Leadership in Administration*, pp. 141–2.

for analysing the different stages of growth in the Church of England's organization. Thus attention has not been focused on one set of hypotheses which have been advanced on structural differentiation—that there would be a fixed sequence of stages[1]—but upon the role of the value system of the institution in determining key aspects of the outcome at every stage. According to the hypothesis, however, the final result in each stage would receive the impress of the basic institutional character and identity of the Church, as it was distilled through the various thought forms, social movements, and modes of organization, of each historical period, and as it was identified with the interests of different groups in the Church. The basic institutional character of the Church of England was taken to be that of an Established Church, or *ecclesia* type of religious body. The genesis of that institutional character lay in the Elizabethan Settlement, which has been described as 'a compromise which included parties and persons of very diverse views in one religious establishment'.[2] The warranty for taking this as the crucial character trait in determining consistency of response in structural terms, lay in the fact that it penetrated even the basic belief system. Hence the comment of a church historian that, 'The formulae of doctrine which emerged from that settlement was couched in studiously ambiguous terms'.[2] And yet this compromise and ambiguity could be developed into an identity prized by many adherents, and considered as worth safeguarding, as the appropriate character for the Church of the English people.

The Church of England's character was of this type and so it was reflected in the manner in which it responded to the different types of circumstances, such as the politico-economic changes, the need for new administrative agencies and norms of operation, and for representative assemblies. It was also a feature of the Church's attitudes to different types of authority in its polity, and especially where these involved a bureaucratic type of organization.

The main factors which have been considered in this

[1] Cf. Neil J. Smelser, *Social Change in the Industrial Revolution*, pp. 14–15.

[2] A. Hamilton Thompson, 'The Reformation', in E. G. Selwyn (ed.), *Essays Catholic and Critical*.

study can now be summarized and related to each other, before discussing them in more detail. First, at the level of the differentiation of institutions and their domains in the society as a whole, every aspect of the Church of England's operation was faced with a dilemma. On the one hand, it had to develop more autonomous administrative governmental agencies, whilst, on the other hand, it sought to maintain its basic identity as a coalition of diverse principles of authority and doctrine, that had given it its character as a national religious establishment, or *ecclesia*. Having discussed the implications of this problem, it was then possible to examine the separate stages of the organizational development, and the underlying dilemma was found to be a major determining factor in shaping the organizational development in each stage. In its ecclesiastical aspect the development was gradually in the direction of producing assemblies, boards, and councils, which resembled those in the denominations. In terms of principles of authority and their administrative entailment this involved the introduction of elements which were based less on tradition, and were more in keeping with the bureaucratic form which is typical of modern Western organizations in all fields. But these elements continued to coexist with older principles and modes of organization, and this coexistence was valued because it preserved the basic coalition of diverse religious parties, and protected various sectional interests, such as those of the parochial clergy.

To characterize the Church of England as an *ecclesia* is to rank it on a continuum of types of religious body: cult, sect, institutionalized (or established) sect, denomination, *ecclesia*, world church.[1] This is an elaboration of the pioneer distinction made by Max Weber, and popularized by Ernst Troeltsch, between church and sect.[2] Troeltsch stated the dichotomy quite simply:

> The Church is that type of organization which is overwhelmingly conservative, which to a certain extent accepts the secular order, and dominates the masses; in principle, therefore, it is universal, i.e. it

[1] J. Milton Yinger, *Religion, Society and the Individual*, pp. 147–55.

[2] Max Weber, *The Protestant Ethic and the Spirit of Capitalism*, and E. Troeltsch, *The Social Teaching of the Christian Churches*.

desires to cover the whole life of humanity. The sects, on the other hand, are comparatively small groups; they aspire after personal inward perfection, and they aim at a direct personal fellowship between the members of each group. From the very beginning, therefore, they are forced to organize themselves in small groups, and to renounce the idea of dominating the world.[1]

Yinger claimed that this dichotomy was inadequate to describe the full range of data, and so he produced the six-step classification on the basis of two criteria—the degree of inclusiveness of the members of society, and the degree of attention paid to the function of social integration as contrasted with the function of satisfying personal need.[2] The three types most relevant to the discussion of the Church of England are the world church, the *ecclesia*, and the denomination. The world church is relatively successful in supporting the integration of society, whilst at the same time satisfying, by its pattern of beliefs and observances, many of the personal needs of individuals on all levels of society, and so it is able to combine church and sect tendencies. In heterogeneous societies this balance is likely to be achieved only very rarely and is not likely to be maintained for very long. The best example of the criteria of a world church being fulfilled, in Yinger's estimation, occurred in the thirteenth-century Roman Catholic Church. The *ecclesia*, like the world church (or universal church), reaches out to the boundaries of the society, and seeks to include all classes, but it lacks the supra-nationality of the world church which can put itself above the classes of any one society. The *ecclesia* is less successful than the universal church in incorporating sect tendencies. It becomes so well adjusted to the dominant elements that the needs of many of its adherents, particularly from the lower classes, are frustrated. It is more successful in reinforcing the exisiting

[1] Troeltsch, op. cit., vol. i, p. 331.

[2] Elaborations of the church-sect typology were also made by Howard Becker, who distinguished four types: the *ecclesia*, denomination, sect, and cult (H. Becker, *Systematic Sociology*, 1950 edn., pp. 624–42; and *Through Values to Social Interpretation*, pp. 114–18). Joachim Wach concluded that there were three major forms: ecclesiastical bodies, independent bodies or denominations, and sectarian bodies (J. Wach, *Types of Religious Experience: Christian and Non-Christian*, pp. 190–6).

pattern of social integration than in fulfilling the personality needs of individuals of all classes. There tend, therefore, to be widespread indifference, sectarian protests, and secular opposition.

The denomination is a larger body than a sect; it has accommodated to most of the standards of the secular culture, and is organized as a body independent of the State, and living in a competitive relationship with other similar bodies, whilst respecting their freedom.[1] A constant theme of many studies of different types of religious bodies has been that there is a tendency for sects, which begin as small, exclusive, groups of the elect, standing in opposition to the accepted values of the wider society, to develop into denominations.[2] It is clear, however, that some sects do not evolve in this way, and that there can also be a development in the opposite direction along the continuum.[3] Friedrich Fürstenberg utilized three types similar to those of Yinger to show that there had been developments in this latter direction in Germany. Corresponding to the world church is the *Bruderschaftskirche*, the original type of church organization of pre-Reformation days; for the *ecclesia* he used the terms *Volkskirche* and *Staatskirche*, the kind of religious body that emerged after the Reformation and which was dependent on the State; the equivalent of the denomination is the *Verbandskirche*, a voluntary association, politically independent, and institutionalized around its own doctrinal and ecclesiological position. The development was in the

[1] This characterization is based on Yinger, op. cit., and Becker, op. cit.

[2] H. R. Niebuhr, *The Social Sources of Denominationalism*, pp. 19–21; Liston Pope, *Millhands and Preachers*; Earl D. C. Brewer, 'Sect and Church in Methodism', in *Social Forces*, vol. xxx, 4 (May 1952), pp. 400–8; O. R. Whitley, 'The Sect-to-Denomination Process in an American Religious Movement: The Disciples of Christ', in *Southwestern Social Science Quarterly*, vol. xxxvi (1955), pp. 275–81.

[3] Neil J. Smelser has summarized the different grounds of criticism of the sect-to-denomination process as: (*a*) It is too limited a statement of the possible adaptations of religious groups, even within Christianity. (*b*) It is limited to particular countries such as the United States. (*c*) It does not take account of the distinctive influence of the sect's original values, its initial level of insulation or isolation from the parent society (Smelser, *Theory of Collective Behaviour*, p. 360). Cf. B. Johnson, 'A Critical Appraisal of the Church-Sect Typology', in *American Sociological Review*, vol. xxii (1957), pp. 88–92; H. W. Pfautz, 'The Sociology of Secularization: Religious Groups', in *American Journal of Sociology*, lxi, 2 (September 1955), pp. 121–8; and B. R. Wilson, 'An Analysis of Sect Development', *American Sociological Review*, vol. xxiv (1959), pp. 3–15.

direction of the *Verbandskirche* as the Church's relationship with the State was called into question and as society became highly pluralistic.[1]

Talcott Parsons maintained that this process was an appropriate organizational response to the modern pluralist society whereby the religious and secular aspects of life were differentiated although not necessarily separated.[2] Other writers on church organization, such as James M. Gustafson and Robert Lee, have maintained that in spite of differences in formal polity, denominations tend to assume the same organizational shape.[3] However, it has seemed reasonable to assume, for present purposes, that there might be variations in the organization of bodies which have come from different ends of the continuum and which still contain some of the elements of their former position. Thus charismatic leadership may be more prevalent in a sect-originated denomination, and traditional leadership in church- or *ecclesia*-originated denominations. In the sect, theology presses immediately on polity, either to minimize the degree of formal polity, or to closely regulate its nature. Consequently it has few or no bureaucratic characteristics. In the sect-originated denomination, the correspondence between theology and polity is greatest at the congregational level, but less at the extra-parochial levels. National organization tends to grow up in a vacuum to meet instrumental organization needs, hence the only authority at that level is of the rational-pragmatic type described by Paul M. Harrison in the American Baptist Convention.[4]

The Church of England appears to be closer to the

[1] Friedrich Fürstenberg, 'Kirchenform und Gesellschaftsstructur', in *Sociologisch Bulletin*, iii (1960), pp. 100–12. Cf. Glenn M. Vernon, *Sociology of Religion*, p. 176, who describes the Church of England as moving towards a denomination status.

[2] T. Parsons, 'Christianity and Modern Industrial Society', in E. A. Tiryakian (ed.), *Sociological Theory, Values, and Sociocultural Change*, pp. 35–70; and 'The Patterns of Religious Organization in the United States', in *Daedalus*, lxxxvii, 3 (summer 1958), pp. 65–85.

[3] J. M. Gustafson, *Treasure in Earthen Vessels*, p. 38; and R. Lee, *The Social Sources of Church Unity*, p. 94.

[4] Harrison describes this as an 'expediential authority', not fully legal nor based on ecclesiastical tradition, but arising out of the immediate needs of the denominational organizations (P. M. Harrison, *Authority and Power in the Free Church Tradition*, p. 14).

ecclesia than to the denomination type, although this study has shown the advance of denominational tendencies. It would be expected that any denomination which developed out of an *ecclesia* would show substantial traces of its origins. In the Church of England there remain substantial elements of its traditional inclusive aspirations and structure (for example, the territorial parish system). It also contains a relatively heterogeneous membership, and a more complex mixture of theological and ecclesiological principles than most denominations of the sect-originated type. Consequently it has a constant problem of balancing differing groups or parties. Because the spectrum of doctrinal and organizational principles is wider within such a body there is a tendency to resist systematic rationalization both in theology and in organization. Accumulation of power and authority in any one section is feared because it might lead to the exclusion of other sections or principles. The present study has demonstrated that in the case of an *ecclesia* traditionally supported in various ways by the State, when state administrative and financial aid is withdrawn there is a readjustment in the course of which it develops its organization increasingly in the direction of greater autonomy. This innovation in structure effects most immediately the norms of operation of the organization, but it also leads to a reassessment of the values which those norms embody, and of the belief system which makes those values viable and rational. Structural reform may, as in the case of the Church of England, give rise to theological party conflict, especially if the new structure is influenced by the methods and patterns of organization employed in secular government and commerce. Such patterns of organization are held to symbolize values inappropriate for a religious body, which must conflict with efforts to reaffirm the institution's autonomous values as it adjusts to its new position in society.

In the case of the Church of England, different groups in the Church responded to these external and internal changes by either appealing to the dominant values of contemporary society to legitimize the Church's functions and its necessary structural changes (thus emphasizing the continued interdependence of Church and State), or else by reviving and reasserting dormant elements in its own value system, thus tending to legitimize and accentuate the Church's autonomy. The former response was typical of an *ecclesia* in its attempt to reinforce the existing pattern of social integration and to co-operate with the governing class in exercising social control. The Church's leaders had been trained according to the traditional assumptions of the Establishment that it was their duty to co-operate with the leaders of secular government to reform the Church when necessary so as to preserve its social utility. The second response occurred amongst men who did not bear those responsibilities, and it sought to reassert principles appropriate to a universal church, which had transcended nations and classes. In the Oxford Movement this sometimes led to religious teachings and practices characteristic of the medieval Catholic Church, and in its political aspect to paternalistic High Toryism or, later, socialism. To the leaders of the *ecclesia* this reaction seemed potentially sectarian (the Roman Catholic Church was a sect in relation to the Establishment), and politically unrealistic.

The basic division, therefore, with regard to the developing organization was between those who were concerned with instrumental adaptation, to enable the Church to go on fulfilling its responsibilities as an *ecclesia*, and, on the other hand, those who were concerned to stress the Church's autonomy as an institution, with its own distinct values. Those who occupied the latter position looked beyond the *ecclesia* to the universal church for their principles, even though the practical consequence of this standpoint might reduce the Church of England to a less inclusive body of the denomination type (or sect type, as their opponents invidiously termed it). Changes in organizational structure brought to the surface long-standing differences over authority in the Church of England. The conflict over authority loomed so large in the Church in the nineteenth and early twentieth centuries, that it sometimes appears, from contemporary sources and church history books, as if the ritualist controversies and the problem of clergy discipline were both the major cause and effect of the differences over authority. In fact those controversies were but one symptom of the painful adjustment required of an *ecclesia* in a society in which institutional differentiation was occurring.

The present discussion has centred not on the problem of authority in itself, but on the relation of the different types or principles of authority to administrative processes in the Church. The crucial question here has been concerned with the reactions of different parties and interests in the Church to the phenomenon of bureaucratization. This has been studied in relation to the basic theory of Max Weber, that the key to understanding the authority relations of any social system lies in the basis of legitimacy claimed for persons in authority. It was his contention that the nature of this claim was an important determinant of the scope of authority as well as the mode of organization. Since no social system can operate over an extensive period of time on the basis of power alone, the leaders seek to establish a legitimate right to exercise their power.[1] Weber claimed that such legitimacy may be rooted in devotion to tradition, law, or the charismatic qualities of the leader himself. He believed that modern, Western organization could be characterized as possessing legal authority with a bureaucratic administration; it involved the exercise of control by the occupants of legally sanctioned offices on the basis of factual knowledge, which gave it the dual nature of rational-legal authority.[2] An organization administered on such a basis is committed to striving for technical efficiency, precision of operation, control by experts, speed, continuity of policy, and an optimal return for the labour and money expended. This constitutes the formal rationality of bureaucratic organization, and it is claimed that it need carry no invidious connotation. In common usage, however, the word 'bureaucracy' has at least four meanings: (1) bureaucracy as a particular form of organization, (2) bureaucracy

[1] A distinction is drawn between power and authority: power is more comprehensive than authority in that it can exist apart from institutional sanction. It is the ability to influence or control the actions of others even without institutional sanction (cf. Marion J. Levy Jr., *The Structure of Society*, p. 333; and Weber, *The Theory of Social and Economic Organization*, p. 152). Authority is thus the expected and legitimate possession of power (Harold D. Lasswell and Abraham Kaplan, *Power and Society*, p. 133).

[2] Max Weber, op. cit., p. 339.

as an ailment of organization, obstructing effective operation, (3) bureaucracy in the sense of 'big government' or centralization, and (4) bureaucracy as a blight, always for the worst, falling on liberty and individuality.[1] Different groups in an institution undergoing bureaucratization invest the term with those meanings which most emphasize their immediate concerns. A group concerned with stressing the distinctive values of the institution is likely to object to bureaucracy as a form of organization, because it threatens to undermine those values. The group responsible for providing instrumental leadership will confine the term 'bureaucracy' to those defects of organization which obstruct its effective operation. Groups with local interests view bureaucracy as 'big government' or centralization, which over-rides those interests. Individuals who prize their professional independence and freedom feel anxious about the effect of bureaucracy on their liberty and individuality.

Critics of bureaucracy in the organizational changes which took place in the Church of England were using the term in any or all these ways. They objected to it as a form of organization because of the primacy which it gave to formally rational criteria to the exclusion of considerations of tradition, divine ordinance, and the symbolic appropriateness of the means employed in relation to transcendental values and ultimate ends. Thus to Pusey, the only criterion appropriate to discussions of cathedrals was their 'sacredness' and the Ecclesiastical Commission's application of the criteria of 'utility' seemed to him inappropriate. The increasing use of formal rationality in the Church's administrative agencies was made necessary by the need for internal central budgeting, as the Church lost external sources of support such as church rates, government grants, and as tithes were commuted and then centrally administered. This fulfilled the condition laid down by Weber by which,

> A system of economic activity will be called 'formally' rational according to the degree in which the provision for needs, which is essential to every rational economy, is capable of being expressed in numerical, calculable terms, and is so expressed. . . .[2]

[1] Fritz Morstein Marx, *The Administrative State*, p. 16. Cf. Michel Crozier, *The Bureaucratic Phenomenon*, p. 3.

[2] Max Weber, op. cit., p. 184.

However, the spread of formally rational organization only accentuated the problem, always difficult for a religious body, of making the activities of such organization substantively rational in terms of absolute values and ultimate ends. As an *ecclesia* the Church of England had sought to reach out to the boundaries of society, to include all classes, and to incorporate all religious tendencies. Inevitably, therefore, there were inconsistencies in its doctrine and polity, and over its values and aims. These differences were exacerbated by changes in the Church's organization, especially as these occurred as part of the process by which the Church gained a certain amount of institutional autonomy, which required it to reassess its goals and values.

Thus there were difficulties with regard to the rational element in the rational-legal authority of Church bureaucracy. But there were also difficulties with regard to its legality. Rational-legal authority rests on a 'belief in the "legality" of patterns of normative rules and the right of those elevated to authority under such rules to issue commands'.[1] In the Church of England there were differences between parties and sections in the Church about the nature and locus of authority. Although the episcopal system was maintained by the Elizabethan Settlement, there was disagreement both about the nature of that authority and its extent. Weber noted that in its pure form charismatic authority exists only in the process of originating, it cannot remain stable because it is specifically foreign to everyday routine structures, and, therefore, it becomes either traditionalized, rationalized, or a combination of both.[2] Episcopal authority in the Church of England was just such a mixture: on the one hand, it was part of the traditional social structure, as befitted an *ecclesia*, and the bishops were state-appointed and sat in Parliament as the Lords Spiritual; on the other hand, for those who looked back to the once universal church, it also rested on a routinized charisma of office transmitted through ritual means, as the Oxford Movement stressed in the doctrine of Apostolic Succession. Broad Churchmen and Evangelicals were more accustomed to regard episcopacy in its traditional aspect and, as such, it

[1] Max Weber, op. cit., p. 328. [2] Ibid., p. 364.

possessed only limited authority, since it could not change anything without the approval of the State—a limitation made more apparent in a period in which circumstances required changes to be made. Even the High Church clergy did not wish for government solely by the bishops, they believed that the bishops should govern in consultation with their clergy, and it was to this end that they worked for the revival of Convocation. The principles on which they justified the authority of Convocation were those of the universal church in which clerical synods had provided the autonomous government of the Church. To other churchmen Convocation without a lay element was an anachronism as a governing body; it had less the character of a synod and more the feudal character which it had possessed when it represented the clerical estate and imposed clerical taxes. Broad Churchmen and Evangelicals took this stand. They opposed any exclusive claims for a charisma of office. If the Church was to develop a governing body it would have to include representatives of the laity, but this brought into conflict all the different principles of authority, and it was only after a succession of experiments had been tried that agreement was reached on a form of Assembly that could be submitted to Parliament and receive delegated powers. Even then, the approach to Parliament was made only reluctantly by Church leaders such as Archbishop Davidson, who wished to preserve the *ecclesia* status. The compromise that was agreed upon resolved none of the previous differences over authority, and excluded none of the different principles. Convocation's authority was jealously safeguarded, as was that of the bishops and of Parliament. Only the most fervent believers in preserving the *status quo*, of whom Hensley Henson was the chief, suggested that changes such as the new church franchise turned the *ecclesia* into a denomination. That there had been some movement in that direction was shown in the resemblance which the Church Assembly organization had to those structures common in the denominations. But the Church Assembly was only one component in the organization, and it had to coexist with other elements which possessed different characters.

Each of the central agencies of church administration

and government which formed part of the Church of England's organizational response to social change reflected the balance both of interests and of principles of authority that coexisted in the religious Establishment. Convocation represented the interests and authority of the clergy and could be used as a platform for denouncing state encroachment on the prerogatives of the spirituality. But although this might be the role envisaged for it by the High Church clergy, it was kept firmly within the *ecclesia* tradition by the large proportion of *ex officio* members, who owed their appointment to the State. Queen Anne's Bounty was the next oldest body; it had come into existence in 1704 when the interpenetration of Church and State was still extensive. Consequently its governors included Privy Councillors, Queen's Counsel, Lord-Lieutenants, and Mayors. Although it played a part in developing the formally rational organization of the Church in the nineteenth century by supplying central statistical and budgetary services, its concentration on helping the poorest clergy from its small funds, and the prominent part played by the bishops on its board during most of its life gave it an authority which was more a traditional paternalism than rational-legal.

The Ecclesiastical Commissioners were set up in the period between the eighteenth century with its pattern of administration, which was almost completely independent of Parliament, and the more closely controlled administration of the later Victorian era. This gave rise to a reputation which was to stay with it even after it took in Queen Anne's Bounty and became the Church Commissioners—that of a quasi-government department, but one responsible to nobody in particular. In the absence of a governing body in the Church, the legality of the Ecclesiastical Commissioners' authority derived from Parliament and the civil service regulations upon which it patterned its internal structure. Other elements of authority based on different principles were introduced with the enlargement of the board, in 1840, to include more bishops, and the inclusion of Church Assembly representatives at a later date, but real control remained in the hands of the three Church Estates Commissioners. Consequently the Church's main financial agency conformed to neither the pattern of the Scandinavian state churches in having a ministerial department of Ecclesiastical Affairs, nor to the denominational pattern of making the instrumental agency into a department of the representative assembly. These two patterns, whilst appropriate to the ideal types of *ecclesia* and denomination, did not correspond with the ambivalent and transitional status of the Church of England. This very independence was to become valued for its contribution in preserving a division of powers that prevented the consolidation of a uniform bureaucracy. This was an instance of the commonly observed sociological phenomenon, that a factor that appears as an unintended consequence of a particular system becomes one of its most valued functions.[1]

The Church Assembly administration did not receive any legality from the delegated legislative powers of the Assembly itself (its constitution as submitted to Parliament made no mention of executive functions). Nor did it have any civil service connections. It incorporated some traditional authority from the presence of bishops on its boards and councils (as they had been on the voluntary societies which, in some cases, were absorbed by the Assembly organization). There were efforts to regularize the precarious legality which administrative activities could claim under the procedural rules of the Assembly, but often the full-time staff had to depend on a rational-pragmatic or expediential authority. The Assembly itself did not attain sufficient authority within the Church to be able to bestow an unequivocal authority on its administrators. This was most noticeable in the case of the Church Information Office, which was constantly undergoing changes in its constitution. A typical criticism was that,

> The office has come to assume the function of an official propaganda department. This has placed it in an equivocal position, for effective propaganda will touch on matters of faith and doctrine. These may

[1] In this case it may simply have been that a function which was manifest to only a few at first (i.e. the Whigs who advocated it as a useful division of powers) lost its character as a latent function and became more and more one of the primary manifest functions of the system. Cf. for a discussion of manifest and latent functions, Robert K. Merton, *Social Theory and Social Structure*, pp. 49–61.

involve pronouncements and judgements which do not properly belong to administration.[1]

This only revealed the basic flaw in the compromise which gave rise to the Church Assembly: the belief that spiritual and non-spiritual matters could be kept separate.

Pusey had predicted that it would be impossible to maintain such a distinction if once the laity were admitted into a synod. He had been prepared to resist the growing power of the laity for that reason, but his successors found that neither church defence nor reform could be undertaken without such a concession. The creation of the Church Assembly had involved a concession in that direction, but acquiescence of the Catholic party had only been secured at the price of a compromise that denied the Church Assembly an unequivocal authority. The new era of discussions on the best way of resolving this dilemma, which began in the 1950s, received its terms of reference from the motion passed by the Church Assembly in 1953, requesting the archbishops to appoint a Commission: 'To consider how the clergy and laity can best be joined together in the synodical government of the Church and to report'.[2] It remains to be seen whether the proposed new General Synod will resolve the dilemma.

The dilemma over authority was reflected in the problem of legality in the administrative agencies. But criticisms of bureaucracy in the Church were directed not only against the form of organization, at its rationality and legality. They were also concerned with it as an ailment of organization, which obstructed the attainment of goals. This is one of the dilemmas in the institutionalization of religion. It is the dilemma of administrative order, in which there is a dichotomy between elaboration and effectiveness:

It is characteristic of bureaucratic structure to elaborate new offices and new networks of communication and command in the face of new problems. Precedents are established which lead to a precipitation of new rules and procedures. One result may indeed be that the structure tends to complicate itself. This state of affairs evolves in order to cope

[1] Archdeacon Guy Mayfield, *Like Nothing on Earth*, p. 132.

[2] Quoted in *The Convocations and the Laity*, the report of the Church Assembly Commission, C.A. 1240, p. 4.

with new situations and new problems effectively. Yet such self-complication can over-extend itself and produce an unwieldy organization with blocks and breakdowns in communication, over-lapping of spheres of competence and ambiguous definitions of authority and related functions.[1]

The process by which the separate administrative agencies grew up in the Church of England presented this dilemma in a severe form. Committees which investigated the various agencies emphasized the failure in communication, both between the different levels in the Church—parish, diocese, and centre—and within and between the agencies themselves. In the nineteenth century, Parliamentary committees commented on the lack of communication between Queen Anne's Bounty and the Ecclesiastical Commissioners. The report of the Committee on the Administration of the Church Commissioners for England (the Monckton Report), in 1963, said that one of the main problems which the Commissioners faced, in common with other Church agencies, was that of communication.[2] The problem of communication was also made acute by the post-war policy of decentralization, which increased the functions performed at the diocesan level.

This placed a large burden on diocesan administration, which depended on a committee system with only a small professional staff. Both in the Monckton Report, and in the debate on that report, it was suggested that there should be a policy of secondment between the Commissioners' staff and those of the dioceses. It was also suggested that the dioceses would need to spend more money on their administration if the central bodies were to have confidence in them, and that communication was hindered by the lack of standardization in diocesan administration.[3]

[1] Thomas F. O'Dea, 'Five Dilemmas in the Institutionalization of Religion', in the *Journal for the Scientific Study of Religion*, 1 October 1961, pp. 32–9, and in Louis Schneider (ed.), *Religion, Culture and Society*, pp. 580–8 (p. 584). Cf. Osmund Schreuder, 'Church and Sociology', in *Social Compass*, xi, 5, 1965, pp. 5–19 (p. 18).

[2] *Monckton Report*, op. cit., para. 93.

[3] *P.C.A.*, vol. xliii, no. 3, November 1963, p. 573. These difficulties apart, the process of partial decentralization had a certain degree of success, which may constitute a process of debureaucratization such as Eisenstadt suggested could occur within sections of an organization, despite the fact that the overall organization itself became more of a bureaucracy in the context of the larger process of extensive

The Church Assembly organization from its inception experienced difficulty in communicating with the dioceses. In 1943, the Central Board of Finance proposed that there should be a new Chief Officer of the Assembly, whose specific task would be to maintain communication and liaison with the dioceses, but nothing came of this proposal.[1] The Organization and Methods Division of the Treasury found a serious lack of communication within the Church Assembly organization; and the Committee on Central Funds in 1956 found that there were overlapping spheres of competence and ambiguous definitions of authority, and a general lack of co-ordination. Despite the recommendation of this and other committees that the powers and functions of the Secretary of the Church Assembly, who was the senior permanent official, should be more clearly defined, no such definition was made, and, in 1966, the Secretary himself commented that the ambiguity of his position was typical of all positions of leadership in the Church of England.[2]

The problem of communication is closely related to that of authority. Terence K. Hopkins has attempted to show that the emphasis on authority in Max Weber's discussion of bureaucracy, and the emphasis on communication in the organization theory of Chester L. Barnard, are but two sides of the same coin.[3] Whereas Weber examines the status of the administrator (the office), attributes authority to this unit, and explains the effective exercise of authority mainly in terms of other attributes of the office or in terms of attributes brought to it by officials. Barnard, in contrast,

differentiation of institutional spheres in society (S. N. Einstadt, 'Bureaucracy, Bureaucratization and Debureaucratization', in *Administrative Science Quarterly*, vol. iv, 1959, pp. 302–20). Also, in the classic case of decentralization, that of General Motors, decentralization was only possible after a period of tighter, central control, which was necessary if the organization was to be reoriented during a period of extensive change when the Du Pont interest took over (Peter F. Drucker, *Concept of the Corporation*, pp. 41 ff.).

[1] *Interim Report on the Proposed Establishment of a New Chief Officer*, C.A.F. 180, printed for the Central Board of Finance, 1943.

[2] Personal interview with Sir John Guillum Scott, Secretary of the Church Assembly.

[3] Terence K. Hopkins, 'Bureaucratic Authority: The Convergence of Weber and Barnard', in A. Etzioni (ed.) *Complex Organization*, pp. 82 ff.; Max Weber, *The Theory of Social and Economic Organization*, op. cit.; and Chester L. Barnard, *The Functions of the Executive*, pp. 163–71.

examines the role relation (channel of communication), attributes authority to communications (which thus become more or less authoritative), and explains effectiveness in terms of other attributes of communications or in terms of attributes of role relations that transmit communications. An acceptable communication for Barnard must have four characteristics: from the recipient's point of view the communication must be understandable, consistent with the purpose of the organization, compatible with his personal interests, and capable of being executed. Later he adds that the communication must be authenticated—the recipient must believe that it comes from a particular position and that this position has the right to send such a communication. Unless these conditions are satisfied the communication will not stimulate response.[1]

The problem of communication experienced in the Church of England's organization illustrates the close relation between communication processes and authority. It has been seen that communication between the central administration and the parishes was hindered by the reservations which many parochial clergy had about the types of rationality and legality with which the central agencies were invested. The communications of the central administration were often unacceptable because the clergy did not find them consistent with the purpose of the organization as a religious body, and they did not accept the authority of the communicators. Thus the Hon. Secretary of the Parochial Clergy Association was reported as having addressed a meeting of clergy in Birmingham on 22 March 1965 which was reported in the Association's journal *Parson and Parish*:

> The Hon. Secretary gave a brief history of the build-up of the central organization of the Church—which was costing around £1,000,000 per year—but did not necessarily add one soul to the Church. It was more than ever essential today for the existence of an organization like the P.C.A. to resist this crushing machine . . . and reassert the freedom of the Clergy to proclaim the Church as a spiritual organism.[2]

Criticisms of bureaucracy in the Church have been

[1] Barnard, op. cit.

[2] *Parson and Parish*, July 1965, p. 7.

discussed in terms of objections to bureaucracy as a form of organization, and as an ailment of organization obstructing the attainment of goals. It remains to discuss criticisms of bureaucracy in the sense of 'big government' or centralization, and as a blight, always for the worst, falling on liberty and individuality. In criticisms such as those of the secretary of the Parochial Clergy Association all the various meanings are combined, and this was typical of criticism which was directed not only at the principles of bureaucracy, but also at the threat which bureaucracy presented to the sectional interests of the parochial clergy. These sectional interests were not mere material interests (the clergy tended to benefit materially from bureaucracy) but the interests involved in preserving what the clergy considered to be vital aspects of their professional role and status. Two aspects were involved: a change in the clergy role, and a loss of financial independence. Both aspects created insecurity for the clergy with regard to their status.

Some of the concern can be traced to the changes in the clergy role which stem from the discrepancy which arose between the traditional ideal of that role which had existed in the rural environment, and the actual role which the clergy found they were increasingly forced to play in the urban parishes which became the norm as a result of nineteenth-century urbanization.

This change in role creates conflict in several different ways: there is a conflict between the ideal with regard to the basic nature of the Church and the clergy's role and the practical requirements of the urban parish; conflict arises over the break with the traditional social definition of the clergy role which the new role represents; and there can be conflict between the role which the ordinand trained for in the theological college and that which faces him in the parish; and between the expectations which the parishioners have of the clergy role and that which the clergyman believes they should have. The subject of clergy role conflict has been widely discussed by sociologists of religion and its main aspects investigated.[1] The aspect which is most

[1] Samuel W. Blizzard, 'The Minister's Dilemma', *Christian Century*, lxxiii (25 April 1956), 508–10; Jerome E. Carlin and Saul H. Mendlovitz, 'The American

relevant to the discussion of the relations between the clergy and central administration is that mentioned by J. H. Fichter and Charles H. Page.[1] This aspect explains the proliferation of supraparochial organizations, and the consequent increase in specialization and the structural need for co-ordination and supervision, and it can be characterized as the gradual transformation of the parochial ethos from communal (*gemeinschaftliche*) to associational (*gesellschaftliche*). In the urban parish, where the sense of community and neighbourliness on a territorial basis has largely vanished, the parish has become a secondary, associational type of social structure. The main structural response of the Church centrally and locally has been to sub-divide its activities, to correspond to the specialized interests and needs of its members. This increases the functions of co-ordination and supervision, and of administration generally. The clergyman as administrator and co-ordinator of diverse activities and personnel is contrasted in the minds of both clergy and parishioners with the traditional image of the shepherd and his small flock of intimates, all participants in a knowable and well-integrated community. This role conflict impedes communication between the central administration and the parochial clergy because the clergy, on the whole, tend to devalue their association with the administrative system. Consequently the role relation between parochial clergy and central administrators is strained and does not function effectively as a channel of communication.

Not only is there role conflict, which affects the relations between the clergy and central administration, but there is also severe status insecurity. The effect of the loss of ancient sources of revenue during the nineteenth century, which had

Rabbi: A Religious Specialist Responds to Loss of Authority', in Marshall Sklare (ed.), *The Jews*, pp. 377–414; Anthony P. M. Coxon, 'A Sociological Study of the Social Recruitment, Selection, and Professional Socialization of Anglican Ordinands', unpub. Ph.D. thesis, Univ. of Leeds, 1965; David O. Moberg, *The Church as a Social Institution*, pp. 495–8; Bryan R. Wilson, 'The Pentecostal Minister: Role Conflicts and Status Contradictions', in *American Journal of Sociology*, lxiv, 5 (March 1959), pp. 494–504.

[1] J. H. Fichter, *Social Relations in the Urban Parish*, and Charles H. Page, 'Bureaucracy and the Liberal Church' in *The Review of Religion*, vol. xvi, nos. 3–4, November 1951, pp. 137–50.

previously been attached to the benefice and so made the incumbent financially independent, was to reduce the independent status of the clergyman, and to make him more dependent on central and diocesan paymasters. The necessary redeployment and redistribution of its financial resources, which the Church undertook in response to nineteenth-century social changes, led to a process of centralization of which the Ecclesiastical Commissioners and the Church Assembly were the chief examples.

The Archdeacon of Aston, in the Church Assembly debate on the Monckton Report, in 1963, suggested that one common factor in nearly all criticism made by the clergy of the Church Commissioners was that of dependence. The clergy had become increasingly dependent upon the Church Commissioners, and dependence never made for clarity of thought. The Archdeacon thought that the only cure was for the clergy themselves, through their representatives in the Church Assembly, to take control of their own money.[1] The Bishop of Lichfield objected to such a plan on the grounds that the central organization which would be set up would have complete control over the clergy and the independence of the dioceses would be gravely affected.[2] Since the Second World War, there had been a policy of partial decentralization down to the diocesan level. But even this raised fears that the clergy would remain dependent on administrators. As a result of this policy the endowment income for the benefices was only one-fifth or one-quarter of the total income, and the rest of the money came from augmentation grants which were at the discretion of the bishop and the diocesan board of finance.[3] The clergy still felt that they were losing their liberty and assuming a salaried status. Thus the Archdeacon of Lincoln commented in his article in *The Times*, on 19 June 1957 that,

> By a quiet revolution, the parochial clergy of the Church of England are becoming transformed into the salaried members of a diocesan staff, living in houses provided and maintained for them, on incomes fixed and guaranteed by the diocesan stipends fund.

[1] *P.C.A.*, vol. xliii, no. 3, November 1963, pp. 577–8.

[2] Ibid., p. 585.

[3] Ibid., p. 578.

In view of this increasing financial dependence the clergy clung ever more resolutely to what they considered to be the remaining safeguards of their professional status, especially that which was conferred by the freehold which every incumbent possessed, by which they received their office as a property from which they could not be alienated except by processes of law difficult to operate apart from proved criminal offences. It was partly for this reason that most of them opposed the proposals made by Leslie Paul in his report on *The Deployment and Payment of the Clergy*, which he produced in 1964 at the request of the Central Advisory Council for the Ministry. The view proclaimed by the Parochial Clergy Association was typical; it maintained that most of the reforms in the Paul Report were 'designed in such a way as to deprive the parochial clergy of their independence and freedom'. And, it was said, the result would be to destroy the Establishment and reduce the Church of England to a denomination.[1]

The economic changes which took place in the Church meant that the ministry has long been moving away from the rugged independence once in theory possessed by more than 10,375 "corporations sole",[2] and Leslie Paul's proposals were intended to provide a system of appointment and tenure that would accept and rationalize the situation, by transforming freehold into leasehold, and instituting central and regional agencies for the purposes of staffing and payment of salaries.

Many of the Paul Report's proposals had been made by the Archbishops' Fourth Committee of Inquiry (one of the five committees set up after the National Mission in 1916) on *Administrative Reform of the Church*, which published its report in 1918, and which had as its secretary William Temple, who probably drafted the report itself. Like Leslie Paul, this Committee recommended that institution to a benefice should be for a limited number of years (ten) and that the Church should take responsibility for the career of the clergyman; that there should be a minimum wage; that

[1] Revd. W. Grimwood, a member of the Executive of the Parochial Clergy Association, in *Parson and Parish*, July 1965, p. 9.

[2] Leslie Paul, *The Deployment and Payment of the Clergy*, p. 109.

there should be more and smaller dioceses and more provinces.[1] One member of the Committee expressed his dissent from its proposal to limit tenure of benefices, and to transfer all property to the Ecclesiastical Commissioners, on the grounds that it was 'motivated in part by the desire to get rid of all independence in the clergyman's position'.[2]

These administrative proposals were in keeping with the twin aims of many members of the Life and Liberty Movement, which were to provide the Church with an organization in keeping with its more autonomous institutional status as brought by the process of social differentiation, and to remove those aspects of its former position in the Establishment that had caused it to be identified with the ruling class. The founders of the Life and Liberty Movement were radical enough to be prepared to face the fact that the logic of their demand for an independent and autonomous Church might entail disestablishment and the reduction of the Church of England to a denomination. In order to secure the passing of the Enabling Bill, however, a compromise was arrived at that preserved the most important elements of the Establishment and so prevented the unhindered growth of a denominational pattern of organization. And yet, despite the structural links with the Establishment, the pluralistic character of modern society has increasingly caused the Church to act as one social group among many and, whilst aware that it has lost its old constitutional role, the Church of England has not discovered a new identity. This was the problem to which Leslie Paul addressed himself.

But his solution would have produced a bureaucracy such as has been described as being typical of the American denominations. As one churchman put it, 'if Mr. Paul's recommendations are carried out we shall in the eyes of the nation at large become as the Baptists, the Congregationalists or the Seventh-Day Adventists'.[3] According to another,

1 *Administrative Reform of the Church*, the report of the Archbishops' Fourth Committee of Inquiry, London, 1918. Similar proposals were made in the influential publication, *Putting Our House in Order*, London, Longmans, 1941.

2 The Dean of Carlisle, in *Administrative Reform of the Church*, op. cit., p. 31.

3 Ivor Bulmer-Thomas, 'Not for the North', in G. E. Duffield (ed.), *The Paul Report Considered*, 47–54 (p. 49).

it would make the Church of England 'a well organized sect rather than the Church of the English people'.[1] It ignored the various conflicts in the Church over interests (such as those of the clergy over against what they considered to be the onward march of bureaucracy), and those over doctrine. The Evangelicals, as the minority party, were particularly alarmed over the latter, and *The English Churchman* said that it constituted a threat to Evangelicals, whilst the editor of *The Church of England Newspaper* confined himself to pointing out that not enough weight had been given to differences of doctrine within the Church.[2]

The temptation in using the typological method of analysis is to assume that when change takes place in a religious organization it must result in a complete change of type—in the case of the Church of England a change from *ecclesia* to denomination. (Churchmen were particularly susceptible to this, as was seen in the pronouncements of Henson and also some members of the Catholic party, on whether the Church of England had changed type as a result of the Enabling Act.) A similar observation has been made with regard to studies of organization, which state that a particular organization is or is not a bureaucracy, rather than considering whether the organization is, or is believed to be, more or less bureaucratic.[3] Like several other European state churches, the Church of England developed certain structures and attitudes typical of the denominational type, but it also clung tenaciously to elements

[1] The Rt. Revd. Eric Treacy, 'Approaching the Report', in Duffield, op. cit., pp. 7–12 (p. 10).

[2] Quoted in Duffield, op. cit., p. 5.

[3] 'But the general view appears to be that the bureaucratic form is a particular *type* rather than a variable: an organization is or is not a bureaucracy, and a sub-unit is or is not a bureaucracy, rather than considering an organization to be more or less bureaucratic' (D. S. Pugh, *et al.*, 'A Conceptual Scheme for the Empirical Study of Work Organizations', an unpublished paper by the Industrial Administration Research Unit, College of Advanced Technology, Birmingham, n.d., p. 6).

In the case of work organizations such as this research unit studies, it is possible to ignore participants' values and prejudices with regard to 'bureaucracy', and they can concentrate on 'an empirically based multi-dimensional analysis of structural variables of organization'. A similar long-term reseach project might be undertaken into the separate administrative agencies in the Church of England, in order to quantify such variables as specialization, standardization, formalization, centralization, configuration, and flexibility.

characteristic of an *ecclesia*. Joachim Matthes has shown that a similar process was taking place in Germany, where there was a progressive decomposition of religiously homogeneous regions which had existed since the seventeenth century. He added, however,

> On the other hand, there has been no significant change in the situation of the two Christian churches as *Volkskirchen*; although Church and State were separated with the constitutional act of Weimar in 1919, both churches were still privileged institutions (*Körperschaften des öffentlichen Rechts*), the church tax-system has not been abolished, and more than 95% of the population still belong to one of the two Christian churches and fulfil certain minimum standards of religious practice.[1]

This did not necessarily contradict Fürstenberg's finding that there was a development in the direction of the *Verbandskirche*, because although some of the structural elements of the *Volkskirche* remained, Matthes noted that German Protestantism, formerly a religious majority oriented toward the whole of state and society, had developed a new self-image of a religious minority since the separation of Church and State in 1919. This development, in which a relatively small group of confessing Protestant Christians found itself opposed to a greater number of merely registered Christians, did not have to take account of internal theological party divisions as wide as those in the Church of England. Consequently the minority self-image could be worked out more thoroughly in theology and policy into a concept of the church as one special social group among others, representing specific interests and intentions.[1] In the Church of England there were minority groups, such as the Evangelicals, who wished to preserve the *ecclesia*-like orientation towards the State, because it protected them from domination by a majority party, which they believed would immediately ensue if the Church of England became an independent denomination. Other groups valued the *ecclesia* ideal for more positive reasons: some because it preserved the Church of England from becoming a class-based

[1] Joachim Matthes, 'Religionszugehörigkeit und Gesellschaftspolitik über Konfessionalisierungstendenzen in der Bundesrepublik Deutschland', in *Internationales Jahrbuch für Religionssoziologie*, vol. i, 1965, pp. 43–68.

church or denomination, others because it made possible that *via media* in doctrine and organization which was the basic characteristic of the Church of England.

The desire to maintain an *ecclesia*-like orientation toward the State limited the extent to which the Church of England developed in the direction of a denomination. *Ecclesia*-like administrative agencies were also maintained alongside the newer, more denominational administration of the Church Assembly, because here too compromise protected certain interests, especially that of the independence of the parochial clergy. The Church of England remained an institution subject to a large number of checks and balances, with several power and authority structures. There was the hierarchy of archbishops and bishops, the provincial and diocesan ecclesiastical courts and offices, the Convocations, Church Assembly, Church Commissioners, Parliament and the Crown, a widely diffused patronage system, and the parish priest with his inalienable freehold. The basic dilemma which had faced the Church of England in its organizational response to social change had been to adjust itself to the process of differentiation of institutional domains, whilst at the same time maintaining its basic identity as a coalition of diverse principles of authority and doctrine. Over the period which has been discussed the Church moved some way along the church-sect continuum in the direction of the denominational type, but in this respect, and with respect to the bureaucratic type of organization, it preserved many elements which have been directly related to its *ecclesia* origins. Organizational developments brought an increment of denominational and bureaucratic characteristics, but these continued to coexist with other, older modes. A parsimonious explanation would be that there could be no alternative to such coexistence if the Church was to continue to include parties and persons of very diverse views in one religious establishment.

Anglican participants in the ecumenical movement judged it differently, and claimed for the Church of England's *via media* in organization and doctrine a special place in the Divine Economy.

IX

SUMMARY

THE task essayed has been to examine the organizational response of the Church of England to wider social changes, taking as a focal point the creation of the Church Assembly by the Enabling Act of 1919. Analytically these developments were viewed as part of a process of differentiation of institutional domains within the social structure. The Church, like other institutions, gradually gained increasing autonomy and had to develop its own administrative and governmental organization. At the same time it had to engage in relations with other institutions, and so its developing organization was influenced by the patterns and modes prevalent in those other organizations. This raised problems with regard to the basis of legitimacy which such apparently secular principles could hope to claim in a religious body. Instrumental efficiency could best be attained by the fullest use of the criteria of formal rationality, but this had to be balanced against the need to follow a substantive rationality which took account of the ultimate goals and values of the institution. This, in turn, posed difficulties in a religious body which possessed goals and values which transcended mundane considerations; the means employed to further these could not be evaluated for their effectiveness by logico-experimental criteria. Modes of organization and the means they employed were evaluated, by those who wished to assert the transcendental nature of the Church's distinctive goals and values, according to their symbolic appropriateness. Thus bureaucratic forms of organization appeared to symbolize principles and values inappropriate for a religious body, and those who exercised power in such an organization were often denied a legitimate authority. As the developing administrative agencies in the Church often acquired some of the characteristics of the bureaucratic form of organization, the problem of legitimate authority, and control over their activities, was a constant subject of debate. The debate involved conflict over diverse principles and sectional interests. These were particularly acute in the Church of England because it contained such a rich diversity by virtue of thc Elizabethan Settlement, which had sought to include parties and persons of diverse views in one religious establishment. This comprehensiveness was the most prized characteristic of the Church of England, and the effort to maintain it affected the final outcome in each stage of its organizational growth. Theologically and with regard to principles of authority, this involved compromise and an avoidance of systematic rationalization, which by excessive definition might have excluded certain elements and reduced the Church to a more exclusive type of religious body. Organizationally, and with regard to the distribution of authority, it involved the maintenance of a complex division of powers.

The history of the development of autonomous administrative and governmental organization in the Church was divided into three periods: (1) the nineteenth century was summarized as a period of *ad hoc* growth of organization, in which instrumental reform and the reassertion of distinctive religious values and principles of authority proceeded separately and sometimes were in conflict; (2) the period from the last decade of the nineteenth century up to the passing of the Enabling Act was viewed in terms of attempts to combine these different concerns in one church reform movement; (3) the period from 1920 onwards was discussed in terms of the formation and development of the Church Assembly and its relation to other elements in the Church's organization.

The attitudes of the different church parties towards change and adaptation were examined in relation to their respective orientations to different system problems. Liberal or Broad Churchmen were found to have had a primary orientation to the function of adaptation of the church system, and to have had as their major concern the articulation of that system with the larger community. The Evangelicals had a similar orientation towards reform, although their attachment to the church system depended on such factors as whether there was social unrest, whether they were under attack within the Church, and according to their own party strength in different periods and areas. The Tractarians were oriented towards asserting the values of the universal church as they had existed in their pristine purity, and wished to preserve whatever patterns had traditionally expressed those values. Instrumental reformers, who held positions of leadership and responsibility in the Church, were primarily oriented towards the attainment of specific goals as defined by church functionaries like themselves, and they felt responsible for maintaining the established status of the national Church. Conservative churchmen in general (and the old High Church party in particular in the early nineteenth century) were primarily oriented towards the integrative functions of the Church and were fearful of changes which might disrupt its existing pattern of organization.

The development of central budgeting and planning agencies in the Church, especially the Ecclesiastical Commissioners set up in the 1830s, and the older Queen Anne's Bounty, were a product of social changes which deprived the Church of state financial aid and administrative arrangements of an older communal type. Although bureaucratization took place within the central financial organization which grew up, there was a constant criticism of that organization for introducing alien principles into the Church, and repeated efforts to relate those agencies to more acceptable centres of authority. There was a conflict between the requirements of efficient administration and the need for control of that administration by a legitimate authority. In the meantime the maintenance of a division of powers prevented the development of a uniform bureaucracy, and preserved the compromise between the various principles and sectional interests which coexisted in the one religious establishment.

In the second half of the nineteenth century the Church's need for a solution to its problems with regard to authority led to a series of experiments for the purpose of developing an acceptable system of representative assemblies. However, the various councils and conferences which appeared between 1850 and 1890 were not based on any agreed theory shared by all parties, but rather received their shape from the defensive stand which the Church had to make against external attack, and they could attribute their failure to gain much authority to the fact that they arose in a period when party divisions within the Church were at their worst. They also failed to address themselves to two of the most important problems which faced the Church: the problem of securing the interest and involvement of the working classes in the Church's government, and the internal problem of correlating the legislative and executive functions within the Church's organization.

A new period of church reform occurred between the last decade of the nineteenth century and the passing of the Enabling Act setting up the Church Assembly in 1919. In contrast to the *ad hoc* reforms of the previous period, and the feverish organization for defensive purposes, the new reform movement sought agreement on a minimum programme of reform which would commend itself to all parties in the Church, and which would also offer some hope of attracting the support of all classes in society. It was facilitated by changes within the Evangelical and Catholic parties brought about by the spread of a new liberalism within those parties, and the development of an organized Christian social movement which was devoted to making the Church appear more relevant and acceptable to the working classes. These different streams flowed together in the Church Reform League and later in the Life and Liberty Movement, which paved the way for the setting up of the Church Assembly. The result was less extensive in its effects than had been hoped by its more radical promoters, however. The plan for a Church Assembly, and the authority vested in that body, were limited by the compromises which alone made possible the recruitment of a sufficiently wide support in the various sections and parties in the Church. Among the concessions made were the dropping of the proposal for special provisions to ensure that working-class representatives were elected to the Assembly, and the preservation of the clerical Convocations with all their powers intact. The most important effect of the Enabling

Act was that it gave the Church of England certain delegated legislative powers, by which it could prepare measures for submission to Parliament, which could then either reject or approve them but no longer itself initiate or amend such church legislation. The ultimate veto still remained with Parliament, however, and this satisfied those church parties which had feared that a greater transfer of power to an autonomous church government would lead to the eventual exclusion of minority parties from the Church. In this respect it preserved the comprehensive, *ecclesia*, character of the Church of England, although opinions varied as to whether the baptismal franchise and registration on electoral rolls constituted a change in a denominational direction by introducing an element of exclusiveness.

Convocations maintained their separate powers with regard to matters of doctrine, ceremonial, and clergy discipline, and these powers were jealously protected in the early years of the Assembly when it was feared that Church Assembly was eager to acquire a degree of authority which would upset the balance of power and extend its own authority to cover all aspects of the Church's life. The parochial clergy were fearful that the Assembly would develop a bureaucratic organization which would rob them of their remaining independence and undermine their professional autonomy. Many of the measures passed by the Assembly in its early years seemed to bear hard on the clergy and a deep suspicion of the Assembly and its organization grew up. The result was that the clergy failed to provide the essential link in communicating information about the Assembly to the parochial level so as to develop an informed and sympathetic support for that body, and in consequence the Assembly was unable to bestow an unequivocal authority on its administrators and their activities. From the first there were accusations that its administration was becoming 'bureaucratic', in the various derogatory meanings of that term. Any suggestions for the consolidation of the central administration of the Church into one agency, were rejected. The Ecclesiastical Commissioners remained a separate body both richer, and larger in staff, than the Church Assembly organization. Whereas the

Ecclesiastical Commissioners' Office was patterned on civil service lines, with a more specialized staff and its own career structure, the Church Assembly departments received much of their character from the voluntary societies which they absorbed, and their staff was small, relatively unspecialized, and without a definite career structure. In both bodies the tension between the requirements of effective administration and the need for representative control and legitimate authority presented a constant problem.

The desire to maintain the Church of England's basic identity as an *ecclesia*, which incorporated diverse elements in one religious establishment, limited the extent to which it developed an autonomous administrative and governmental system along the lines found to be typical in the denominations, which are sometimes described as the appropriate form of religious organization in modern societies, where institutional domains are highly differentiated. The Church of England has developed a certain degree of autonomy, and is inclined to accept some of the implications of denominational pluralism, but it still prizes its own comprehensiveness and internal diversity, which it preserves by following a *via media* with regard to doctrine, principles of authority, and organization. This is the crucial limiting factor on any development in its organization towards the 'ideal types' of denomination and bureaucracy.

SOURCES AND BIBLIOGRAPHY

General Sources of Information

Interviews were carried out with senior members of the Church Assembly staff, and with Sir John Guillum Scott, the Secretary of the Church Assembly. Information with regard to the staff of the Church Assembly departments was compiled with the assistance of the Central Board of Finance.

BIBLIOGRAPHY

(Only works actually referred to in the text and footnotes are included)

Unpublished sources

In the Church Assembly archives, Church House, Westminster:

Archbishops' Committee on Church Finance, Minutes, 1909–14.

Central Board of Finance Executive Council Minutes.

Central Board of Finance Special (Diocesan Relationship) Committee Minutes, 1920–1.

Church Assembly Staff Salary Lists.

Church Assembly Standing Committee, Minutes, 1920–3.

Church Reform League, Minutes and Papers.

Committee to Consider the Relationship Between the National Assembly and the Central Board of Finance, Minutes, 1920.

Report of the Organization and Methods Division of the Treasury on the Organization and Procedures in the Church Assembly Departments, July 1955.

In Lambeth Palace Library:

Davidson, Archbishop R. T. Letters and papers. (Special permission to consult those papers which came within the Library's 50-year rule was given by the Archbishop of Canterbury. In 1966 the papers were in the process of being catalogued, and were kept in boxes under subject headings, e.g. 'Church Finance', etc.)

Tait, Archbishop A. C. Letters and papers.

Temple, Archbishop W. Letters and papers. (Special permission to consult these papers was given by Mrs. Temple, the widow of Archbishop William Temple. The papers had only recently been transferred to Lambeth Palace in 1966, and were contained in two suitcases, uncatalogued.)

Reports referred to in the text

Report of the Commissions of Inquiry into the Ecclesiastical Revenues of England and Wales, 1835 (*P.P.* 1835, vol. xxii, pp. 15–1060).

Reports from the Commissioners appointed to consider the State of the Established Church, with reference to Ecclesiastical Duties and Revenues:
First Report, 1835, *P.P.* 1835, vol. xxii, pp. 1–13.
Second Report, 1836, *P.P.* 1836, vol. xxxvi, pp. 1–44.
Third Report, 1836, ibid., pp. 47–60.
Fourth Report, 1836, ibid., pp. 61–78.
Fifth Report, 1837, *P.P.* 1837–8, vol. xxviii, pp. 9–22.

Report from the Select Committee on First Fruits and Tenths, and Administration of Queen Anne's Bounty, 1837 (*P.P.* 1837, vol. vi, pp. 1–75).

Reports from the Select Committee on the Ecclesiastical Commission, 1847 and 1848 (*P.P.* 1847, vol. ix, pp. 1–282; *P.P.* 1847–8, vol. vii, pp. 523–end).

Reports from the Royal Commission appointed to inquire into the State and Condition of the Cathedral and Collegiate Churches in England and Wales, Three Reports, 1854–5 (*P.P.* 1854, vol. xxv; *P.P.* 1854–5, vol. xv).

Reports from the Select Committee on the Ecclesiastical Commission, 1856, Three Reports (*P.P.* 1856, vol. xi).

Report from the Select Committee on the Ecclesiastical Commission, 1862–3 (*P.P.* 1862, vol. viii; 1863, vol. vi, pp. 43–301).

Report from the Select Committee on Queen Anne's Bounty, 1868 (*P.P.* 1867–8, vol. vii, pp. 467–615).

Report from the Joint Select Committee on Queen Anne's Bounty, 1900–1 (*P.P.* 1900, vol. viii, pp. 79–254; 1901, vol. vii, pp. 313–479).

Report of Canterbury Convocation Committee on Lay Co-operation, in *Chronicle of Canterbury Convocation*, 1872.

Report of the Islington Clerical Meeting, 1901: 'The Old Century and the New—Experiences of the Past, and Lessons for the Future', London; W. Gordon, 'Record' Office, 1901.

Report of the Joint Committee of the Convocation of Canterbury on the Position of the Laity in the Church, London; National Society, 1902, republished S.P.C.K., 1952.

Report of the Archbishops' Committee on Church Finance, London, Longmans, Green, 1911.

Report of the Archbishops' Committee on Church and State, London, S.P.C.K., 1916.

Report of the Archbishops' Fourth Committee of Inquiry, on Administrative Reform of the Church, London, S.P.C.K., 1918.

Report of the Committee of the Representative Church Council on the Report of the Archbishops' Committee on Church and State, London, S.P.C.K., 1918.

Report of the Special (Diocesan) Relationship Committee, N.A.F.1, Central Board of Finance, 1921.

Report of the Committee on the Relations Between Convocation and the National Assembly, no. 546, in *Chronicle of Canterbury Convocation*, vol. iv., no. 3, 1922.

Report of the Commission of Enquiry into the Property and Revenues of the Church, London, Press and Publications Board of the Church Assembly, 1924.

Report of the Committee Appointed to Consider the Appointment of a New Chief Officer, C.A. 741, London, Press and Publications Board of Church Assembly, 1944.

Report of the Commission to Enquire into the Expenses of the Assembly and its Organization, C.A. 910, London, Church Information Board, 1949.

Report of the Committee on Central Funds, C.A. 1181, London, Church Information Board, 1956. (The Committee made a further report, C.A. 1207, in 1957.)

Report of the Committee appointed by the Archbishop of Canterbury on the Administration of the Church Commissioners for England (the *Monckton Report*), London, Church Commissioners for England, and distributed by the Church Information Office, 1963.

Reports of proceedings of councils, assemblies, and boards

Chronicle of Canterbury Convocation (abbreviated as *C.C.C.*).

Chronicle of York Convocation.

Proceedings of Church Congress (*P.C.C.*).

Proceedings of the Representative Church Council.

Proceedings of the Central Council of Diocesan Conferences.

Proceedings of Church Assembly (*P.C.A.*).

Annual Reports of the Central Board of Finance.

Annual Reports of the Church Commissioners.

Other works referred to

ARNOLD, T., *Principles of church reform*, London, B. Fellowes, 1835.

BARNARD, CHESTER L., *The functions of the executive*, Cambridge, Mass., Harvard University Press, 1938.

BARNES, HARRY ELMER (ed.), *An introduction to the history of sociology*, University of Chicago Press, 1948.

BECKER, H., *Through values to social interpretation*, Durham, N.C., Duke University Press, 1950.

BECKER, H., *Systematic sociology*, Gary, Ind., Norman Paul Press, 1950 edn.

BENSON, A. C. *The life of Edward White Benson*, London, Macmillan, 1899, 2 vols.

BENTHAM, JEREMY, *Church-of-Englandism and its Catechism examined*, London: Effingham Wilson, 1818.

BEST, G. F. A., 'The Evangelicals and the Established Church in the Early Nineteenth Century', in *The Journal of Theological Studies*, vol. x, pt. i, April 1959, pp. 63–78.

—— 'The Constitutional Revolution 1828–32 and its Consequences for the Established Church', in *Theology*, vol. lxii, no. 468 (June 1959), pp. 226–34.

—— *Temporal Pillars*, Cambridge University Press, 1964.

—— 'The Whigs and Church Establishment in the Age of Grey and Holland' in *History*, vol. xlv, 1960, pp. 103–18.

BIBER, G. E., *Bishop Blomfield and his times*, London, Harrison, 1857.

BLIZZARD, SAMUEL W., 'The Minister's Dilemma', in *Christian Century*, lxxiii (25 April), 1956, pp. 508–10.

BLOMFIELD, A., *A memoir of Charles James Blomfield, D.D., Bishop of London*, London, John Murray, 1864.

BOOTH, CHARLES, 'Religious Influences' series of the *Life and Labour of the People of London*, London, 1902–3.

BOULDING, K. E., *The Organizational revolution*, New York, Harper, 1953.

BRADY, Sir ANTONIO, *Lay organization*, Salford, Church of England Laymen's Defence Organization n.d.

BREWER, EARL D. C., 'Sect and Church in Methodism', in *Social forces*, xxx, 4 (May 1952), pp. 400–8.

BRILIOTH, YNGVE, *The Anglican revival: studies in the Oxford Movement*, London, Longmans, 1925.

BROSE, OLIVE J., *Church and Parliament, the reshaping of the Church of England, 1828–1860*, London, O.U.P., 1959.

BROWN, FORD K., *Fathers of the Victorians*, Cambridge University Press, 1961.

BURLEIGH, J. H. S., *A Church history of Scotland*, London, O.U.P., 1960.

BURNHAM, JAMES, *The Managerial revolution*, New York, John Day, 1941.

CHADWICK, OWEN, *The mind of the Oxford Movement*, London, Adam and Charles Black, 1960.

CHURTON, EDWARD, *Memoir of Joshua Watson*, 2 vols. London, Parker, 1861.

COLERIDGE, S. T., *On the organization of Church and State according to the idea of each*, London, Hurst, Chance, 1830.

COLLINS, W. E. (ed.), *Typical English churchmen from Parker to Maurice*, London, S.P.C.K., 1902.

CONEYBEARE, W. J., 'Church Parties', in *Edinburgh Review*, xcviii (October 1853), pp. 273–342.

Crockford Prefaces: The Editor Looks Back, London, O.U.P., 1947.

CROZIER, MICHEL, *The Bureaucratic phenomenon*, London, Tavistock, 1964.

DAVIDSON, R. T., *The testing of a nation*, London, Macmillan, 1919.

—— *Life of Archibald Campbell Tait, Archbishop of Canterbury*, 2 vols., London, Macmillan, 1891.

DEARMER, NAN, *The life of Percy Dearmer*, London, Jonathan Cape, 1940.

DILLISTONE, F. W., *The structure of the divine society*, London, Lutterworth Press, 1951.

—— (ed.), *Myth and symbol*, London, S.P.C.K., 1966.

DRUCKER, PETER F., *Concept of the Corporation*, New York, John Day, 1946.

DUFFIELD, G. E. (ed.), *The Paul Report considered*, Abingdon, Berkshire, The Marcham Manor Press, 1964.

DUGMORE, C. W. and DUGGAN, C. (eds.), *Studies in Church History*, vol. i, London, Thomas Nelson, 1964.

DURKHEIM, EMILE, *The division of labour in society*, trs. by G. Simpson, Glencoe, Ill, The Free Press, 1947.

EISENSTADT, S. N., 'Bureaucracy, Bureaucratization, and Debureaucratization', in *Administrative Science Quarterly*, vol. iv, 1959, pp. 302–20.

ETZIONI, A., *A comparative analysis of complex organizations*, Glencoe, Illinois, The Free Press, 1961.

—— 'Two Approaches to Organizational Analysis: A Critique and a

Suggestion', in the *Administrative Science Quarterly*, vol. v, no. 2, September 1960, pp. 257–78.

Etzioni, A. (ed.), *Complex organization*, New York, Holt Rinehart & Winston, 1962.

Fichter, J. H., *Social relations in the urban parish*, Chicago, University of Chicago Press, 1954.

Francis, R. G. and Stone, R. C., *Service and procedure in bureaucracy*, Minneapolis, University of Minnesota Press, 1956.

Fulweiler, H. W., 'Tractarians and Philistines: The Tracts for the Times versus Victorian Middle Class Values', in *Church History* (the Historical Magazine of the Protestant Episcopal Church of America), vol. xxxi, March 1962, no. 1, pp. 36–53.

Fürstenberg, Friedrich, 'Kirchenform und Gesellschaftsstructur', in *Sociologisch Bulletin* (Holland), iii (1960), pp. 100–12.

Glock, Charles Y. and Stark, Rodney, *Religion and society in tension*, Chicago, Rand McNally, 1965.

Gore, Charles (ed.) *Essays on church reform*, London, John Murray, 1898.

Gouldner, A. W. 'Metaphysical Pathos and the Theory of Bureaucracy', in *American Political Science Review*, vol. xlix, 1955, pp. 496–507.

Gustafson, James M., *Treasure in earthen vessels: the Church as a human community*, New York, Harper, 1961.

Halevy, E., *A history of the English people in the nineteenth century*, London, Ernest Benn, 1927, Paperback edn. 1961, 6 vols.

Harrison, P. M., *Authority and power in the Free Church tradition*, Princeton University Press, 1959.

Harvey, G. L. H. (ed.), *The Church and the twentieth century*, London, Macmillan, 1936.

Heady, Ferrel, 'Bureaucratic Theory and Comparative Administration', in *Administrative Science Quarterly*, vol. iii, no. 4, March 1959, pp. 509–25.

Henley, Lord, *A plan of church reform*, London, 1832.

Henson, H. Hensley, *Cross-bench views of current church questions*, London, Edward Arnold, 1902.

—— *Retrospect of an unimportant life*, London, O.U.P., 1942–3, 1950, 3 vols.

Hoare, Henry, *Hints on lay co-operation*, London, F. & J. Rivington, 1858.

Howley, Archbishop, *Primary charge*, London, Rivington, 1832.

Hume, Revd. S. J., *Church boards. A letter to Albert Grey M.P.*, Oxford, Parker, 1881.

Hunter, L. S. (ed.) *Scandinavian churches*, London, Faber, 1965.

Iremonger, F. A. *Life of William Temple*, London, O.U.P., 1948.

—— *On the need for a G.H.Q. for the Church of England*, O.U.P., 1945.

Jackson, M. J. and Rogan, J., *Thomas Arnold: 'Principles of church reform' with an introductory essay*, London, S.P.C.K., 1962.

Jeffcock, John T., *Convocation made fairly representative*, London and Derby, Bemrose & Sons, 1881.

Johnson, B., 'A Critical Appraisal of the Church-Sect Typology', in *American Sociological Review*, vol. xxii (1957), pp. 88–92.

Kemp, E. W., *Counsel and consent*, The Bampton Lectures, 1960, London, S.P.C.K., 1961.

KITSON CLARK, G. *The making of Victorian England*, London, Methuen, 1962.

LASKI, H. J., *Studies in the problem of sovereignty*, New Haven, Yale University Press, 1917.

LASSWELL, HAROLD D. and KAPLAN, ABRAHAM, *Power and society*, New Haven, University Press, 1950.

LATHBURY, D. C., *Correspondence on church and religion of William Ewart Gladstone*, London, John Murray, 1910, 2 vols.

LEE, REVD. FREDERICK GEORGE, *The Ecclesiastical situation in 1899 from a Tractarian standpoint*, London, Thomas Baker, 1899.

LEE, R., *The social sources of church unity*, New York, Abingdon Press, 1960.

LERNER, DANIEL (ed.), *The human meaning of the social sciences*, New York, Meridian Books, 1959.

LEVY, MARION J., *The structure of society*, University of Princeton Press, 1952.

LIDDON, H. P., *Life of Pusey*, London, Longman, Green & Co., 1894, 4 vols.

LIPSET, SEYMOUR M., *Agrarian socialism*, Berkeley, California, University of California Press, 1950.

LLOYD, ROGER, *The Church of England in the twentieth century*, London, Longmans, 1946, 2 vols.

LOCKHART, J. G., *Charles Lindley Viscount Halifax, Part 2, 1885–1934*, London, 1936.

LUCKMANN, T., 'On Religion in Modern Society: Individual Consciousness, World View, Institution', in *Journal for the Scientific Study of Religion*, vol. ii, 2, spring 1963, pp. 147–60.

MACAULEY, LORD, 'Gladstone on Church and State', in the *Edinburgh Review*, April 1839, vol. 69, pp. 221–80.

MACINTYRE, ALASDAIR, *Secularisation and moral change*, The Riddel Memorial lectures, 1964, London, O.U.P., 1967.

MACNUTT, F. B. (ed.) *The Church in the furnace*, London, Macmillan, 1917.

MAGNUS, PHILIP, *Gladstone*, London, John Murray, 1954.

MANNHEIM, K., *Freedom, power and democratic planning*, London, O.U.P., 1950.

MANNING, H. E., *The principle of the ecclesiastical commission examined in a letter to the Rt. Rev. The Lord Bishop of Chichester*, London, J. G. & F. Rivington, 1838.

MARX, FRITZ MORSTEIN, *The administrative State*, Chicago, University of Chicago Press, 1957.

MATHIESON, W. L., *English church reform 1815–1840*, London, Longmans, Green, 1923.

MATTHES, JOACHIM, 'Religionszugehörigkeit und Gesellschaftspolitik über Konfessionalisierungstendenzen in der Bundesrepublik Deutschland', in *Internationales Jahrbuch für Religionssoziologie*, vol. i, 1965, pp. 43–68.

MAYFIELD, GUY, *Like nothing on earth*, London, Darton, Longman & Todd, 1965.

MERTON, ROBERT K., *Social theory and social structure*, Glencoe, Illinois, The Free Press, 1949.

Michels, Robert, *Political parties*, trs. by E. and C. Paul, Glencoe, Illinois, The Free Press, 1949.

Moberg, David O., *The Church as a social institution*, Englewood Cliffs, N. J., Prentice–Hall, 1962.

Mudie-Smith, R. (ed.), *The religious life of London*, London, Hodder & Stoughton, 1904.

Neal, Sister Marie Augusta, *Values and interests in social change*, Englewood Cliffs, N.J., Prentice-Hall, 1965.

Newman, J. H., *Apologia pro vita sua*, London, Longmans, 1864.

Niebuhr, H. R., *The social sources of denominationalism*, Hamden, Conn., Shoe String Press, 1954.

Oastler, Richard, *Convocation: The Church and the people*, London, C. W. Reynell, 1860.

O'Dea, Thomas F., 'Five Dilemmas in the Institutionalisation of Religion', in the *Journal for the Scientific Study of Religion*, vol. i, October 1961, pp. 32–9.

O'Dea, Thomas F., *The sociology of religion*, Englewood Cliffs, N.J., Prentice-Hall, 1966.

Page, Charles H., 'Bureaucracy and the Liberal Church', in *The Review of Religion*, vol. xvi, nos. 3–4, November 1951, pp. 137–50.

Palmer, W., *A narrative of events*, London, Rivington, 1883 edn.

Parsons, Talcott, 'The Patterns of Religious Organization in the United States', in *Daedalus*, lxxxvii, 3 (summer 1958), pp. 65–85.

—— *et al.*, *Theories of society*, 2 vols., Glencoe, Illinois, The Free Press, 1961.

—— *The social system*, Glencoe, Illinois, The Free Press, 1951.

—— *The Structure of Social Action*, Glencoe, Illinois, The Free Press, 1949.

Partridge, F. (ed.), *The Church Assembly and the Church*, London, Church Information Board, 1930.

Paul, Leslie, *The deployment and payment of the clergy*, London, Church Information Office, 1964.

Pfautz, H. W., 'The Sociology of Secularisation: Religious Groups', in *American Journal of Sociology*, lxi, 2 (September 1955), pp. 121–8.

Phillpotts, Henry, *Charge delivered to the clergy of the diocese of Exeter*, London, John Murray, 1836.

Pickering, W. S. F. (ed.), *Anglican-Methodist relations, some institutional factors*, London, Darton, Longman & Todd, 1961.

Pope, Liston, *Millhands and preachers*, New Haven, Yale University Press, 1942.

Port, M. H., *Six hundred new churches*, London, S.P.C.K., 1961.

Ramsey, A. M., *From Gore to Temple*, London, Longmans, 1960.

Reckitt, Maurice B., *Maurice to Temple: a century of the social movement in the Church of England*, London, Faber & Faber, 1947.

Rigg, James H., *A comparative view of church organisations*, London, Charles H. Kelly, 3rd edn., 1897.

Roberts, David, *Victorian origins of the Welfare State*, New Haven, Yale University Press, 1960.

Rogers, T. Guy (ed.), *Liberal evangelicalism*, London, Hodder & Stoughton, 1923.

SANDERS, C. R., *Coleridge and the Broad Church movement*, Durham, North Carolina, Duke University Press, 1942.

SCHNEIDER, LOUIS (ed.), *Religion, culture and society*, New York, John Wiley, 1964.

SCHREUDER, OSMUND, 'Church and Sociology', in *Social Compass*, xi, 5, 1965, pp. 5–19.

SELBORNE, LORD, *A defence of the Church of England against disestablishment*, London, Macmillan, 1886.

SELWYN, E. G. (ed.), *Essays Catholic and critical*, London, S.P.C.K., 1926.

SELZNICK, P., *T. V. A. and the grassroots*, University of California Press, 1949.

—— *Leadership in administration*, Evanston, Illinois, Row, Peterson, 1957.

SKLARE, MARSHALL (ed.), *The Jews*, Glencoe, Illinois, The Free Press, 1958.

SMELSER, NEIL J., *Theory of collective behaviour*, London, Routledge & Kegan Paul, 1962.

—— *Social change in the industrial revolution*, London, Routledge & Kegan Paul, 1959.

SMYTH, CHARLES, *Simeon and church order*, Cambridge University Press, 1940.

STANLEY, A. P., *Life and correspondence of Dr. Arnold*, London, Teacher's edn., 1901.

STEPHEN, LESLIE, *The English Utilitarians*, London, Duckworth, 1900, 3 vols.

STOCK, EUGENE, *The history of the Church Missionary Society*, London, C.M.S., 1899, 3 vols.

STOKES, ERIC, *The English Utilitarians and India*, Oxford, Clarendon Press, 1959.

SWEET, J. B., *A memoir of the late Henry Hoare*, London, Rivington, 1869.

TEMPLE, W., *Life and liberty*, London, Macmillan, 1917.

TILLOTSON, G. (ed.), *Newman, prose and poetry*, London, Rupert Hart-Davis, 1957.

TIRYAKIAN, E. A. (ed.), *Sociological theory, values, and socio-cultural change*, Glencoe, Illinois, The Free Press, 1963.

TOMKINS, OLIVER, *The life of Edward Woods, Bishop of Lichfield*, London, S.C.M., 1957.

TREVOR, MERIOL, *Newman*, 2 vols., London, Macmillan, 1962.

TRILLING, LIONEL, *Matthew Arnold*, London, George Allen & Unwin, 1939.

TROELTSCH, E., *The social teaching of the Christian Churches*, 2 vols., trs. Olive Wyon, London, Allen & Unwin, 1931.

VERNON, GLENN M., *Sociology of religion*, New York, McGraw Hill, 1962.

VIDLER, A. R., *The orb and the cross*, London, S.P.C.K., 1945.

—— *The Church in an Age of revolution*, London, Penguin Books, 1961.

WACH, J., *Types of religious experience: Christian and non-Christian*, Chicago, University of Chicago Press, 1951.

WARBURTON, WILLIAM, *The alliance Between Church and State*, London, J. & P. Knapton, 3rd edn., 1748.

WARRE CORNISH, F., *The English Church in the nineteenth century*, 2 vols., London, Macmillan, 1910.

WARREN, JOHN, *An address to members of the Church of England; both lay and clerical on the necessity of placing the government of the Church in the hands of members of its own communion*, London, Simpkin, Marshall, 1837.

WEBB, C. C. J., *Religious thought in the Oxford Movement*, London, S.P.C.K., 1928.

WEBER, A. F., *The growth of cities in the nineteenth century*, London, P. S. King, 1899.

WEBER, MAX, *Theory of social and economic organisation*, trs. by Talcott Parsons and A. M. Henderson, London, O.U.P., 1947, Free Press Paperback edn. 1964.

—— *The Protestant ethic and the spirit of capitalism*, trs. by Talcott Parsons, London, Allen & Unwin, 1930.

—— *The methodology of the social sciences*, trs. by E. A. Shils and H. A. Finch, Glencoe, Ill., The Free Press, 1949.

WEBSTER, A. B., *Joshua Watson*, London, S.P.C.K., 1954.

WELCH, P. J., 'Blomfield and Peel: A Study in Co-operation between Church and State, 1841–46', in *Journal of Ecclesiastical History*, vol. xii, 1961, pp. 71 ff.

WHATELY, E. J., *The life and correspondence of Archbishop Whately*, London, 1866.

WHITLEY, O. R., 'The Sect-to-Denomination Process in an American Religious Movement: The Disciples of Christ', in *South western Social Science Quarterly*, vol. xxxvi (1955), pp. 275–81.

WILLIAMSON, E. L., *The Liberalism of Thomas Arnold: a study of his religious and political writings*, University of Alabama Press, 1964.

WILSON, BRYAN R., 'An analysis of sect development', in *American Sociological Review*, vol. xxiv (1959), pp. 3–15.

—— 'The Pentecostal minister: role conflicts and status contradictions', in *American Journal of Sociology*, lxiv, 5 (March 1959), pp. 494–504.

—— (ed.), *Patterns of sectarianism*, London, Heineman, 1967.

WINCH, PETER, *The idea of a social science*, London, Routledge & Kegan Paul, 1958.

WOLMER, VISCOUNT, *The failure of the House of Commons in ecclesiastical legislation*, Church Self-Government Papers, no. 10, London, S.P.C.K., 1919.

YATES, RICHARD, *The Basis of national welfare . . .*, London, F. C. & J. Rivington, 1817.

YINGER, J. MILTON, *Religion, society and the individual*, New York, Macmillan, 1957.

Pamphlets

National Church Reform Union Pamphlets:

The people's interest in the national Church.

The Church and the people.

Why should you support the Church Reform Union?

(Undated: nos. 73402–4 in Pusey House, Oxford, Pamphlets Collection.)

Life and Liberty Movement Leaflets and Pamphlets:

The social message of the Church. (Leaflet G in a series of leaflets A–O, published between 1917–19. A series of pamphlets 1–19, was published by S.P.C.K. between 1918–20.)

Administrative reform. A guide to study and discussion (compiled by F. A. Iremonger), 1920.

Tracts for the times (published at intervals between 1833–41), London, Rivington.

Theses consulted in part or in whole (in some cases they were proceeding contemporaneously with this study)

Coxon, A. P. M. 'A Sociological Study of the Social Recruitment, Selection, and Professional Socialization of Anglican Ordinands.' Unpub. Ph.D. thesis, University of Leeds, 1965.

Ridley, S. 'The Background of the Life and Liberty Movement and its achievement in the years 1917 to 1920.' Unpub. B.D. thesis, University of London, 1966.

Rudge, P. F. 'The Study of Ecclesiastical Administration, Using the Methods and Insights of Public Administration.' Unpub. Ph.D. thesis, University of Leeds, 1966.

Wilson, F. M. G. 'A consideration of the experience in Britain of administrative commissions represented in Parliament by non-ministerial commissioners, with special reference to the Ecclesiastical Commission, the Charity Commission and the Forestry Commission.' Unpub. D.Phil. thesis, University of Oxford, 1953.

INDEX

PRINTED IN GREAT BRITAIN
AT THE UNIVERSITY PRESS, OXFORD
BY VIVIAN RIDLER
PRINTER TO THE UNIVERSITY